A WORLD OF MY OWN

JASON CRUMP

His triumph in the Grand Prix series of 2004 brought Australia a first solo speedway world champion for more than half a century. It came after a succession of near misses and frustrations which might have dampened the spirit of a lesser performer. Jason, however, was born to race and destined to be a winner. His early titles include those of Australian Under 16 champion, Australian and World Under 21 champion. He also starred when Australia won the World Team Cup in 1999, 2001 and 2002. For more than a decade he has been an outstanding performer in the leagues of Great Britain, Poland and Sweden and now spends most of his time in Europe. This is his first book. Jason and his wife Melody live near Northampton, with their children Mia, who is turning seven, and Seth, three.

MARTIN ROGERS

One of the foremost administrators and journalists in British speedway until he and his family moved to Australia in 1988. Martin and his wife Lin were promoters at Leicester, King's Lynn and Peterborough. Of 19 sporting titles he has written and/or edited, *Briggo*, the Barry Briggs story, and the *Illustrated History of Speedway*, are two of the all-time best-selling speedway books. Others include *Stars and Bikes* with Bruce Penhall, *My Story* with England cricketer John Emburey, *In My View*, and, most recently, *Forty Years On: King's Lynn Speedway.* Martin, who has known the Crump family since Jason's father Phil came to England in 1971, is an associate editor of the *Gold Coast Bulletin* newspaper in Queensland. Martin and Lin's son, also Martin, is a London *Daily Mirror* sports journalist.

A WORLD OF MY OWN
Jason Crump with Martin Rogers

First published in Great Britain and Sweden in 2006 by Galathco Publications under licence from Front Page Books

Pre-press production by Bob Johnson
Cover and colour section by Jonathan Nash

Printed and bound in Great Britain

A CI P catalogue record of this book is available from the British Library

ISBN 0 948882 98 0

A WORLD OF MY OWN

JASON CRUMP

with MARTIN ROGERS

ACKNOWLEDGEMENTS

WRITING a book, like winning a world championship, involves a large cast list of helpers but in the end the author or authors will be judged by their own efforts.

However, *A World of My Own* would not have been possible without the assistance of a great number of people in Australia, England, Sweden, Poland and around the speedway world.

Melody Crump and Lin Rogers have as usual provided the necessary inspiration to keep their respective menfolk focused on the task in hand.

Bob Johnson has been a wise, calm professional co-ordinator of all the technical pre-press operation. Jonathan Nash, likewise, proved a tower of strength in orchestrating cover and colour page design.

Thanks must go to the following whose contributions have been so important and to anybody else whose help may inadvertently been overlooked:

Neil Bird, Neil Campbell, Mark Carter, Peter Collins, Bob and Marj Crump, Carole Crump, Phil Crump, Richard Clark, Rod Colquhoun, Bob Cowley, James Easter, Dave Fairbrother, Brendon Gledhill, Christer Gustavsson, Jonas Holmqvist, Per Jonsson, Bill Key, Brian Karger, John Krause, Mark Lemon, Ola Lindblom, Jim Lynch, Steve Magro, Ivan Mauger, Tony McDonald, Jithendra Nair, Darryl Nicol, Peter Oakes, Gareth Parry, Mike Patrick, John Perrin, Mick Poole, Bob Radford, Philip Rising, Alun and Julie Rossiter, Alex Schroeck, Dave and Margaret Schooling, Susan Shields, Andrew Skeels, Drew Street, Graham Street, Neil Street, Wojtek Szoltysek, Ian Thomas, Nigel and Jill Tremelling, Lucasz Treszckowski, Bert Upson, Helen Wheatland, Peter White, Vic White, Bo Wirebrand.

The co-operation of the publishers and staff of *Speedway Star*, *Backtrack* magazine, *Peter White's Speedway World*, and *Speedway Racing News* has also been invaluable as have countless published sources.

CONTENTS

FOREWORD

by Per Jonsson

(world speedway champion 1990)

I AM very happy to have enjoyed Jason Crump's friendship and support since my own career ended. He has all the talent and dedication to be the best.

It was a thrill for me to become world champion in 1990, and now 15 years on to be asked to contribute to Jason's book is a real pleasure.

Back in 1984, straight after my 18th birthday, I came to ride for in the British League. Although I rode for Reading my UK base was always Swindon, and from the start I was really lucky to have people around me who would help in their different ways.

It was my old friend Bob Radford who quickly took me up to meet Phil Crump, who I knew was a top-line rider. Jason was then 10 years old and Phil was Swindon's top rider by a mile. I spent a fair amount of time at their home and it helped me settle into my life in a new country.

We'd enjoy barbeques, have a few drinks, talk about anything and generally relax with the whole family. In my first year I didn't race in the Swedish League and the friendship really was welcome.

There were no Tuesday night tracks in the British League then and that became a regular night – even though bell ringers at the local church proved annoyingly noisy when we sat outside the house in Grange Park. So much for speedway's noise problems!

I think Jason was always interested in speedway though I first remember him tearing around on his pushbike. He actually started to help his father in the workshop and the pits very early on, but then Phil retired from the British scene in 1986.

I met up with them all again when a Swedish team went to Australia, and visited them there which was fun. By then it was obvious that Jason wanted to become a rider. He was doing very well on the junior scene out there, and he often practised on the local salt flats which gave him a hard, flat smooth surface.

He'd grown up with speedway all around him. His grandfather Neil Street had a long career and stayed involved in speedway and Phil was a great rider by any standards. Yet who could have guessed then that this young teenager would go on to be even better than his father and the best rider in the world?

You can have great teachers, but if you don't have the desire and the talent it means nothing...

Jason and I always got on well, we just liked each other. When he came back to Britain to race I'd go to watch him riding for Swindon in what was

INSPIRATION ... Jason with Per Jonsson, Reading, 1994, after injury had halted the champion Swede's racing career

Division Two. I saw then how well he rode the bike, looking for different lines to race on, so that was when I first thought he could be world champion one day.

Although he won individual Grand Prix rounds early on Jason has had to work so hard to be number one. Quite a few riders have shown that potential, but not many constantly look at how they might make themselves better, and in speedway it is mainly down to you. You have to want it so much!

He worked on set-ups, even saw a sports psychologist – something all the young Swedish riders in my day did. It is so very easy to get fed up, blame the bike or the track – and many do that – but it you want to be number one I believe the desire and determination comes from within yourself.

Even during those three long years as world number two he was always searching and striving to improve. Yourself, you have to want to win so much and there is no doubt that Jason always had that. I am happy he achieved his aim to be the best, and I know he can go on to win more titles in the future.

LNB
POLAND
LNB
POLAND
2
POLAND
POLAND
POLAND
FUCHS

Winners are grinners

> It was Jason Crump's destiny to become world champion. If he really wants it, he can be a force for some time to come. Possibly he was not ready to win (before 2004) but he has all the ingredients. He has always been a racer through and through.
>
> – Ivan Mauger, OBE MBE, speedway's 'man of the 20th century'

IF winners are indeed grinners, Jason Crump should wear a perpetual smile.

One of speedway's most exciting, fiercely competitive, driven and colourful performers, celebrated in Great Britain, Poland, Sweden, Australia and wherever the sport has a foothold, he has been winning races since he first stepped on to a motorcycle, and getting paid for it since he was 16.

As a regular on the European circuit since 1992, and an international presence from a very early stage of his career, he probably has around 4,000 race wins, and counting.

Of course, nothing brought him greater joy than entering the exclusive club of world solo champions. Among his most significant performances, victory in the 2004 Grand Prix series stands supreme.

It was a triumph all the more remarkable for the years of toil and trouble which preceded it – notably in the same Viking Ship stadium in Hamar, Norway 12 months earlier when seemingly the title was within his grasp but slipped away

That was just the latest in a catalogue of examples designed to emphasise that even the most fiercely burning ambition isn't enough. To climb to the very top you have to be prepared to negotiate all sorts of obstacles along the route.

For several years a spectacular public star battled his private demons to become a player of consequence at the highest level. For three frustrating years he had to settle for runner-up. He had been a national junior and senior title winner, the world's Under 21

AFFIRMATION ... at last, the speedway world championship gold medal in Jason's safe keeping

champion, then three times a World Team Cup winner.

Still he could not nail the one he sought most of all – a 'world' of his own.

Jason Crump, so the critics argued, could win anything and everything and routinely and regularly did so. But for what must have seemed like an eternity, he appeared cast as the perennial 'nearly' man.

It's because of some of the disappointments which littered an extended learning curve that the smiles have been punctuated by the black moods, the uncertainty and the frustration which haunt even champions.

Yet to have won the sport's highest prize after a series of gut-wrenching near misses means that Jason today is a happier man, a consuming ambition achieved. But his career still is very much a work in progress. More titles beckon and the next few years will show if history is to honour and remember him among the great champions or simply as a very good one.

Jason's pursuit of world championship success is a continuing passion. His motivation, like that of the true champions, is to keep on developing, to improve and progress. He's had ups and downs and life experience to equip him for further challenges, and plenty of them.

After finally securing the world title, Jason was quick to declare it a career landmark rather than an end in itself when he opened up to Richard Clark of England's *Speedway Star* magazine.

"Nothing changes, everything's the same. But it's a good feeling, it's nice to know that you've finally achieved what you set out to do.

"I guess for me personally it takes a bit of pressure away, because it was a long road, a long time coming, a lot of highs, a lot of lows, and finally to do it, it's worth it.

"Of course there were a lot of times when I wondered if it would ever happen, but luckily for me I kept going with it – and anybody who wants to win anything in life can see now that you can actually do it if you keep going.

"There were a lot of times when I didn't really want to keep going with it, but I did.

"After Norway 2003 I could have done anything really. But it just takes a little bit of time to come to terms with things and you generally make the right decision in the end.

"You realise what the important things in life are, what you think are important, and I guess you take strength from them.

"After I lost in Norway, we started to change things right away.

"There were things I didn't even realise I had changed, but through the course of the year you look back and think 'oh, I reacted in a pretty good way to that' or did something different here or there to what I would normally have done, subtle changes.

"That comes down to a lot of the work I do with people away from speedway tracks. That's become a very important part of my set-up now. The mental preparation is crucial. I took a big step by cutting

WE'VE DONE IT ... Drew Street and Seth Crump join in the celebrations at Hamar, 2004

out Sweden, and I'm very happy with the way it worked out.

"That was all part of the plan that was put together, and it was good. You find out what works for you."

If a world title has mellowed this one-time stormy petrel, he's smart enough to understand that tall poppies are never going to be universally loved.

"I'm not the most popular rider out there," he said.

"But I'm not out to be popular, just to win."

The fact that 2005 produced another of those runner-up medals has not dented his resolve or credentials. In attempting to win back to back last year, Jason faltered, singed by the Tony Rickardsson blow torch. But he still managed to place in the top two for the fifth year in a row, a statistic even the remarkable Rickardsson has not managed. For this sort of consistency you have to go back to Hans Nielsen who between 1984 and 1989 won three titles and was runner-up three times.

Pending elevation to the short list of multiple winners, he stands out as the single most successful one-off champion among the 19 from Australia's Lionel van Praag on to have climbed aboard the victory rostrum.

Jason's four second places in five years (2001, 2002, 2003 and 2005) set a new, possibly unwanted statistic yet he can take heart from the fact that many of the sport's greats also had to sample the sour taste of silver on several occasions.

Those who have figured so consistently at or around the top usually sign off with a few titles to their name.

Crump devotees will feel optimistic that their man, already in quite rareified company, can make a further such impact on the history books. His persistence so far speaks volumes for his current status and the final reckoning may prove to be significantly more impressive.

Ian Thomas, one of England's longest-serving promoters, who has Jason as his captain and No.1 at Belle Vue, already ranks him among an all-time top 10.

That is a big call, coming from someone who has had Ivan Mauger and Barry Briggs riding for him at club level and bossed national sides which revolved around the likes of Peter Collins.

"It is difficult trying to compare riders from different eras," says Thomas.

"I have had a lot of riders pass through my hands. Jason rates up there alongside the very best. I've only worked with him for the one season but there is no doubt about that in my mind."

ALUN Rossiter, now combining duties as promoter at Swindon with the role of mine host at the New Inn in Stratton St Margaret, reckons that in one regard Jason Crump is no different today from the teenager who burst on to the scene in 1992.

"He calls it as it is, always has," says Rossiter, a former Poole and Swindon team-mate, who for an extended period was also Jason's landlord.

"I think people now realise where he's coming from but for a long time he was very misunderstood. Some people seeing him angry at meetings criticised his temperament without properly appreciating how important his performances are to him.

"Sheer will and determination make him what he is. And he's very up front, he won't lie to you. People who speak the truth often aren't liked for it, but that always has been his way.

"He is a terrific bloke and friend but at speedway he makes no bones about it, he's there to do the business. He doesn't go out there to play around. He will always make the effort and that's why a lot of people, riders and mechanics, those who are close to it, do really respect him.

"He's been a good world champion, he will be again, and he's grown up a lot and learned to be a bit more diplomatic. But his attitude towards racing won't ever change. It doesn't matter whether it's a Grand Prix, a league match or someone's testimonial meeting, Jason is there to win."

Peter Oakes, sometime promoter, team manager and the most prolific and informed speedway journalist, cites the excitement factor as the defining signature of Jason's contribution to the sport.

"The fans of today don't realise how fortunate they are to see such a spectacular brand of speedway, with riders hanging off the bike at all angles, and Jason was one of the first and best exponents of that sort of style," says Oakes, who hired the 16-year-old boy at the start of his British career, and four years later paid a record £35,000 for his transfer from Poole to Peterborough.

"He just never knows when he's beaten. He's always been the same. He rides to the limit and no matter what the occasion, there is never anything less than 100 per cent effort. How highly Jason will be rated is something we will find out after a few more years but he's got every chance of putting himself up there among the very best."

Provided he does win again, it will be another landmark move into the ranks of the elite. Of 31 winners of the world championship, only a dozen have managed to repeat the performance.

From a historical perspective Jason needs a second title to move into the company of his compatriot Jack Young, Freddie Williams, Ronnie Moore, Peter Craven and Bruce Penhall.

The next target would be three-time winners Ole Olsen, modern-day director of the Grand Prix series (1970s) and Erik Gundersen (1980s).

If desire has anything to do with it, Jason has every chance of leapfrogging over even such exalted names.

Alun Rossiter, who made the transition from riding to running Swindon last year, and has been a longtime friend and confidant, identifies 'sheer will and determination' as explanation enough for a distinguished record he believes will become significantly better yet.

Certainly time should be on his side in the quest to win again. Ivan won four of his world titles after turning 30, TR has won three of his after passing that birthday, Hans a couple.

What they all had in common was a combination of experience and enthusiasm which is something Jason is hopeful he will be able to achieve and retain for a while.

Anyone with realistic ambitions of joining the club of multiple winners has some work to do, though. The learning curve Jason had to follow declares that maybe it's not such a mystery why it took him so long to become world champion.

If ever there was a rider seemingly born to the role, schooled in the approved manner, marked down from the start of his career as somebody destined for great things, it's Jason Philip Crump.

The pedigree was there, the credentials seemingly just right. Yet at 29 years and 57 days when he won in 2004, he had been a full-time professional racer for 13 years, and was the oldest first-time winner since Egon Muller in 1983.

Even Mauger, a notoriously late developer, was a month short of his 29th birthday in 1968 when he took out the first of his six titles.

It seems premature, then, to be talking of Jason Crump in quite the same breath as the sport's iconic champions. The jury deciding upon his place in history will be out for a few years. Few observers though will be surprised if he does continue to provide reasons why he should secure a place among the pantheon of all-time greats.

The weight of expectation and the expectant wait before he was crowned as Australia's first world champion in more than half a century might have been crippling to a man of lesser intellect and mental toughness.

A teenage debutant in the last one-off World Final, the youngest winner of a Grand Prix (21 years 23 days at Hackney in 1996), he soon displayed the mercurial talents which in another era may well have brought him sooner to the biggest prize of all.

Old-time titles, certainly, were won by men who arguably were not the best in the world at the time, even if they proved equal to the test on one night and, in some cases, later grew in stature and accomplishment.

But since the Grand Prix series became the approved method of establishing just who should wear the crown, a different kind of demand is placed upon those who would be king.

It seemed inevitable that Jason would get there in the end, so relentlessly consistent was he in all types of competition around Europe.

Maturity, nevertheless, was a while in coming. For several years the young man in a hurry appeared to be too impetuous, too prone to moments of spectacular misadventure and misjudgement. He had the ability to beat the best, and to win meetings, offset by a knack of finding new and ever more bizarre ways to lose.

It didn't matter in the end, according to Mauger, because Jason refused to be deflected from his passionate ambition.

"You can't put devil into a speedway rider. It has to be there in the first place," says Ivan.

"Sometimes youthful enthusiasm and determination can go over the top but that's fine.

"It's possible to temper it and channel all that energy into becoming a champion and that's what Jason has done."

It's tough to argue with the suggestion that holding it all together over a series of half a dozen, or nine meetings – and once, 10 – has proved to be a much more searching test even than the old-fashioned world championship qualification method of domestic and continental rounds.

All that really mattered in the old days was to be able to gather sufficient points to move on to the next stage. Ove Fundin, Briggo, Mauger and the legends of yesteryear regularly won such big meetings but almost invariably their over-riding focus was to qualify.

CHAMPION ... JC and longtime guru Ivan Mauger, a man who knows a bit about winning world titles

One of the most emphatically successful championship campaigns in history was that of Dave Jessup who in 1980 won a swag of lead-up events but still finished second to Michael Lee on World Final night.

Vic White, secretary of the Veteran Speedway Riders Association which counts most of the living greats among its numbers, sparked intense debate by claiming that a 'true' world champion was one who traditionally had to fight through the old-time qualifying rounds and then deliver on one big night.

Increasingly though, contemporary opinion suggests that it's an accolade which has never been tougher to win than under the present-day system.

While its critics argue the Grand Prix is virtually a closed shop, an exclusive club, in many ways that is a measure of its strength, its competitiveness and relevance.

Every point won or lost takes on a significance – the more so since the system was amended last year – which underscores why modern observers claim the racing and the intensity of the entire series is more ferocious than anything Wembley or other one-off finals produced, its demands a uniquely contemporary test of mettle.

Jason has come to believe that he needed to sample all shades of fortune and the full scale of emotion

A TOUGH DAY AT THE OFFICE ... Cardiff, 2005

before he was ready to claim the top prize. The frustration and volatility of earlier years has been replaced by a greater understanding of himself, of the world he inhabits and the psychological steel required to get the job done.

Bob Radford, longtime journalist, administrator and Crump family friend, is one of many in awe of how Jason shrugged off years of disappointment.

"There has never been any doubt that he so desperately wanted to be world champion – so much at times it almost hurt," says Radford.

"His mental strength must have been both immense and strained during those three years as world number two."

That was never more so than in 2003. To all appearances a more assertive and organised rider than in previous near-miss campaigns, he would be haunted and finally undone by misadventures in three Grand Prix rounds.

He fought back into contention after a wretched night in Sweden but in Krsko he ran out of fuel on the last lap of a semi-final which not only ended his participation but let in a reprieved and relieved Nicki Pedersen.

An incandescent Jason sacked mechanic Ben Powell on the spot but the damage could still be repaired if he got everything right in Hamar. In the event he didn't, when a controversial exclusion after a semi-final third-bend crash with Rune Holta handed Pedersen the championship.

Conspiracy theories abound in speedway and there are individuals close to the Crump camp who believe but could never prove that the exclusion robbed him of the 2003 title.

The rumour mill buzzed with suggestions that the agenda of the sport's power brokers was better served by having a Scandinavian champion than one from unfashionable Australia.

You won't find anyone going on the record but there are those who feel that referees at times find themselves put under pressure – and certainly Polish official Marek Wojaczek's decision to exclude Jason following the infamous coming-together with Holta drew raised eyebrows in some quarters.

Tony Steele, the greatly-respected British referee who has taken control of more Grand Prix meetings than anyone, knows the sort of challenges which confront officials and insists 'it would not be right for me to agree or disagree with any decision made by a colleague'.

Yet even he and other impartial observers recognise that a decision taken from one position, possibly aided by a television replay – also from one position – may not necessarily be a correct one. Steele called it 'refereeing by incident'.

"The referee seemed to have little option from the pictures shown," he said.

"But if you look at how the race was progressing and watch the lines the riders were taking you could come to a different conclusion. You could take the view that Rune had entered bend three too wide and was scrubbing speed off to come back down to the white line.

"Jason was positioned on the inside line and entered the corner at greater speed but was met by the slower rider moving down on him. In such circumstances it is usually the slower-paced rider who comes off the worst.

"The question that has always remained in my mind is: who made the mistake? Jason was riding the traditional tried and tested line. What actually did he do wrong? Could you put forward the view that

Rune made the mistake and was out of position?"

Well, you could. But the technology – a feed from the local television station – rarely has the degree of sophistication available in some other major sports. It's one angle and one man and Wojaczek called it as he saw it.

"Luck does have a habit of working itself out. Jason's commitment and dedication finally brought home the world championship. Many would argue that this was very much overdue. His record is one to be very proud of but I can't help thinking how much better it would be had not the hand of fate stepped in at some very inappropriate moments," said Steele.

Riders have to accept the bad with the good and Jason refused to isolate that exclusion as being his downfall in 2003. Instead he pointed to earlier, avoidable incidents which undermined his position. Significantly, it was a thinking response rather than a reactive one.

Radford is a detached observer with his own take on why maturity, and the world title, was a long time coming.

"When he moved into the senior league Jason was a number one rider immediately, and the pressure thus was always on. I think this contributed a lot to his early hothead or ginger whinger image – had he had senior role models in the teams he rode for it might have helped him adapt to those pressures.

"I think he might have become world champion rather earlier had his choice of clubs been different."

It is a point of view, though not necessarily one in tune with the dictates of today's schedules which expose elite riders to a variety of experiences unknown to their predecessors of generations past.

Club affiliations remain important, though not perhaps as

THE record books show that Tony Rickardsson outpointed Jason Crump in the honours stakes over a period of several years. But day in, day out, Jason has never been short of outstanding – and unsurpassed in the judgment of John Perrin, who as his Belle Vue promoter for three of those years had plenty of first-hand evidence to back his claims.

"You can't argue with what Rickardsson did last year but overall I think Jason has been far better than Rickardsson. His record over a long period of time is remarkable, he doesn't get fazed by any other rider, and he wants to be the best.

"It's great for a team to have someone like that to look up to, a front man who keeps on delivering the goods.

"He wouldn't have been flattered by winning the world title earlier. He had some terrible luck. A couple of really dodgy exclusions, the time his fuel ran out – I believe he was the best rider going around in 2003 as well as 2004.

"You never can tell if he'll win it again but I think he will never be short on ambition."

relevant to a rider's upbringing and development as was the case before Sweden and Poland became at least as competitive, meaningful, star-spangled – and cosmopolitan – as the British League.

These days one essential yardstick of class is measured by a rider's ability to perform at the highest level in all of those Elite Leagues. Few have come close to Jason's record of excellence in this regard, although his focus on the biggest prize of all prompted a decision to cut back on his Swedish involvement in the past couple of years.

That's a loss for the fans because wherever speedway is staged, he is a huge drawcard, his record of achievement matched by a fierce determination to give everything of himself each time he slings a leg across a bike.

He was a crowd-puller in England and Australia from day one, and Swedish and Polish supporters swiftly embraced him. Even though Jason left Vargarna a couple of years ago after a lengthy stint, he remains a massive favourite there.

And in Poland, as in the UK, he's a great drawcard irrespective of having gone through clubs at fairly regular intervals.

It's largely because of an on-track presence as compelling as any rider of his era. Rod Colquhoun of Australia's *Speedway Racing News*, briefly rode with and against Jason before becoming a writer and commentator, and he it was who coined the typically Aussie description of 'the rottweiler on wheels'.

"Jason is the undisputed king of giving 100% and deserves everything he has won," says Colquhoun, who for a couple of years was a Motorycling Australia commissioner.

"I am a huge fan and I love the way he clenches his fist after every race win. It shows he wants it as much as his fans want it for him. He's a star and great with young kids starting out."

Certainly Jason has developed a keen understanding of the relationship between individual ambition and the common good. Yet speedway remains a searching test of personal mettle and nerve. Riders race a high proportion of their meetings in a team environment but in the end, they are solo performers. While the public and private process of growing up will be influenced by people and circumstances, so much of it is up to the individual to shape his own personality and ultimately, his destiny.

Setting yourself a target, and then falling wretchedly short, is a critical examination of character. Jason, often battling to contain a self-confessed volatile nature, grew to know all about of such tests as first he toiled to establish himself among the world's elite, and then, for three or four years, knocked on the door of greatness only to be knocked back time after time.

Observers conscious of his sometimes fiery temperament were prone to tiptoe around the subject. Eventually impatience gave way to a more measured attitude, past disappointment and frustration became an added driving force.

Those who knew how desperately he wanted to be top gun watched him grow mentally stronger.

Crump-watcher Radford detected a new maturity as the ascent to world champion reached its last few steps.

"On the night he won the world title the former top Norwegian star Dag Lovaas made a rare appearance. He'd been very friendly with Phil and wanted to just say hi. An hour from the start Jason not only shook hands, but told Dag that he's heard a lot about him – a nice touch from a sportsman under the most intense pressure at that moment."

Pressure, some say, is when you fear you might not be up to the challenge.

"I did feel I was ready," said Jason when the champagne corks were popping in his honour.

"Everything that went before just made me stronger and more determined."

Life would never be quite the same. Winning a world title is like being an Olympic medalist or an Ashes winner. It's for life.

Membership of such an exclusive club, of course, brings with it new responsibilities which also last more or less indefinitely.

Speedway racing, in common with so many sports, demands a great deal of its champions. They are expected to be clean-cut ambassadors, confident yet gracious, telegenic, all things to all people.

This is especially true of those disciplines which fight a constant battle for recognition, desperate to be spoken of in the same breath as the traditional big-ticket events.

Speedway can point to a long history and loyal support in the United Kingdom and Sweden. It is an authentic and now a huge, high-profile sport in Poland. Reluctantly, its devotees are forced to acknowledge it has become all but invisible in Australia – its birthplace and supposedly spiritual home.

Jason Crump, born in the UK, fashioned by Australia, citizen (as well as champion) of the world, now understands how high are the expectations of speedway folk often unreasonably paranoid that their flag bearer should be a 'good' world champion.

Far from being daunted by the demands which come with the territory – the realisation that every time he jumps on a bike, everybody wants to beat him ... the pressure to be a coherent and convincing spokesman and ambassador whether dealing with a corporate heavyweight or a five-year-old autograph hunter – this is another test he has passed with flying colours.

It is a considerable achievement for one who has negotiated a long and difficult road. Like many a fierce competitor who wears his heart on his sleeve, he hasn't always been a paragon, The journey, however, took him from boy wonder through some fractious years to the pinnacle of the sport and earned him a respect and status he values much more than if it had simply fallen into his lap.

Phil Crump's analysis is that there are few riders in the world better able to lift themselves for the

PHIL Crump was never obsessed with the idea of seeing his son following in his racing footsteps. Given the nature of the Crump family lifestyle in the 1970s and 1980s, though, it did not come as any great surprise that Jason should get involved.

"Looking back, I suppose it was pretty inevitable he would want to ride because he had always been around speedway, going everywhere, travelling to all the tracks," said Phil.

"I wasn't bothered one way or the other – I didn't mind if he did and I really didn't mind if he didn't. But that was the world he knew, he was comfortable with the set-up, and was used to mixing with and talking with riders and referees and tuners.

"The first bike we got him in Mildura was a little Z50 from when I had a Honda motorcycle dealership for a couple of years. It was the most amazing bike, which kept going for years. Jason must have loved it to death because he made enquiries all over the place to get one just like it for Seth – and someone stole it before he'd even had the chance to ride it.

"It's funny how things fall into place. The first bloke to do an engine for him way back was Peter Morris who is now the GM importer for Australia. I knew him because he is John Boulger's cousin and a mate of Mark Gilbert, and we got on well.

"When he was starting to show some promise in juniors Jason asked Peter if he would sort out something and all these years later they still maintain contact and work together with new ideas. Peter does a few sprintcar engines for some American drivers and a bit of that sort of technology is coming into speedway now.

"But Jason always had the ability to get on with people. Riders like Jimmy Nilsen, Bo Petersen, Marvyn Cox and Jeremy Doncaster came out to see us when we were back in Mildura and Jason would be out back racing against them on the junior bikes. He also managed to scam lots of gear from most of them – helmets, gloves, anything that was going.

"We built a house on a 10-acre block of land we had bought and he laid out quite a decent little track behind the property. Even if there was nobody else around, he was in his element because he could ride round there all day long without being a nuisance to anybody."

big occasion than Jason. It is a source of pride for a man, who, according to many pundits, ended up with a world championship record which did not properly recognise his capabilities.

"He's always had that inner ability, being able to get himself up like when he won his first couple of British GPs," said Phil.

"Over time he has developed the knack of going to that next level which you need to do well in the Grand Prix.

"When he had those three years of finishing second anybody could be excused for wondering if he would finally crack it, but from way, way back, I felt he could.

"When he won in 2004 I didn't go crazy or anything, it was just a feeling that this was a proper outcome because a hell of a lot of effort had gone into arriving at that point.

"Last year was a different challenge and I don't think Jason was quite prepared for the amount of scrutiny you're under as a world champion. He worked really hard all year and rode pretty well, and I don't see any reason why he wouldn't world more world titles.

"You would definitely back him against anybody when there is a bit more dirt around.

"But he has learned to deal with things as they are, not as you would ideally like them to be. The

THE daughter of one speedway rider, then wife to another, Jason's mother Carole Crump was sceptical, if eventually resigned to the prospect of seeing Jason embrace speedway as a career.

"I just worried about how it would go," she says.

"It is an exciting life while it lasts but for many riders, they have everything at a young age and then little or no preparation or direction when it comes to life after speedway.

"For most people, they struggle to establish themselves when they are young and then start to consolidate and enjoy more rewards as they get older. Professional sport is not like that at all. And nobody tells you how to deal with things when it all comes to a halt.

"I had seen both sides. My father has had what I am sure he considers to be charmed life, a really great life, racing, then as a tuner and mechanical innovator, and as team manager of Australia. He loved all of those different phases and speedway has given him a very fulfilling time.

"But Phil, like many riders, was really at a loose end when he stopped racing. I wanted us to stay in England after he finished in '86 but for years he had dreamed about coming back to Mildura and that's what we did.

"With what he is doing now, spending the season in England, doing engines and being involved, no doubt it's much better for him. But we don't have any contact. We went our separate ways several years ago and that's how it is."

Carole, who still lives on the Gold Coast, combines a job with Australia Post with studies which, she hopes, may lead to a psychology degree.

"I've moved on, as you have to do," she said.

"The kids were very upset for a while. It was difficult for all of them when I left Phil but I had spent half my life doing what was expected of me and as soon as Gabi was 18 it was time to do what I wanted and needed to do for myself.

"Of course I miss the opportunity to get close to Jason and Melody's kids, especially with them being in England virtually all the time. It is very tough but hopefully there will be some catching up in the not too distant future."

Jason's younger sister, Gabi, 23, lives at home and is forging a successful career as a nail technician and beautician. Justine, 27, lives close by, has two daughters with Nick Sowter, a movie lighting expert, and a good position with National Australia Bank.

opposition, the way the tracks are, all of that stuff you can't influence or control, you have to be able to put to one side and just get on with it.

"That's something he has got better at doing each year."

Jason is a modern man, a star of his generation and one whose reputation will endure. Quirkily enough, the place where he finds himself today is very much what many folk have been anticipating for years.

Almost everybody who was anybody in British or Australian speedway circles in the 1980s got to know Jason Crump, or, at the very least, they knew who he was.

He was the bright-eyed kid with the ginger hair who could be spotted in the pits, chatting to riders and officials, at ease with them all, comfortable in the rareified atmosphere which is peculiar to a race meeting.

Like it or not (and he didn't too much) he was 'Crumpy's kid'.

Phil was an established star of his time, a highly-respected, much decorated and extremely professional rider who for the best part of two decades regularly beat the best and rightly was accorded gun status.

And in the middle and latter part of his father's career, Jason was a regular member of the support team, eager to help, diligent when it came to attending to duties such as fuelling and oiling, changing wheels, carting equipment in and out, and always hugely supportive.

From a very early age his was a perfect vantage point from which to observe and experience the highs and the disappointments, the travel from one hemisphere to another, the hectic demands of a European season, the hours spent in the workshop.

While many of his attitudes and attributes were fashioned and refined in country Victoria, he also enjoyed the huge benefits of a racing education on the run, so to speak, for as long as Phil Crump was a much prized British League and international rider.

Much in speedway has altered in the 35 years since Phil first ventured to England. It went through one of its most significant technological changes in 1975 – the year Jason was born – when Neil Street master-minded and Phil did so much to advance the cause of the four-valve engine.

These days much of the equipment of that era is virtually stone age technology, supplanted by the development of lay-down engines, leading front forks, not to mention dirt deflectors, air fences and other symbols of modernity.

The international schedule of British and colonial racers way back then might have included a few weekend trips to the continent. Now the boys criss-cross Europe for a series of high-profile world championship events, and routinely include weekly club meetings in Poland and Sweden. Before long, you can add Russia to that list.

And yet, in this, the 12th year of the Grand Prix – attended by riders in multi-coloured gear adorned by the names of their sponsors, back-up teams wheeling one glittering machine after another from the expensively kitted motor homes – in many ways the more things change, the more they stay the same.

Jason Crump, as professional, focused and committed as any of his famed predecessors, if better rewarded than many of them, remains true to the sentiments which made his portable classroom a magic place to be when he was still in short trousers. He just loves to go to the races. And loves to win.

It's not just about getting on a bike and going flat out. It isn't about collecting a fat pay cheque at the end of another successful meet.

It's the way of life.

It is a tough gig, and not one of the 31 men whose names have adorned speedway's world championship trophy had a longer, more detailed examination of their credentials. The learning curve seemed to go on for ever.

"I had my doubts, of course I did," says Jason.

"I got so close to winning the world title a few times and kept missing out. However focused and confident you are, you're bound to end up wondering whether you might have missed your chance.

"But what would you be if you didn't keep trying?

"It is very, very tough, and whatever the old timers say, I think almost everyone recognises that it's never been tougher than since the Grand Prix come in.

"In the days of the one-off World Final, quite a few people won the title in their early 20s. The trick was to be able to beat everyone on one given night.

"I won my first Grand Prix less than a month after turning 21, but I was still pretty much a kid. If I had been world champion at that point I don't think there is any way I would have achieved what I have over the past few years – I didn't have a clue about what was involved."

As he has been from his earliest racing days, Jason of course is being hard on himself.

At 21 he was as talented, as educated in the ways of the sport and as plausible a candidate for the highest honours as Peter Collins had been at the same age. Whatever some of the old-timers and traditionalists may say, the road he took to become the world's No.1 is convincing evidence of an unprecedented contemporary cutting edge of competition.

Jason Crump stood out from the beginning as much for his hair colour as his heritage.

If you're ginger, it seems, nothing can protect you against the inevitability of comments about your appearance and the perceived character traits that go along with it.

Which, to all the world's non-redheads, gives rise to the assumption that underneath the carrot thatch, there's a short fuse burning. Mind, if you're hit with that line a million times, there would seem to be some justification for making it a self-fulfilling prophesy.

Subsequently he could console himself with the thought that famous redheads have included names like Boris Becker, Ginger Spice, Billy Bremner and Sir Winston Churchill

WINNING INSTINCT ... on the way to victory in Malilla, 2005

and for them, red hair proved no disqualification to achievement.

Underneath a racing helmet, the physical traits are not obvious but body language and attitude say a lot. Whether it's in front of 40,000 at Cardiff or a couple of thousand at a country track in the middle of nowhere, Jason Crump is a racer and a fierce competitor, very Australian in his attitude to getting the job done.

The Australian sporting psyche has attracted worldwide attention. If you think Polish followers are demanding, be aware that Aussies are even more so. They're hard markers. Any tributes from his fellow-countrymen, then, can be taken as the real thing.

Grandfather Neil Street, whom Jason credits as possibly the greatest influence on his rise to the top, might be accused of bias.

Those who know him, however, recognise his opinions to be as sage and balanced as any and the respect is entirely mutual.

The input of the wise old man of Australian speedway has been immense as Jason learned to be fatalistic about circumstances he could not control ... referees, track conditions, an unfavourable draw and the rest.

Arguably the best rider in the world in at least two or three of the years in which he missed out on the ultimate accolade, he was determined not to fall into that over-subscribed category of riders successively branded 'the best never to win the world title'.

Street did not doubt him and made sure he didn't doubt himself too much.

"He had the all-round ability, the attributes required to win, and was so consistent in England, Sweden and Poland for a number of years," said Street.

"Running second in the Grand Prix for three years in a row was a sign of strength, not weakness. He never forgot the lessons of those disappointments, and learned to handle things. I was sure he would come good.

"He's always had a bit of fire, always anxious to do his best. Like most riders he would get wound up and chuck things around a bit.

"But he's worked at it and he had to find a way that worked for

FROM the back yard in Mildura to the stadiums of the world – Jason's grandfather Neil Street has seen it all, and has been a constant source of encouragement and advice. He has fond memories of a chirpy, engaging youngster who always was comfortable on and with bikes and riders.

Neil, who had been such a mentor for Phil Crump and later became his father-in-law, frequently spent a few weeks of the Australian summer fruit picking at the family property in Mildura.

"Jason was usually riding his little 125 around the back yard, doing practice starts with me as the starter. He was so enthusiastic, as kids often are. You can't stop them. They never miss anything – it's like they have a big sponge in their head at that age. At race meetings, Jason knew exactly what every rider had done that night.

"And when Phil was riding, he had no difficulty getting along with the other riders. I have this picture in my mind of him at Cradley one time, I don't know how old he was but he was about the same size as Erik Gundersen and the two of them were just sitting there together discussing things like a couple of little old men.

"It was no surprise that he wanted to race. And when he did, he went about it properly, learning how to do things. Of course he was always aggressive, always ready to have a go.

"His parents helped him but in different ways. I'm sure Phil's career had a big influence on Jason but he wanted to do things his way. And his mother was a huge support. She regularly drove him to Adelaide in the pick-up because Phil was still riding in Australia at that time.

"He was a fairly remarkable kid who didn't just think of himself. He was racing in South Australia one time and although it was a long trip home, he insisted on going to see Todd Wiltshire who was in hospital after a pretty major pile-up.

"As a kid he always had compassion, and as a big brother he was very protective and caring with his sisters. My mother, who was a well-read and worldly woman who had a bit of psychic power, said she had never seen a boy who looked after his siblings with such sensitivity.

"He could be a bit of a handful at times, like all lively young boys, but Carole never did her block with him – she gave him such a lot. She's a reasonable, intelligent and businesslike person and there's a lot of that in him."

him, which you have to say he has done pretty successfully.

"The way he accepted Cardiff last year when the referee shot him to pieces, that was all class."

It was in the British GP of 2005 that Jason, as the reigning world champion, realised his tenure on the title was likely to be short-lived, this after starting the year favourite to regain the championship. His refereeing nemesis Mr Wojaczek saw to that, controversially excluding him three times in the qualifying heats. But given the nature of his earlier experiences, he quickly filed that one away as just another day at the office. There's always another chance.

"In earlier years he probably would have blown up at everybody," says Alun Rossiter, who sat outside the back of the Cardiff pits with him as Jason came to terms with the enormity of one of his most spectacular GP disasters.

"But in the last couple of years he has grown up so much."

Arguably his greatest accomplishment so far has been to demonstrate to himself – as well as the doubters – that he had the steel and personality required to negotiate a succession of trials and tribulations. For a few years, there were those who wondered if he could and some who had serious doubts.

Peter White, veteran editor of Australia's *Speedway World* magazine, a champion of Aussie riders for almost four decades, and a keen student of history, admits it was a long wait he feared might prove fruitless.

"I have been his greatest proponent for years and it got to the point where I reckoned he might have hiccupped once too often," he says.

"It was not a matter of being disloyal, you just could not help wondering how many disappointments he could take. I'm so glad to have been proved wrong.

"Jim Shepherd – who has been writing about solos for even longer than me – believed Jason's destiny was to be world champion, that it was written in the stars, and he was right."

Mick Poole, one of Australia's most accomplished and best-respected riders of recent years, has long been quick to defend Jason against critics as well as being at the head of the queue of those whose congratulations have been genuine and heartfelt.

"I might sound a bit biased towards him but he is a mate and I am the first to jump to his defence when somebody is bagging him," says Poole, whose 14-year-old son Taylor is cutting a dash in junior speedway.

"When the racing starts the bullshit stops in no uncertain terms for Ginger. He is very, very serious about what he is out to do and obviously is not afraid to show it, unlike some other riders who can be cool, calm and collected.

"He does get a lot of bad press about his personality especially over here, but if you book Ginger to ride you are guaranteed to get a good crowd as he is a bit different to all the other guys and people want to see what he is all about. It`s not a show he puts on to make him more hardcore – it`s just plain and simple the way he goes about trying to be the best speedway rider which he believes he is.

"Everybody knows when you ride against him that if you make the start on him you had better go for it. He will be all over your back wheel, trying to get past and will not give up. All the times I rode against him he always gave you room. Sure there have been times when he has pushed and barged but if you can show me one rider who hasn`t done it and been successful I will shake his hand.

"You always hear the cliche 'the sport needs a character'. I think we have one larger than life in Jason, He has done a lot for speedway over the last ten years or so.

"Has there ever been a world champion willing to drive 12 hours overnight to ride for no payment at a track, then ask that track to make a donation to the junior speedway club, run a free training school the next day and give new goggles to all the kids who participated?

"He came to present the trophies at the 2005 Australian junior speedway titles at Somersby and roamed around the pits chatting to all the kids.

"You can imagine what the kids think of him. That's the kind of bloke Jason is."

Brendon Gledhill, administrator and doyen of the Mildura Motorcycle Club where Jason had his first rides, is another who speaks with pride of the boy who became a champion.

He, and the Mildura junior club, were beneficiaries of the generosity to which Poole referred.

"Jason had taken some flak from some quarters, based on a perceived attitude to not riding in Australia. I have always acknowledged and publicly stated and written that these guys are in Australia on their 'annual leave' when they are here for just a few weeks, basically to have Christmas with their families.

"Some of them now have commitments with kids and school all of which needs to come into serious consideration. They also use the opportunity to repair their bodies and freshen up their minds before heading back to another gruelling season in UK and Europe.

"As a youngster Jason could be a bit of a hot head and even now you will find people who will bag him and don't like him – there's always someone ready to knock a champion, it goes with the territory. But I've only ever found him to be a good lad. I think he's just been incredibly hard on himself, he really beats himself up when things go wrong.

"People who have got on the wrong side of him often haven't appreciated that there's a time and a place for everything. It's best to pick the right moment. In that respect Jason is not so different too most top sportsmen."

Former school mate Darryl Nicol also pays tribute to Jason's ability to re-connect with his roots.

"I think a true sign of the type of person he is, was reflected in the way he handled himself on return

THANKS MATE ... Jason with Neil ('Bill') Street, his grandfather, mentor and 'best mate'

visits to Mildura during the off season in England," he said:

"He would always be straight on to the phone when he arrived arranging to catch up for a beer with his old mates. We would all go out to the Sandbar pub and have a laugh about old times.

"People would come up and chat to Jason about speedway and his successes and he would always be polite and be prepared to give them some of his time.

"I think that champions have the potential to forget where they have come from, but this is definitely not the case with Jason."

While his mates always had Jason marked down as a star in the making, his father had reservations.

"For some reason, I just didn't think he would be good enough," said Phil.

"I didn't think he would make a speedway rider until he started to impress as junior level, along with a lot of other Australian youngsters of that era.

"Once he started racing, though, I could see he was going to be bloody good. He was always very fast and could make a lot of speed somehow.

"I'm obviously very proud of what he has achieved so far."

With the best will in the world, though, fathers and sons can be an incendiary cocktail, especially in the pressure-cooker atmosphere of elite sport. Jason's determination to succeed on his own terms and Phil's natural wish to see him do well have not always followed a parallel or harmonious path.

They have had some spectacular disagreements over the years.

Early in the piece, or after half a lifetime, parents still tend to think they know best.

Phil, however, has been based in England for the past four or five speedway seasons and is a part of a sparky but generally harmonious back-up team at the Grand Prix meetings, along with Jason's uncle Adrian (Drew to almost everybody).

Drew, Neil Street's younger son, has been on the scene since he drove a 16-year-old new arrival to and from his first senior meetings. No shrinking violet himself, he has managed to exert an easy and usually calming influence which Jason is always keen to acknowledge.

"He and his father are still fighting," says Drew with a shrug of resignation.

"Jason can be fiery, that's always been the case, but Phil can't help himself sometimes, getting frustrated and saying the wrong thing at the wrong moment.

"What he forgets is that what worked for him does not necessarily work for anyone else. Everybody has to do things their own way.

"I have lost count of the number of times I've had to be the peacemaker. That sort of stuff is not good when you're trying to focus all your energies on the job in hand.

"When Jason is set on a particular course of action, whether it's changing gear, or choosing a gate position, I let him bounce things off me but very rarely do I try to influence him. He's watching everything, he can assess what is going on.

"But it's still a test to put it all together on the night. I think it took until about 2003 before Jason really got the hang of it."

His maturing as an individual as well as a speedway rider capable of translating his enormous potential into crowning achievement was played out against a background of a family scenario fractured when Phil and Carole went their separate ways.

It was a traumatic time and one which, according to his grandfather and uncle, probably affected Jason more than he was prepared to admit. He didn't relish being caught in the middle of the situation or the difficulties it imposed on what had been a close relationship with his mother and two sisters.

For support outside the family circle, he was able to turn to a handful of trusted friends on either side of the globe, sometime manager Neil Bird being one such.

It was almost like turning back the clock as Bird, who spent 12 years working on the road racing grand prix circuit, had been a rock of support as Jason negotiated his teens and early twenties.

"Sometimes it is difficult for youngsters to talk to their parents but we always got on well. Years ago Phil or Carole would ring me to see if I could talk to him about different things. He's actually always been mature for his age."

Bird has no doubt about the

hugely positive contribution of Jason's wife and longtime partner Melody in helping him deal with both the personal and professional tribulations.

"She has been a tower of strength."

At Jason's side as the constant calming presence in his life, the slim blonde with the fashion magazine looks has been enormously influential. They've been together for nine years, have two bright-as-a-button kids (Mia, who will be seven this year and Seth, who is turning three) and a desirable home base in the country near Northampton in England's south midlands.

After spending so many days at speedway, so many hours traveling by road and air, this is the haven to which the hard man of the track can retreat, to gather his thoughts and prepare for the next challenge. And at home, he is far removed from his public image.

Not all wives are thrilled to have their man about the house but Mel, who isn't afraid to tell it as it is, says Jason is 'fantastic' with the children, a doting, loving, hands-on father, a considerate husband, can whip up a mean pasta and is by nature a generous, giving person.

Many elite sports personalities live cocooned in a world of their own – it goes with the territory to a certain extent. But Jason is not one to permanently isolate himself. He is articulate, will happily sustain a conversation with people from all walks of life, and debate with vigour on any topic which grabs him.

This is not to say that he is everybody's friend. He does not suffer fools gladly, is unfraid to voice an opinion which might clash with the widely accepted order of things. He has been accused of arrogance, bad temper and poor manners and in that respect he is on par with just about every public figure who ever lived.

In Neil Bird's words 'with Jason you either love him or dislike him' and on track or away from it, he creates an impression few will ignore. By the time he's stopped beating all the best speedway riders in the world, perhaps, he will become more widely loved and of course, he'll cop it however it goes.

Having absorbed the lessons and met the challenges of his defining years, Jason Crump now has the opportunity to establish himself, not just as one of the best of his time, but one of the best riders the sport has seen. The demons have been exorcised, the monkey is off his back, but the passion and the hunger is undiminished.

He embraces the philosophy which points out that once you have scaled the mountain, you have to keep climbing just to stay at the same altitude.

"I can't say how long it will be but as long as I continue to be competitive enough to win in the Grand Prix, I'll keep trying to improve, to learn, and to be the best I can be," he says.

Any young pretenders may as well reconcile themselves to the fact that their wait could well be as lengthy as the one which ultimately prepared Jason Crump for his towering achievement.

3 SUNDAY
277/089 Week 40

TAS and New Zealand Daylight Savings starts.
Move clock forward one hour at 2am.

7:00

8:00

I've just put the phone down from Domino's Pizza in Northampton.

9:00

I'm lying back in 'my' couch watching Football Sunday on the television.

10:00

'Did you order me a mini pizza Dad?' Mia asks, concerned but secretly aware of the reassuring answer. Do you think I would have forgotten?

11:00

She smiles and runs off to play with her brother.

12:00

What happened last night has not been mentioned for around 4 hours. The bags are unpacked. Melody is checking if Mia's school uniform is sorted for tomorrow morning and the kids are laughing about some game they're playing.

1:00

It could be any day in any household. The only tell tale reminder of what had occurred less than 24 hours beforehand was the pizza delivery boy's extreme enthusiasm when I gave my name over the phone and his then assurance that my delivery would arrive swiftly.

2:00

3:00

I slouch down even further into the couch I so look forward to returning to, beer in 1 hand, t.v. remote in the other.

4:00

I grin to myself, as of around 10:00pm last night I became 'Jason Crump – Speedway World Champion'

5:00

Life's good!

6:00

I could stay like this forever.

7:00

January

S	M	T	W	T	F	S
				1	2	3
4	5	6	7	8	9	10
11	12	13	14	15	16	17
18	19	20	21	22	23	24
25	26	27	28	29	30	31

February

S	M	T	W	T	F	S
1	2	3	4	5	6	7
8	9	10	11	12	13	14
15	16	17	18	19	20	21
22	23	24	25	26	27	28
29						

March

S	M	T	W	T	F	S
	1	2	3	4	5	6
7	8	9	10	11	12	13
14	15	16	17	18	19	20
21	22	23	24	25	26	27
28	29	30	31			

April

S	M	T	W	T	F	S
				1	2	3
4	5	6	7	8	9	10
11	12	13	14	15	16	17
18	19	20	21	22	23	24
25	26	27	28	29	30	

May

S	M	T	W	T	F	S
						1
2	3	4	5	6	7	8
9	10	11	12	13	14	15
16	17	18	19	20	21	22
23	24	25	26	27	28	29
30	31					

JASON CRUMP world champion

Some people spend all their life chasing a dream and I'm fortunate enough to have realised mine, which was to become world speedway champion.

From an early age, that was what I wanted. Not just a speedway rider, but the best.

I have never been afraid to say what I think, or backward in coming forward. If others have a problem with that, it's their problem, not mine. At times it quite amuses me, actually, being criticised by people who really don't know me or understand what makes me tick.

Chasing that No.1 spot, that's always been what it's about.

I loved the various successes along the way, national titles, the World Under 21, then three World Team Cup wins with Australia.

Still, what I most wanted was a 'world' of my own.

'Jason could finish up as one of the greats. I know it took him until he was 29 to win the thing, but what pressure he must have been under after being runner-up for three years in a row. But there was this goal, this target he had grown up dreaming about and going for since he was a little kid. He has this burning desire and he's just been fantastic in recent years'

– former world champion Peter Collins OBE

GOING FOR IT ... Eskilstuna GP, 2005

Once one target is achieved, though, you have to re-set your goals. It was a lot of hard work, a long, tough road, a real learning curve. I would do it all over again, in a minute.

If I never add to the title I won in 2004, it won't destroy me – but it would be a long way short of the truth to suggest that I am anything but fired up to produce a repeat performance or two.

I've had a heck of a run in the world championship, spent the past five years in the top two, and there are no plans to walk away from it any time soon. My ambition is to remain competitive, to be organised, motivated and healthy enough to give myself the opportunity to win again.

There is a saying in sport that the more you win, the more fun it is. As any competitor will tell you, there is no fun greater than winning. Coming second – a habit I have sometimes found difficult to shake – never, ever, tastes remotely as sweet.

But in 2005, I tried my hardest to be a credit to the sport and to the role of world champion. It was new territory, being the defending champion rather than the guy chasing for that elusive top spot. However, that's what comes with the deal, which also includes a lot more attention from all sorts of directions.

There were demands on my time and energy which I worked hard to fulfil. More press, more expectations, more everything. I don't think it seriously impacted on my title campaign but possibly it did in some small ways. Only nine guys of the 31 who have been speedway world champion have ever won back to back, but each case is different.

Of the others, some outstanding riders have managed to come back and win again, including a few who rank among the greatest names in the business. Ove Fundin, Ole Olsen, Tony Rickardsson. They all 'failed' to defend the title after their first victory, but it didn't affect their ability to return to the winners' circle in subsequent years. In fact, they all returned better, stronger, and more accomplished.

Maybe you have to give up a world title to fully appreciate what it means to win one.

When it comes right down to it, I didn't 'lose' the world title. You start with a clean slate every year and from most aspects, last year was another year of considerable achievement.

I was pretty consistent, had a decent number of good meetings, including victories in Eskilstuna and Malilla, and qualified for seven finals. In almost any other year it would have been enough to take out another world title.

But the nightmare at Cardiff, where I was excluded three times, pretty much put paid to my hopes of keeping in touch with Tony Rickardsson. That night, along with the gut-wrenching disappointment in Norway in 2003, when a title was there for the taking, goes down among my all-time bad memories.

In all the other years since the Grand Prix replaced the old one-off World Final it had been possible, if not advisable, to have the odd poor meeting. This time the pace being set was so unbelievably hot, there was no way of recovering from such a disaster.

However the fact that I won the title once, after some near misses and many years of trying, doesn't make me any less keen to show that I can do it again, provided everything comes together. Just because my 30th birthday has come and gone doesn't mean it's time for carpet slippers, armchair and a pipe by the fire.

Achieving a long-standing ambition can sharpen your hunger for more or tempt you to snuggle up in a comfort zone. If you think you have reached a peak and it can never get better than this, then you probably won't repeat the performance. If, on the other hand, you know there are more mountains to climb, more rewards on offer, it's all the motivation you need.

The whole point of racing speedway at the highest level is to expose yourself to the toughest challenge of skill, character and staying power. Negotiate one hurdle, there will be another one along in just a minute. Pass one test, then prepare for the next. Do your best to make every post a winner.

And if, as has been the case with me on several occasions, you don't succeed, then you need to do whatever it takes to sort yourself out and then come back for more, positive, focused and energised, and with your attitude – and appetite – even stronger.

This year it will be important not to lose the plot or become distracted by any sideshows.

Realistically, even though it is the great sporting cliché, you really do have to take things one step at a time.

The years in which I went close, then closer still, but seemed always to be a tantalising step away from that elusive world title, I now realise were all about learning – gaining experience, developing coping mechanisms and working out which piece came next in what always was going to be a complicated jigsaw to complete.

It has been much more than my opposition that I have had to contend with in the past few years. There is so much to learn and experience before you can start thinking about winning the big prizes, and that includes coming to terms with your own strengths and weaknesses as well as those of everybody else.

Of course the initial pleasure of moving myself out of the ranks of the also-rans into those of the contenders for the world championship gave way to some frustrations. You think of the effort that has gone in over time, the ifs and buts and maybes and might have beens. You replay races, meetings, entire seasons and tend to think that it took only a bit of luck here or a different call there and everything might have come together much earlier.

But those near misses, the disappointments which accompanied them, must have taught me something. The big lesson is that if you have a goal, you just need to keep going, to maintain your belief, to learn from the lessons, to go to each race that little bit wiser and better prepared than before.

It's too easy and way too self-indulgent to brood over a missed opportunity or an unlucky break. Time tends to put it all into perspective. You get a bad draw one day, you'll make up for it on another occasion. There are meetings when everything runs like clockwork but however well organised you are, inevitably there'll be others in which things don't work out according to plan.

At this stage of my career I hope and believe that I have absorbed the lessons, grown stronger from the various experiences, have found the best way to manage myself, my workload and my life. If you can't make every post a winner, at least there is an opportunity to learn something from everything that happens, and that includes coming second again in 2005.

The champions of the past probably didn't lose too much sleep about the opposition and nothing has changed. You can't afford that luxury. What matters is that there will be more opportunities for me, and I want to prepare myself the best way possible and give myself the maximum chance of being competitive when it counts. I am enjoying the challenge and look forward to being involved in quite a few more title bids.

I'm not under any illusions about things getting easier. The same goes for the rest of the guys, and, as one year follows another, there will be others older, wiser and also giving themselves a better chance than before.

Very likely the competition will become even greater and it is the development and emergence of new challengers that keeps sport interesting from season to season. When the top guns of a previous era have moved on,

CONFIRMATION ... Jason Crump with the world championship trophy he pursued so relentlessly for so long

there has never been a shortage of newcomers putting up their hand to be the next big thing.

In one sense, chasing the big prize is why we get out of bed in the morning. Yet in another way, just having the chance to go racing, to pit your skills and your wits against top competition, to meet and deal with a succession of challenges and challengers, that's the business we're in.

In the Grand Prix it's so much about individual ambition and achievement – that much said, it is impossible to think about taking out a world championship without having some fantastic support and a back-up team similarly driven and focused on the task in hand.

It is all such a highly-charged, personal thing and it demands a single-minded and often selfish approach; it's good to be able to share the moment with people who commit themselves to the cause and make important contributions in so many ways.

For much of the time, though, we're involved in club competition, striving for team success which means so much to all concerned. I've been in championship and cup-winning sides in England, Sweden and Poland and it is important to be in a happy, cohesive set-up where people are pulling in the same direction.

JIM Lynch, initially a sponsor, later Jason's promoter at Peterborough, and now newly in charge at Reading, is one of a band of admirers who consider that his elevation to world champion was a belated, if appropriate acknowledgement of his special talent.

"Winning the world title was something that had to happen. People tend to forget that he was the best rider going around for three years before he won it,' says Lynch.

"It was such an achievement to get there after all he had gone through, and although he didn't go back to back, he was a great ambassador as world champion. He took the responsibility seriously, made himself available, spoke frankly and honestly and very well.

"Jason is more than just a fantastic rider, he's always been a showman and I have never known a rider who is better with kids.

"The amazing thing is that he is nothing like the person a lot of people think he is. He is one of the nicest people I have ever been associated with.

"He so appreciates what people have done for him. He just doesn't forget. When he won the world title he took out an advertisement to acknowledge those who have helped him along the way and the list included people who had maybe done one small thing for him years before.

"There are those who have complained that he is very insular, very self-centred to the point of rudeness. But when it is time for business, he is all business. When he puts the kevlars on and it's 7.25pm, he's entirely tuned in to one thing and that's racing.

"He's funny though, he has a real dry sense of humour and he doesn't mind at all taking the mickey out of himself. He understands that part of the deal is to have fans who boo you and give you stick but that it's all show business. He could be upset by it but in fact he finds it particularly amusing that he gets the criticism he does and provokes a reaction from people who really don't know him at all.

"Not all riders have the balanced persona that Jason does, and Mel, she's a perfect foil, an absolute joy."

For most people who regularly go to watch speedway, just like a large number of us who race, the programme contains 80 to 90 per cent domestic meetings. So it is important not to under-estimate the importance of the so-called 'bread and butter' stuff.

The intensity of the Grand Prix rounds is something you have to learn to come to terms with, to prepare for, to be fantastically organised and detailed in your professionalism. Racing anywhere, at any level, is a highly-charged, emotional business and at the big events it's magnified to a degree you can't begin to explain.

It would be intolerable to be subjected to the same degree of pressure all the time. Bit it's never going to be a case of turning up and expecting things to just happen. Winners want to cultivate and maintain the winning habit because you need to be in some kind of groove before you step into the really big occasions.

Your run of the mill league match might contain a couple of Grand Prix riders on either side, although it's not the same as having three of them lining up beside you in every race. That is not to say that any match, or any opponent, can be taken for granted because lurking in the reserve berth of the other team there's probably some ambitious new young spark who is just bursting to make a name for himself.

And that's fine, because that is what racing is all about. Just getting on a bike and having a skid round the back paddock or on a practice run is good fun, it's something we all do instinctively and most of us have been doing so for years. That's the way we are. Put two or three guys alongside, and it's on for young and old.

I'll have fun charging around with a couple of mates with nobody watching and I'll enjoy going shoulder to shoulder with a world-class rival in front of 20,000 in a Polish League match. Battling for Belle Vue against Coventry with a league title or cup at stake or riding in a highly-charged local derby in Sweden, it's all part of the same package.

Never let anybody tell you that what we do is anything but exciting. Of course there's a load of stuff attached to it – tracks which are not always ideal for racing, knocks and bangs, a relentless travel schedule, hours on the road or in a plane, promoters, supporters, bikes which break down, jealousies, rivalries and petty politics.

And then there's the other side, the special days when everything comes together, wins materialise like clockwork, an engine which pulls like a rocket, seeing the sights, dealing with professionals on and off the track, bringing pleasure to fans who support their favourites through thick and thin.

Weighed up, all those plus factors so far outweigh the minuses. We can all get pretty cranky at times when things are not going right, and like most things worth doing, you don't get it right without having to commit a great deal of yourself to the process. It's still better than doing some humdrum job for an average weekly wage and toiling your seemingly never-ending way towards a pension and a gold watch.

For quite a few years I could never quite be sure whether it was a gift or a curse to be a professional racer. There are such highs and lows, it plays with your emotions and it can play with your mind. It's easy to have something of a love-hate relationship with it. Then again, you're a long time retired.

Winning the world title has at last enabled me to stop for a moment, to take stock of what I have done, where I came from, where I've been and where I am going. And I have been incredibly privileged to come this way. The sport has brought me life experiences which most people can only fantasise about, and a standard of living which, if I'm smart, should set me up for the future.

At the end of the day, though, it isn't splitting the atom of finding a cure for AIDS. Even in sporting terms, it's not remotely on the same scale as, say, playing soccer for Manchester United, or cricket for Australia. It definitely isn't like being on the golf tour or the tennis circuit and winning a million dollars in a single tournament.

Yet speedway appeals to thousands of people and we get to race in front of enthusiastic spectators in all sorts of places. As a youngster starting out, I used to love telling my mates that I'd just been in Germany or Sweden or some other location which to many was no more than a spot on the atlas.

But in a funny sort of way, being a big fish in a reasonably small pond, which motorcycle racing is on the global scale of things, has kept me in touch with reality. I am happy with my lot, happy with my life, thrilled with a family who I love and who love me whether I've won a big race or run a last.

A quiet night in, a good book, a rough and tumble game with the kids – these are the real prizes in life and every bit as much of my existence, more so in fact, than sitting at the starting tapes with a motor revving its head off, and then, perhaps a minute later, punching the air as the chequered flag is shown.

Maybe that doesn't sound like a fired-up, ferocious racer who takes no prisoners and eats raw meat but it is a necessary part of maintaining some balance. If according to some people I prowled around like a bear with a sore head for years, then the growing-up did not come a moment too soon.

There are some ways, however, in which I won't change as long as I am racing. Every single race is a challenge to the ego, a chance to test yourself. It's what we do. Each Grand Prix is like a mini-World Final in itself, the tensions, the atmosphere, the ferocious competition all designed to sort the men from the boys.

It can be intimidating but basically, if you're stimulated by it, if you're up for it, then you know you are in the right business. When it stops providing that sort of reaction, it's time to go.

So coming second in the world once more has sharpened rather than lessened my ambition. There is no point anybody wasting time and energy by wishing they had been around in a slightly different era. You're who you are when it's your time. Guys like Ole Olsen would be the first to say that if it

PARENTAL GUIDANCE ... Phil, Hamar, Norway, 2004 ... Carole, Broadford, Victoria, 2002

hadn't been Ivan Mauger in his way then it could easily have been someone else making things difficult for him and the rest.

To look at things from a broader perspective, Tony Rickardsson has been a boon for speedway because he has been able to do a massive amount of good for its projection and image. In a time when television has put the sport into places it never penetrated before, he has done plenty to lift its profile.

It's a shame that as the first Australian to win the championship for more than 50 years, I couldn't have had a more definite and positive impact there.

I can hear some people in Aussie saying that this sounds rich coming from someone who breezes in and out only occasionally and hasn't made a major play on the scene over there in recent times.

But I am not the one responsible for the state of solos in Australia. The problems and the low-key image it has is part of a situation that has existed for many more years than I have been around.

If I had ridden more there in the past few years it might have made some limited impact but would not have done anything to influence the big picture.

The cold hard truth is that in spite of the sentimental and historical connections which according to the record books kicked off in 1923 at West Maitland Showground – just down the road from where my wife Melody and her folks come – 'world' speedway these days is in truth all centred in and around Europe.

It would be great if the Grand Prix took in Australia (as it did in 2002) and New Zealand, but sadly I don't think it is going to happen in the foreseeable future. It would be terrific if the United States featured on the GP roster, too, but things went backwards there at a great rate after the 1982 Los Angeles World Final.

For now, Europe is it, and with things situated as they are, Tony Rickardsson has been an ambassador, a flag bearer and a major player as speedway, and especially the GP, has stretched its boundaries. It's no exaggeration to suggest that he has taken things to another level just as Ivan Mauger did in the 1970s.

Life goes on and with a bit of luck I can win again – on merit – as I did in 2004, and it would give me the greatest pleasure to be No.1 again. And again. You just never know what fortune has in store.

EUROPEAN EXTRAVAGANZA ... celebration wheelie after the last heat of Torun's 44-46 win over Polonia Bydgoszcz, 2004

There have been some great (as well as some not so special) one-time champions. It possibly would not have taken much for old-time riders such as Peter Collins or Michael Lee to have won more than a single world title and few would have begrudged them another. I think Per Jonsson was a big chance to win a second one before his tragic accident.

As is always the case, when the GP is on again, I won't be the only rider approaching the future with optimism. Critics described last year's world championship as disappointing but probably there are three or four riders who, by upping their level of performance by three or four per cent, put themselves in with a real shout.

There are such small margins between winning and losing in elite sport. The favourite can be off his game by a couple of per cent and the next guy is there waiting to pounce. Even in a head to head confrontation, often it doesn't take much to tip the scales.

I paid my dues and always felt confident that it was my destiny to be world champion. It seemed as if it took for ever yet Ivan didn't win the first of his six until he was almost 29, pretty much the same age as I was – give or take a few weeks. He was close to 40 when he won his final title.

I'm not about to look into any crystal ball but if I am still racing at that age then hopefully it will be because I have continued to be still in with a show.

Time and history will take care of things.

I managed to become more relaxed about domestic speedway and able to handle the odd setback without seriously affecting my ability to win races on a regular basis. There is no good reason why I can't be more relaxed about the Grand Prix series and I don't intend to stress myself out of contention next time because someone happened to knock me off the top spot last year.

It is too easy to be up and down like a yo-yo, to be crestfallen when all the best-laid plans for a race or a meeting go pear-shaped, and then to be unreasonably hyper when on another occasion it all works like a dream. The trick is to maintain some sort of consistent level of performance and mentality, not to get too down on yourself (which I always used to do) or too far ahead of yourself (been there and done that, too).

JASON'S first visit to Poland was memorable in several respects – and never forgotten by James Easter, the Ipswich travel agent who was the Australian team manager at the time.

The year was 1986, elder statesman Phil Crump was winding down his career, and led a youthful team to Leszno to contest a World Team Cup round. Never keen on flying, Phil drove to the meeting with Jason along for the ride to dope and oil for his dad.

"It had rained all night, the track was a mess, and three hours before start time we had no chance of a race meeting. Suddenly five lorry loads of straw arrived, which the local Communist Sports Body spread over the track. Next came a petrol bowser which perplexed us all and this then emptied waste oil all over the straw," said Easter.

"We were all pushed back into the pits, and the buggers set fire to the lot. It was an amazing sight, enjoyed immensely by an 11-year-old red-haired Aussie boy who was excited by the display of naked arson. The straw burnt out, and we had a rock hard track. Next half the town's bus fleet arrived and tyre-packed the place until it was a perfect surface ... an amazing event."

When the meeting got under way, Easter observed the youngster expertly going about his business in the pits, loving each minute of his involvement and absorbing every detail.

"Most of all I remembered arranging his Polish visa, and realising that instead of Mildura, Jason was actually a British-born lad who originated from Bristol."

The item of information was to prove invaluable several years later when Easter, newly installed as co-promoter of Peterborough along with Peter Oakes, signed the now 16-year-old for his first full British season – as a two-point rider on an ACU licence.

TELEVISION'S *Funniest Home Videos* show and the 'what happened next' segment on *A Question of Sport* don't have a monopoly on embarrassing moments.

And it's in the nature of our business that every speedway rider's highlights package contains a few less than memorable occasions. Falling off when you're not even racing isn't the most dignified look.

But sitting spreadeagled on the Viking Ship track in Hamar, Norway, with thousands of people laughing at my pathetic efforts to celebrate winning the 2004 world championship, I just didn't care.

For five seconds or so, time seemed to be suspended. Then I was laughing myself.

After a lifetime of working towards this moment, I was world speedway champion. The hounds who had been on my heels during the season could bark all they liked. I was home free at last.

Three years as the 'nearly' man, runner-up in the Grand Prix in 2001, 2002 and 2003, had made me more determined than ever that it was time to end the sequence.

For once, I got the start to the series which had eluded me in previous seasons, and built up a decent lead. It meant that for a change, it was the other guys who were doing the chasing instead of me.

IN THE GENES ... With Phil at Mildura, aged four in 1979, and then at 16 when father and son raced together on the same programme for the first time, 1991

All I had to do in that last Grand Prix of 2004 was keep my head, not do anything silly, and, at least, qualify for the semi-final. That was even if Rickardsson, the man everyone had been trying to tame for years, kept on winning races.

Tony had made a habit of collecting titles, and is one of those riders who never considers any cause lost. It's never over 'til it's over with him. Statistically, he could still catch me although his task was a lot greater than the one which faced Nicki Pedersen at the final round of 2003.

Nicki had mounted a consistent challenge that year but he was a point behind me with one GP to go. I had to keep him in my sights and whatever either of us did on the night, finish ahead of him in Hamar, as I had done in the three GP rounds before it. I stuffed up, big time. He nicked what could and probably should have been my title. Fair play to him, he rode like a man possessed all year and when his opportunity came, he grabbed it.

This time though, realistically, I had left Rickardsson had little or no chance. He was 17 points adrift coming to another Hamar showdown and I had to implode if he was to overtake me. Crucially I could afford to go to the last round knowing that provided I got through to the semis, I couldn't be caught.

I was nervous as hell, but thanks to a sequence of happenings stuttered through and suddenly, there was no way I could be caught.

I've seen videos of old-time finals when champions have celebrated with both hands off the handlebars and thought how embarrassing it would be if they had lost balance and fallen off in a heap.

But hey, this is the showbiz age, this the era in which you are supposed to pull a big wheelie to celebrate the moment and share your joy with all those who have been along for the ride.

It was all a bit surreal. I'd had a nervous start – third behind

PER Jonsson has been an influential role model and friend to Jason, first when they were neighbours in Swindon, then when the Swede won the 1990 world title.

A shocking crash in Poland in 1994 left him paralysed but he retains strong connections with the sport and a keen and enduring interest in how his protégé is faring.

An anecdote from what was to be one of his last meetings illustrates the camaraderie which riders share.

"I remember testing an engine for Jason, but testing isn't racing so you can't feel totally sure of a motor. I was down at Poole with Reading, and frankly struggling with my equipment.

"Somewhat to the annoyance of the Poole management he opened up his van which had contained three bikes – he wasn't using this one that night. I hopped on it and my fortunes changed and I managed to beat Jason.

"It confirmed that the bike was terrific, though Jason certainly got some earache for lending an opponent a machine – especially a good one!

"I knew then that his bikes were extremely good. I already knew he was a potential world champion."

Rickardsson and Nicki Pedersen – but I scrambled a win in Heat 15. Then came Heat 19, the race which provided the key to the door in a really weird fashion.

Runa Holta moved me over coming off the start, I piled into Nicki, he collected Ryan Sullivan and the three of us ended up in a heap on the first corner. Tony Steele, the referee most of the riders rate as the best of the lot, called it as an unsatisfactory start and put everyone back in.

Incredibly, Holta was excluded for delaying the start in the re-run, pulling back after we'd been put under starter's orders. So then there were three.

Up we come again and this time Sullivan hits the deck. He's out. His yellow exclusion light is on. And in a flash, the realisation hits. With a two-man line-up I'm home and hosed ... I am world champion.

I had turned round to see if Sully wanted a lift back to the pits, and out of the corner of my eye I saw Ted and Helen Jarvis, longtime sponsors from Milton Keynes, up in the stands ... and Helen was punching the air.

EVEN though he has been a part-time participant in Sweden for the past two seasons, Jason Crump's popularity is as high there as in any country of the world. The pleasure he generates obviously is a two-way affair, with some of his finest triumphs coming in Sweden – including two GP wins in 2005.

Bo Wirebrand, one of the wise men of Swedish speedway, a former international rider, team manager and federation official, now the head honcho of VMS Elit, heads the list of admirers ready to sum up his contribution.

"I get in trouble from the supporters at Vetlanda for not using Jason more often," he says.

"But our agreement is firm, he is a very important man for our club even though he does not want to do all the matches. We are happy to have him as much as we do.

"Jason is one of the best riders I have seen in the 40 years I've been in speedway and a top guy, who every time tries to do all he can for the team, the club, our major sponsor, everybody. We have great respect for each other.

"He is such an easy man to deal with, I can't think of anyone better, and he is worth so much more than the points he scores. He is such a professional, always organised and ready, and giving his best even if he has some problems at the time.

"I think he learned so much last year. It took him a long time to be world champion, maybe he put too much pressure on himself before, but I think he is a very big chance to be absolutely top notch again.

"I have known him for many years and tried before to get him to ride for VMS Elit. It's always very good for us when he comes to Sweden because you know he will never give you anything less than his very best."

She had spotted that Sullivan's yellow exclusion light was on and immediately worked out that I couldn't be overtaken.

Whatever happened in the re-run, and in the last few races of the 2004 Grand Prix, I was the No.1. At last.

No wonder that everything went blank for a few seconds. It was my Cathy Freeman moment, you know, when she sat on the track after winning her 800 metres race at the Sydney Olympics and all the years of preparation, hype and expectation produced one life-changing victory.

The next thing I knew Nicki Pedersen, Tony Rickardsson and Leigh Adams were all on top of me, my dad, Phil, was half a step behind them, and I was being bombarded with congratulations and backslapping and lapping up the cheers of the crowd.

They could have stopped the season right there, never mind the meeting, and I wouldn't have cared.

Ole Olsen, the race director, bustled into my corner of the pits to hurry me out for the re-run but in all honesty, I was in auto-pilot. I couldn't tell you much of what I did for the next little while. All I knew was that I had achieved a lifetime ambition, and reached a high point in my chosen sporting career.

Every speedway rider dreams of becoming world champion.

When you're a kid and your career is starting to unfold, anything seems possible. The truth is, it turns out to be an impossible dream for all but a few. I'm one who got lucky.

Whoever it was who said 'it's funny, the harder I work, the luckier I get' sums it up for me.

I never considered it my right, but it always was my goal, and as I tried to take in the emotion of that day, I felt the most amazing sense of relief after a long, tough, and certainly exciting journey.

Since speedway began thousands of guys like me have slung their leg over a bike, fired with ambition and dreams of the big time.

The fulfilment of that dream, in the shape of a world title, had materialised for just 31 of us, including four Aussies. Lionel Van Praag won the first world championship in 1936 and Bluey Wilkinson followed him two years later. Jack Young was champion in 1951 and 1952.

And then, for 52 years, nothing ...

My dad was aged seven months when Youngie climbed on to the rostrum at Wembley on September 18, 1952. Phil was one of the army of would-be champions of later generations, good enough to be third in the world in 1976.

I was a month old when he made his World Final debut at Wembley the previous year, the year Ole Olsen collected the second of his three titles.

Obviously, something was burned into my mind almost from birth. I don't know if you could call it genetic, yet I always knew I wanted to be a racer. And the best I could be. It is something more than instinct, it's a driving force.

Simon Wigg used to say that the goal of becoming world champion was the single most compelling reason for getting up in the morning.

And as I tried to take it all in at Hamar, a thousand thoughts spilling on top of one another as I contemplated my new status as the champion, I thought of what it would have meant to him, and what it represented for so many people.

Simon died at 40 in 2000, one of my greatest mates, mentors and rivals in speedway, one of the most optimistic and inspirational blokes you could ever wish to meet.

Then there was Per Jonsson, my boyhood idol, for whom life as he knew it came to a shocking end when he was paralysed in a track crash.

Per, who had it in him to dominate the world championship in the same fashion as Hans Nielsen and Tony Rickardsson, won the title in 1990 but fate intervened before he could add to that triumph.

Not a day goes by when I don't think of the man who first became a friend when he was starting out in England and I was a teenage kid riding my BMX bike around the Swindon pits and car park.

There's also Krystof Cegielski, much more of a contemporary, who also had a very promising career shattered by injury, a really talented rider and a good friend for several years, a guy who had been one of the boys in the Grand Prix until 16 months earlier.

When you see things like that happen, it sure does make you appreciate everything else in life – not just the winning of a world championship, but the family, the friends, the good times, the very great fortune to be able to take in an occasion and achievement such as this.

At that point, I never appreciated them more – Melody, my longtime partner and soon-to-be wife, crying and laughing all at the same time, our kids Mia and Seth, jumping up and down with excitement, shouting and carrying on.

Phil, the father who did thousands of races in his own distinguished career and then 'rode' thousands more on my behalf. Drew Street, my uncle and longtime mechanic, Bill Street, my grandfather and father figure to generations of Australian riders, all the other members of my support team, sponsors, supporters.

Back in Australia my mum, Carole, and sisters, Justine and Gabi – half a world away because of a combination of different family circumstances, but people who would know as well as anybody what this day meant to me.

It was an unreal time, my life literally flashing past my eyes.

These people had shared the journey, helped to negotiate all the hurdles, pumped me up when required, calmed me down at regular intervals, and continued to believe in me and encourage me even when I was down in the dumps, and from time to time questioning whether all that stuff about destiny was for real.

Even if I did believe I could and would become the world champion, never at any point of my life were there any illusions about how difficult it would be. I saw how much of a toll racing took on my old man, the hours he put in, the punishing schedules, long days which became late nights in the workshop,

IN THE FAMILY ... Neil and Mary Street and their family were hugely influential in Jason's first few years in England

overnight trips across one continent or another, the sheer will power required to front up day after day, another track, another meeting, another queue of guys wanting to beat you.

Phil was a professional racer for the best part of 20 years, one of the best in the world, but he wore plenty of scars and bruises and telltale signs of a tough career. Racing didn't make him a rich man and the transition to life after speedway was difficult, never more so than when he and my mum split up a few years ago.

From early on I recognised that it wasn't all glamour, and today I'm grateful that so many things have worked out really well for me.

But I do think I've paid my dues.

I always figured that if something is worth doing then you do it properly, to the very best of your ability.

I became one of the best speedway riders in the world by working at it, not by accident. It's what I do and it's who I am.

And when I finish I don't want there to be any 'what ifs' and 'might have beens'.

PRACTICE MAKES PERFECT ... Riding the 500 at Mildura and waiting for that looming 16th birthday to arrive

The Mildura Connection

> I think that champions have the potential to forget where they have come from, but this is definitely not the case with Jason.
>
> – School friend Darryl Nicol

RACING from one place to another, flying around the world, chasing summers from one hemisphere to another, didn't seem like such a big deal to me when I was a kid.

It was simply what people did. At least, it was what you did if your dad was a top speedway rider earning his living in England from March until October, and came home for more of the same through the Australian season.

This is what Phil had been doing from the age of 18, and explains how I came to be born in Bristol rather than in Australia.

I can't pretend that being Phil Crump's son has been any disadvantage to me in the long term. It probably helped to open a few doors and growing up in a speedway environment would have given me more of an insight into the business than many riders.

But it meant that there were greater expectations on me when I was starting or making my way in the sport. If Phil had been an ordinary rider it would have been different.

Sons of high-achieving fathers will tell you how tough it is. Kym Mauger, Tony Briggs, Darren Boocock – Jacob Olsen is a more recent example – all found it tough to escape from under the shadow cast by big-name stars like Ivan, Briggo, Nigel and Ole.

Three of those guys were world champions several times over and Nigel was just about the most successful England international of his era. They're big footsteps to follow.

Chris Louis is just about the only top rider I can think of whose record at the top level was comparable with that of his father. There may have been other instances in the distant past but I'm not aware of them.

It isn't surprising. The comparisons, the expectations and the pressures just keep coming from all directions. You need to develop a strong sense of self, a thick skin, and the determination to achieve on your own merits rather than on the back of someone else's reputation.

People started to take me seriously when I qualified for the 1994 World Final at 18, going on 19. A real test in the long run was whether I could be even more consistent than Phil was for so long,. And ultimately, whether I could win a world title which eluded him.

The fact that I have managed both does not diminish my respect for what he accomplished.

In Mildura for years he was the most famous person in the town.

One thing I didn't bargain for when I was racing was having to inherit some of the baggage left over from his racing days. Phil was a tough opponent and left an impression on a number of rivals, including Sam Ermolenko with whom he had one pretty spectacular incident the locals still talk about.

They were going for it at Olympic Park and Sam was all over Phil's back wheel, but he ran out of room and ended up clearing the fence on the Merbein bend and disappearing in the direction of the Murray River, which runs alongside the stadium.

THE year 1952 was a significant one for all sorts of reasons. Queen Elizabeth II came to the throne in February, Phil Crump was born three days later, and in September of the same year, Jack Young won what was destined to be Australia's last world solo speedway title for more than 50 years – watched by a Wembley crowd which included Neil Street, a 21-year-old Victorian on his first racing trip to England.

Jason Crump's father Phil was the eldest of five children of Bob and Marj Crump (nee Hagan) who owned and operated a 50-acre fruit-producing property outside Mildura for half a century and still live in their original home next door.

The Crump family arrived in Australia from Exeter in 1924 and settled on a vineyard at Cardross, five kilometres out of Mildura, in 1926. There were eight children – six girls and two boys. The eldest child, Philip, at the age of 20 was killed in action in El Alamein in the early 1940s.

Robert, the other son, married Marjory Hagan in 1951, and remained on the vineyard producing dried sultanas and currants until 1996 when they sold up and retired. After Phil came Edward, Janet, Ian and Gillian.

Phil was born on February 9, 1952 in Red Cliffs, approximately eight kilometres from Cardross. He purchased his first motorcycle in 1968 which was a BSA Bantam. From this point he joined the Mildura Motorcycle Club where Phil Sedgmen, the President at the time, lent him his BSA speedway bike, and it was from here that Phil's speedway career began.

Brothers Eddie and Ian also rode, briefly, and Gill married Nigel Tremelling,who won the Australian Under 21 speedway title in 1986 and had a season in England with Poole before injury cut short his career. Nigel and Gill's 11-year-old son Jake, though, regards Jason as a role model and has ambitions of racing.

I'm sure Sudden Sam filed that one away in the memory bank because a few years later we always seemed to be clashing. It wasn't as if I had any history with him – he was one of the riders I idolised as a kid – but it was a different story later on. I'm relieved to say we get on nowadays. It was pretty hairy there for a few years.

Of course I heard plenty of stories about how my dad started. There was a guy at the Mildura club called Phil Sedgmen who was pretty handy and he had an old BSA which was converted for speedway. One day he said to Phil to come and throw his leg over his slider and in no time at all, apparently, the pupil was beating the master.

A local motorcycle dealer got Phil organised with a two-valve Jawa and for a couple of summers he used to pack in three meetings on most weekends. He was working as an apprentice boilermaker at the Co op treatment plant and used to work through his lunch break so he could build up enough time to knock off early on Fridays.

Then he would load his bike into his dad's old Holden ute, drive five hours to Adelaide to race at Rowley Park, do another eight hours the next day to get to Melbourne to race at Brooklyn on the Saturday night, and then drive back to

It all sounds familiar to Bob Crump, who was to see his eldest son and grandson achieve such international fame.

"When Gill was born in 1968, it was when Phil got his first motorbike," says Bob.

"Phil came to hospital to visit his new baby sister and told Marj to come home so she could get him some money out of his bank account, 15 pounds, to buy his first motorbike."

Jason's mother Carole, born January 19, 1957, is the first of three children of Neil and Mary Street (nee Gill) who met and wed after the Melbourne-born and raised speedway rider began his English speedway career at Exeter.

The Street family also contained eight children, of whom Neil was the eldest. His two sons, Graham and Adrian, both played a role when Jason first ventured to England to ride, and Drew, as he is generally known, remains a trusted member of his support team to this day.

Phil and Carole's relationship developed in the early 1970s when Street began to take a keen interest in the career prospects of Mildura speedway's rough and ready but obviously talented teenage discovery.

It blossomed during 1973 when Phil, after having made a major impression in his first two seasons as a rider at Second Division Crewe and parent club King's Lynn, returned early to Australia because of a scaphoid injury which was to impact greatly upon his later years as a rider.

Carole, then finishing school, had grown up as a collector of frequent flyer points as her parents made annual trips between Australia and England. When Phil went back to link with Newport – and Neil Street – for the 1974 British League season, she came too.

PROUD PARENTS ... Phil and Carole show off the new-born Jason, Newport, September 1975

Cardross, do a bit of work on the bike and then front up at Mildura on Sunday night.

It was during this time that he met Bill Street and his daughter Carole, who became Mrs Crump. And in 1971, having never been out of Australia, he went off to ride for Crewe in the Second Division in England. He had a couple of really good years there, won the Second Division Riders' Championship in 1972, and moved up into First Division.

Going to Newport in '74, riding in the same team as Bill Street, and being the chief test pilot for the new four-valve engines, was the move which really set him on his way to the top.

Phil and Carole stayed with the Streets at Silverton, a village outside Exeter, before buying their first British home at Nailsea, near Bristol, the following year.

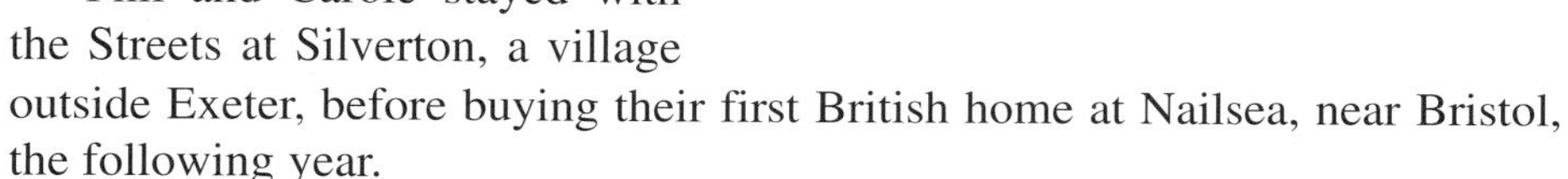

According to my mum, I arrived on the scene at Eastville Hospital, Bristol, at 2.01pm on Wednesday, August 6, 1975, weighing in at 7lb 8oz. Given that six of her dad's siblings had ginger hair, it was not too much of a surprise that I did too. There must be something about August 6. Ginger Spice, the pop singer Geri Halliwell (born in 1972), shares the same birthday.

Phil took his next big step towards stardom a few weeks later when he finished fifth on his World Final debut at Wembley in 1975, and added to his reputation when he came third in Katowice a year later.

He was not just among the best riders in the sport, he was an absolute gun around Mildura and my first speedway memories are of him ruling the roost there. Virtually all the world champions of that time came to Olympic Park and it was almost expected for him to beat them all.

I was a real keen spectator and quickly got the hang of the idea that winning was a lot more fun than anything else.

Not much happens in Mildura and sport has helped give the place some of its identity and reputation. There have been other sportsmen to come from the place, including a few decent AFL players, but because he had success on an international stage, and motorcycles mean so much to people there, Phil was the king.

I do believe though that the best legacy my parents gave me was the opportunity to travel round the world and be comfortable with that sort of lifestyle.

It became routine for us to spend the summers in Australia and then head off to England for the eight-month European season. And of course Phil was a big deal at places like Bristol and then, for a number of years, at Swindon, which is where I first started to get a sense of what being a full-time speedway rider was all about.

Phil was a boy from the bush who had never been anywhere and even when he became a top performer, he possibly still was wondering how the hell he was supposed to compete with all those superstars.

On the other hand, I sort of grew up with those situations and those people, so much so that it probably would have been more weird for the other riders than it was for me when I got out of short trousers and started racing against some of them,.

Even so, most of my very early memories of speedway belong to Mildura, especially when the Americans Bruce Penhall and Bobby Schwartz came there in the Australian summer of 1981-82. Bruce had just won the world title and

PHIL and Carole Crump bought their first British home at Nailsea, near Bristol, in 1975. It was an area expanding so fast to meet the demands of would-be home buyers that for the first year they lived there, Phil and Carole had to make do without a telephone until an addition to the local exchange was built.

It did, however, have a village pub called the Royal Oak where folk singer Adge Cutler and the Wurzels went down extremely well with the cider-drinking locals and had recorded the first of their hit albums a few years earlier.

Phil was preparing to race at Swindon's Silver Plume on Wednesday, August 6, 1975, when the Crump's first child, Jason Philip, made his entry into the world. It was a complex birth as the baby was facing the wrong way and a forceps delivery was required. The new parents were not allowed to pick him up for the first four or five days.

August 6 has had its share of famous birthdays, among them Alfred Lord Tennyson, Poet Laureate of England (1809), Sir Alexander Fleming (penicillin, 1881), tough-guy actor Robert Mitchum (1917) and pop-artist Andy Warhol (1927).

Perhaps the most celebrated sporting name with whom Jason shares a birthday is Poland's 1972 Olympic gold-winning ski jumper Wojiech Fortuna (born in 1952).

It's been a huge day in history, too – Serbia declared war on Germany on August 6, 1914 which signalled the start of the First World War, and on August 6, 1945, the B-29 bomber *Enola Gay* dropped the atom bomb dubbed 'Little Boy' on Hiroshima to effectively end the second great conflict of the 20th century.

Perhaps nobody should have been surprised that the Crump firstborn was destined to write his name in a few history books, too.

Bobby and he were the world pairs champions and I think Phil beat them about four times in the one night round Olympic Park.

When I was about four they had started a junior section of the Mildura Motorcycle Club.

Leigh Adams and his brother Andrew and Jason Lyons were all a few years older than me, and they were among the first kids to begin to make an impression.

Naturally after a while I was hanging out to join them but my parents didn't greatly encourage the notion. Phil seemed to believe that it was better for me to wait and Carole may have thought the best idea of all was if I never did get on a bike. They were fighting a losing battle though, and must have known as much.

The months in England were all business, Phil would be riding three or four meetings a week and everything was geared around his schedule. Back in Australia it was quite different, with the racing at weekends, and of course a lot of the boys were riding motorcycles from an early age.

I just kept nagging away and in the end my parents must have got fed up with the constant requests because I got my first bike when I was 10 – although it was another year or two before I got into regular competition. I wanted to learn to ride first, and the Nowingi salt flats, about half an hour out of town, was a perfect place to practice

I managed to get plenty of holidays because in Australia the summer break ran through December and January and in England I'd have July and August off, so that was pretty cool.

HONDA KID ... Have bike, will travel

SOUTHERN SUMMER ... Bob and Marj Crump's fruit block outside Mildura – plenty of sun, sand and lots of sultanas

One thing I do remember about coming from Australia to England each season was how cold it was. The climate, the air travel, I remember those things more than I do the actual speedway.

Schooling in England is much tougher than it is in Australia, or it was then. There were a few years in Swindon when I had to have a private tutor who came to teach me at the house after school and sometimes on the weekend.

I split my schooling between the two countries. Greendown, the last school I went to in England, was in the middle of nowhere then but now Leigh Adams lives close by and Jimmy Nilsen also had a house there. The last house we had in Swindon is 500 yards from where Leigh is based in the European season.

There are a lot of happy memories from Swindon. As I began to take an increasingly intelligent interest in what was going on, I always liked to watch Bo Petersen, who had a successful spell there. He seemed so organised, immaculately turned out with his colour co-ordinated bikes and leathers and he was a very good rider.

When Jimmy Nilsen and Per Jonsson came, we saw plenty of them. They were young guys in a new country and both of them had Swindon as their British base. Pretty soon they were right up there in my list of favourites.

I loved watching the Americans, too. The Moran brothers were unreal on a bike, Bobby Schwartz always was so friendly and Sam Ermolenko was someone else who impressed me no end. These guys used to give me high fives and hand out stickers, it was magic for a wide-eyed kid.

GOODBYE ENGLAND ... for the time being. Jason with his parents and sisters Justine and Gabi at Phil's farewell dinner in Swindon at the end of the 1986 British League season

That was all pretty neat, and so it was when any of them came out to race in Australia and dropped in to see us. The speedway community, then as now, is just one big international family. Travelling back and forth, that's just what we did. Phil was a speedway rider, and that's how his routine – and that of the whole family – was for years.

The contrast between Mildura and, say, Swindon, could not have been much greater. Swindon isn't the capital of the world, but it's a sizeable city with plenty of amenities, and within easy reach of heaps of other places, a couple of hours up the motorway to London and so forth.

Mildura is a country town in the middle of nowhere, with relatively few facilities. It's in a south western corner of Victoria. Melbourne is seven hours away, Adelaide four.

And the prospect of being full-time in Mildura, instead of simply spending four months of the year there in between trips to England, was a shock to the system. But after the end of the 1986 season, when he was still close to being a nine-point heat leader in the British League, Phil pulled the pin. The scaphoid injury which had bothered him for years was now too much of a problem.

Riding a few meetings in Australia, without any great pressure, was still quite an attractive option for him but the grind of regular league racing overseas had lost its appeal. At that time there were still maybe 20 or more meetings a season to be had in Australia – he was only 34 after all, and still capable of beating anybody – and he wanted a bit more of a normal life.

So just at a time when I was beginning to take a more intelligent interest in what he did, and in bikes, I was back to being a boy from the outback, too. The only contact with the outside world was if we went interstate for a meeting or if some of the overseas riders came to Mildura.

MUMS often worry about whether children who concentrate their energies in one sporting direction are missing out on other aspects of growing up. And parents whose own schedule is dictated by the demands of professional sport tend to fret about the disruption to family life and the absence of what others would consider to be normal routine.

The young Jason Crump had it both ways, but to all appearances he has not suffered or been deprived in any significant sense. He is who is he is because of the lifestyle his folks led and because – when they felt the timing was right – they gave him every encouragement to follow a similar path.

When you are a child growing up in a sporting environment, and your father is a star attraction, and all of his workmates and associates take the time to greet and treat you as one of their own, it's a great way to learn, to develop self-confidence and become skilled at communicating with people.

And when you're in the thick of things, be it at a speedway meeting or off competing in a junior event on your own account, you live for the moment, the excitement, the buzz and the atmosphere. You most certainly don't stop to worry about whether you are missing out on anything else, because you're having simply the best time.

"I didn't really discourage him, but I felt that there were better ways of earning a living," said Carole.

"Jason was a bright child, always a good talker, able to hold his own in an argument, and quick to grasp new ideas. He could have been anything. He's stubborn, like me, and if he believes in something he won't back down. I liked the idea of him becoming a lawyer.

"But although he was a good student, he wasn't that interested in school. There were too many other things which excited him and took his attention, including motorbikes of course."

Although so many of the kids in Mildura were into bikes, officialdom decreed that they could not race until they were nine years of age.

Carole, however, displaying the independent streak which has become one of her son's trademarks, was not about to be told when Jason could or could not ride.

"I didn't intend to be dictated to," she said.

"We were happy enough to have Jason riding but I didn't want to see him in competition until he was about 12, and that's what happened."

It wasn't exclusively about bikes though, and for us kids, it was the chance to find out what 'normal' really meant. Being back in Australia meant that for the first time in our lives we didn't have to flit from one country to another, we could settle into some sort of routine with school and friends and other activities.

And when Phil bought a ski boat we were able to spend days and days water skiing on the Murray River, which runs through Mildura. We had hours of fun on – and in – the water. It was really good. Even school at Mildura Tech (now the Chaffey Secondary College) was fun and I had a lot of mates there.

But despite the various counter-attractions, now that I had a bike of my own this became a central part of my world.

The junior section at Mildura had grown in reputation as riders such as Leigh Adams and Jason Lyons began to make their mark. And there was a

DARRYL Nicol, one of Jason's best mates in Mildura, is always pleased to have a natter and a beer at the Sandbar when his one-time school friend is back in town.

"My first recollection of meeting Jason was riding my BMX bike past his house in Mildura. Jason was out the front riding his bike. I stopped and a conversation started about speedway when I told Jason that my dad Alex used to race speedway for the Berwick Bandits in Scotland," he said.

"Jason was always very competitive at everything he did. There were many passionate battles on the tennis courts at school with Jason desperate to be the winner. More so than the rest of us. Jason was easily frustrated by the prospect of losing. He was certainly a much better player than me, but by simply keeping the ball in play, I would wait for him to make mistakes which would ensure that I often won – at least that's the way that I remember it.

"At school Jason was a very confident person. He was well liked by his teachers, he was intelligent and contributed often in class but at the same time he could really get under their skin. He loved to push the boundaries. You could have described him as a lovable rogue. He had a nickname for most of them, not to mention his school mates.

"Jason had a way with words and was very good at devising plans to make our school lives easier. The best was during science with Mr Nick.

Nick had planned some work-sheets for a double lesson when Jason suggested it was too nice a day to be stuck inside doing science. He suggested to Nick that we go and get a soccer ball and have a game on the back oval.

"Nick explained that the principal most likely wouldn't approve of soccer during science and said no. Jason then came up with the idea of making an experiment out of the game. He suggested we all have our temperature taken before and after the game and compile the effects of exercise on the body in a later lesson. Nick approved and we all enjoyed a great game of soccer out in the sun."

regular interchange with the Sidewinders club in Adelaide which had produced Craig Hodgson, Scott Norman, Shane Parker and where Ryan Sullivan, who is six months older than me, was the new kid on the block.

At Mildura the younger boys coming through were people like Mark Lemon, Cory Alderton and Jason Hawkes.

There were stacks more, kids who came from moto cross and others who went straight into the junior speedway, and the more successful the whole thing became, the greater the interest.

Yet I never felt it was something I had to do. I was never pushed into it. If it had been something other people wanted me to do, then I probably wouldn't have done it.

And I was quite happy to spend a couple of years just practising, learning how to ride a bike, before going into competition.

It certainly didn't hurt me, and nor did the Crump connection. It did have its advantages to me because I could always get into things. There were privileges I got as a kid. Later on, there was a bouncer at one of the night clubs, the Sandbar, who used to be a speedway rider and knew very well that I wasn't 18 but he would let me go in and sneak into a dark corner just because of who my dad was.

You don't know any different. He was famous when I was growing up and still us. If I had lived my whole life in Mildura it all would have been very much more difficult for me.

That said, Phil and I frequently didn't see eye to eye, as fathers and sons often are. When I was getting into racing he had a lot of ideas that I didn't want to take on board.

We probably both have mellowed over time.

I understand that he has a wealth of experience and knowledge and sometimes it's 'do as I say not do as I do'. He's very much a one-pace type of guy whereas I've always blown hot and cold.

His reputation with engines is very good and having him along in the Grand Prix series has been quite a part of the story in recent years.

Where Phil is at his best at those big meetings is his ability to get a job done effectively and quickly. If a quick gear change is needed, something straightened or some other running repairs he doesn't flap and drop spanners like some mechanics do under pressure. He just keeps on keeping on in his own way and you can be sure the job will get done in time.

From a mental point of view though, I owe such a big debt to my mum Carole. From years back she could always talk me through things rationally and make me analyse what was going on. As often as not, she was the driver when the junior speedway trips started. in 1987 because Phil was still riding most weekends.

Our trips were an adventure for me and part of learning. In four or five hours on the road, going to and from meetings, there was always plenty of conversation. Such times are as valuable as the actual racing. You can absorb so much and really start to understand who you are and where you're going.

It meant that Justine and Gabi's ballet activities ground to a halt but they put a brave face on it and pitched in on the outings, which often involved fortnightly trips to Adelaide, interspersed with events at Mildura and elsewhere.

Some of the parents couldn't wait to hurry their boys into it but to be fair, once it was established that I was going to ride, my parents wanted to see me learn to do it properly and get comfortable on a bike before I went into competition.

It was a good policy because by the time I did start to race, I had some sort of a clue about what I was doing and an understanding of how the bike behaved. You couldn't say the same of a few of the lads who were pushed in, white-faced and nervous, before they had any idea of what was required.

For three or four years I virtually lived on a bike. You could get from our place to Mark Lemon's at Palm Court, Merbein, on the other side of town, without going on the road and I'd ride over there after school almost every day. Cory Alderton joined us on the weekends and we were forever trying things, racing, playing with the bikes.

The Nowingi salt flats outside town was always a popular venue and so was the track we built at the back of our property at Ontario Avenue. Anywhere there was a spare bit of dirt was a potential speedway circuit. But my career could easily have been cut short – literally.

Although we were brought up to respect what was going on at the fruit blocks which are everywhere in and around Mildura, we probably did go a bit too fast along the tracks and our enduro bikes kicked up trails of dust. That annoyed one particular blockie who had his fruit out on the drying rack.

The next time we rode past his property he'd strung fish wire across the track and it was lucky that Lemo saw it just in time and baled out. He reacted as all the kids were taught to do when learning speedway and put the bike down in a flash. I was right behind him, and managed to pull up just in time.

When he pointed out the wire we both realised how lucky we were. It could have taken our heads off.

A funny angle to this incident is that Mark's brother Craig, who had a dabble on speedway without making a great impact, had failed his 'lay down' test three times before finally being allowed to have a racing licence.

When I was riding junior speedway, Carole put in a lot of work at the club, helping to organise events and serving on the committee. Because of his other commitments Phil was not involved too much and that was fine by me.

In all sports, there have been some horror stories of parents getting involved, organising events, being on committees and that sort of thing. Probably junior sport would not exist without the input of fathers and mothers but the reality is that there always seem to be hassles and arguments and politics and I didn't want any of that.

Within the best will in the world, petty jealousies and rivalries sometimes get out of hand, and yet when you come right down to it, the kids just want to have fun.

Even so, it was an expensive hobby and I understood that I wasn't going to have everything laid on for me. I was always up for other money-spinners on the side so I could afford to buy new bits for my bike and working at a bakery after school provided another source of income for several of us. The place was owned by the Tappel family whose sons both rode in the junior motorcycle club.

SPEEDWAY administrator and journalist Bob Radford was for several years a near neighbour and Crump family friend in Swindon. He watched Jason growing up, later visited the Crumps in Australia, and has watched his career develop.

"He certainly wasn't a spoiled child – indeed once or twice I thought that Phil was a bit hard with him. Jason always seemed happiest out on his bicycle. He never seemed to be in any trouble at all, and of the those I met I felt he chose his friends wisely. Quite early on it became obvious that he had a keen interest in speedway.

"Two young Swedish riders came in 1984 and 1985 – Per Jonsson and Jimmy Nilsen respectively. I introduced both to the family and both became friends in their own right immediately. The fact that they came to Britain as 18-year-olds almost certainly meant that Jason could relate to them probably more easily than his father.

"There was much sadness when Phil retired from British speedway at the end of the 1986 season. While not at his peak Phil was still mighty close to being a nine-point rider. When HTV did a small feature after his last Swindon meeting, the picture was on Phil and Jason walking off the Blunsdon centre green with a sunset background.

"A few years later I visited Australia twice in the space of six months. By then Jason was riding junior speedway and I saw him in action. In almost every case a half smile and acknowledgement covered quite deep personal dislikes in almost all directions, and not only the Crumps. Phil having been such a big star in a small town, and with a shy-ish personality made them targets, not that they didn't have their own thoughts on others too.

"By then Jason and father Phil were far from a harmonious duo – Jason I think wanted to be seen to be doing it on his own – certainly the two got on each other's nerves as fathers and sons do at that stage.

"The Mildura area had quite its share of good young speedway riders. Though everyone came together for the racing, it soon became clear that there was a small town attitude to the place and plenty of rivalries and petty jealousies.

"I recall going out with Jason and Carole during the day to some salt flats just outside Mildura. I'd never believed you thought you could see water when none was there – unless hallucinating! But it was for real and Jason blasted around proficiently on his 500cc machine. Then I asked if I could move the cones and make the racing shape different – this was to see if he could turn the bike harder – and of course he could. I'd taken out a Reading 1990 league winners race jacket I'd managed to save as a present."

JUNIOR RACING ... Jason tussles with Brett Tomkins, who beat him in the 1989 Australian Under 16 title run-off

I had lots of little jobs, such as separating and bagging up bread rolls after they had come fresh from the oven in their trays of 24; loading and moving loaves; putting the icing on sticky buns and all sorts of other tasks.

The biggest boost to my meagre resources in the later stages of my junior speedway came from Mark Gilbert, who was known around Adelaide as a great enthusiast, someone who had worked for Billy Sanders in England, and had later turned his hand to promoting.

Because Phil knew him from way back, we used to stay over with Mark and when he came along to watch me riding in juniors, he decided that I needed more horse power. That led to the introduction to Peter Morris, a good mate of his and a mechanical wizard who even then had the ability to make motors go fast.

I had been runner-up in the Australian Under 16 championship to defending title-holder Jason Hawkes in 1988, and then to Brett Tomkins in 1989. My uncle Adrian (Drew) was on a trip out from England and that '89 meeting was the first time he had been there to help in the pits. I had hoped to make it second time lucky after the disappointment of the previous year, but drew the outside gate in a run-off and was left behind at the start.

Even at this stage the lesson was there – nothing comes easy, you have to pay your dues and learn how to handle defeat before you learn how to win.

Drew was born in Melbourne, and even after the family put down roots in Exeter, he still liked to come to Australia every couple of years. He came to that meeting with me because Phil and Carole were away for the weekend for some senior event somewhere.

In juniors, you had to have a parent or guardian accompanying you and he got the job.

Straight away, Drew was great in helping me appreciate the positives to be taken out of the occasion and to get over the disappointment. I had two junior bikes and the next day we were out having a play at the track at our property. It was blazing hot, about 45 degrees, but we didn't care.

To be kind to my uncle, he isn't a natural on a motorcycle, so I thought I should take it a bit easy and he won the first in a best-of-three series of races. Of course honour dictated I had to square things up in the second, and then we could have a 'decider'. The problem was that after letting him make the start on me, I was laughing so much at his rather unconventional style on a bike that I fell off!

So for ever and a day I have to put up with the story of Adrian Street, match race champion (retired). At least he had the good grace to retire while he was still ahead!

When Mark Gilbert offered to help me, it was an important step forward for my career. He never asked for any publicity or anything in return, but the benefits of his involvement became evident when I started to set myself up for a third crack at the Under 16 championship in 1990. Now I had the equipment to go with my increasing confidence.

The breakthrough came when I won the Victorian Under 16 title at Mildura and then backed up by going off to Bibra Lake in Perth and winning that Australian title as well.

Ryan Sullivan, who was about four foot one then, was second in WA and Brett Woodifield was third.

That was a special day, with my grandfather along to support me – thanks to Trevor Harding, who sponsored us both with our air fares, a terrific gesture. He is a former rider who in his racing days was nicknamed 'the White Ghost' – hence his nickname of 'Ghosty' – and later put a lot of time and money into supporting Australian speedway.

Just ensuring that my grandfather was with me was a tremendous boost and, not for the first and certainly not the last time, 'Bill' helped me keep my feet on the ground. I was an impressionable kid and he had always emphasised that there was no magic, no secret to doing well in speedway. You just have to work hard, he told me. You must serve an apprenticeship as you would in almost any other job.

Bill Street is a wise and worldly man, and he did it tough when he was growing up. They were difficult times, during and after the war. When he first came to England to ride in 1952, he brought cans of meat with him because rationing was still in force.

He didn't get to all that many of my junior meetings but when he did, there was always a word of advice or encouragement. So to have him in my corner in Western Australia, that was something else.

I had packed up the bike which we sent by interstate courier, and he and I jumped on a flight from Melbourne. It was real Hollywood stuff for a 14-year-old. I certainly didn't need to set the alarm clock for 5am to be sure of making it to the airport in time.

I was definitely ready for more of this. This was the crowning moment for a junior, one I had really wanted, the first real milestone win in my career, and to share it with the man who was and remains my greatest mentor was a fantastic thrill. But I only did another two or three junior meetings after that. In my mind, I was headed for the big stuff.

In 1990, Swindon asked Phil to go back and ride again for them, so after a break of three or four years, there we all were, packing up everything and off to England.

There was no reason to believe that he wouldn't be competitive, but for one reason and another he wasn't. He was 38 and even though he had still been winning races in Australia, Phil possibly did not bargain for the improvement in standards or, especially, the effect the time away had on his ability to step up.

Swindon had a pretty good year but it turned out to be a season too far for the old man. Inevitably I sensed his disappointment but I was having too much of a good time myself to let that spoil the trip.

It was great for me – I rode his bike after the meeting at Blunsdon and at most of the other places we went to as well. They let me have regular rides at Poole, where Justin Elkins and I were the 'next generation' interval attraction as often as not.

An added factor of interest was seeing how my mate Mark Lemon was doing at Poole where he was trying to break into the side. We had shared plenty of good times in Mildura and I identified with his efforts, much more so than, say, Leigh Adams, who was already in his first year in the top flight in the Swindon side.

Leigh had had a few rides at the end of the 1988 season, and then did well enough in the lower league with Poole to step up. Leigh is more than four years older than me, and was on the verge of moving into the senior ranks when I started in juniors. He was one of the 'big boys' at the Mildura club, and our paths would often cross, whether at Olympic Park, or out on the salt flats. I couldn't say we were best buddies at that time though.

It was weird, seeing him out there with all the hot shots at Blunsdon and the other tracks. He very quickly established himself as a force to be reckoned with and averaged over seven points, a big effort in senior company. Leigh was already being hailed as 'the next Phil Crump' even before anyone in England thought of applying a similar label to me.

As far as other emerging riders went, I didn't have any special wraps on anyone apart from Lemo. But watching other young hopefuls chalk up respectable scores and adapt to the big time was great, and must have played

FIRST TITLE ... Australian Under 16 championship at Bibra Lake, 1990. Jason leads Ryan Sullivan and Jason Hawkes

some part in furthering my own ambitions and belief that within a couple of years, it could be me out there.

All up, I had a ball that year. It was a huge buzz and quite easy for me to visualise coming back myself to do it all for real.

Another highlight of the year was watching the World Final at Bradford. I went up in the car with Lemo and another mate, and I was absolutely dazzled when Per Jonsson won after a run-off with Shawn Moran.

It was Sweden's first title for 16 years, with the Danes dominating for much of that intervening period.

There was a great deal of interest in the final from a personal angle – I had never seen one live – with both Per and Jimmy Nilsen expected to be among the contenders. We saw a lot of them when we lived at Swindon and it would have thrilled me for either of them to do well.

Jimmy had finished fourth on debut in 1986, fourth again in 1987, but then went a couple of years without qualifying. Per was fifth in 1987 and 1988 so the chances were they were going to be there or thereabouts.

Hans Nielsen was marked down as the man everyone had to beat, especially when Jan O Pedersen, his closest rival at the top of the Sunbrite League averages and many people's tip as the next champion, was unluckily ruled out with a broken arm.

That, though, let in Henrik Gustafsson, a 20-year-old Swede who both Per and Jimmy had been raving about. And for the first half of the meeting it looked as if he, rather than my two more fancied mates, could come through to pull off a sensation.

At the interval Per and Henka both had eight points, and so too did Todd Wiltshire, also making his World Final debut.

But a puncture wrecked Gustafsson's hopes and in the end Jonsson and Moran were tied on 13, Todd a point adrift in third. Jimmy battled to 10 points but was off the pace.

So it all came down to a run-off.

After a first race third place, Shawn had steamed to four straight wins and if anyone could afford to miss the jump, he was the one ... but Per made a perfect start, resisted any challenge and reeled off four of the most copybook laps you are likely to see.

It was inspirational stuff for a wide-eyed kid.

Mick Poole was riding for Poole Pirates in 1990 and was blown away by his first sight of the then 14-year-old Jason Crump on a 500cc machine at Wimborne Road.

He was swiftly convinced that he was watching a champion in the making.

"I've said this many times to people who often ask – I could tell he would go all the way," said Poole.

"Everything was in the correct position ... legs, arms, head, body weight movement.

"It`s quite amazing how it`s taken 15 years to happen. It goes to show how hard it is to be in that special club of world champions."

Rod Colquhoun, also wearing the Pirates race jacket that season, was impressed with the young man as much as the young racer.

"My first thoughts upon meeting were how modest he was," says Colquhoun, who later became a columnist and, for two years, a Motorcycling Australia speedway commissioner.

"He worked as a mechanic for me once or twice (Ipswich comes to mind) and I had no self-belief and was intimidated to think that a 14-year-old kid could probably get on the bike and do a better job than me. However, these thoughts were entirely my own and Jason couldn't have been more supportive or complimentary.

"I had a strong interest in playing and listening to music and this is where Jason and myself really hit it off. I would make mixed tapes for him and he would give me feedback and we really got close there for a while. He would come over to my house and we'd work on the bikes and listen to tapes.

"I liked the fact he was keen to learn and develop his own identity."

Odsal had seen bigger and better days, but the stadium, in a natural amphitheatre, was as impressive as anything I had seen to that point, and a decent crowd ensured that there was going to be a special atmosphere.

You could taste the excitement, which built from the moment we spotted the first of hundreds of cars and coaches with fans from all over. You could understand why riders worked for occasions like this, and this was the day more than any other which crystallised my thoughts and ambitions about being a champion speedway rider.

And funnily enough, another meeting, at Swindon just a fortnight later, helped to emphasise what a fantastic seam of history preceded the modern-day championships.

Barry Briggs put on one of his Golden Greats meetings at Blunsdon, couldn't resist having a ride himself, of course, and brought along Ove Fundin, Anders Michanek, and a stack of other riders from the past who, to me at least, were just names – but what names!

It was a different kind of atmosphere, and some of the old boys looked a bit creaky and struggled to fit into their leathers, However, what it underlined to me was that this was a unique world I was planning to enter, full of remarkable people with tremendous records and fantastic stories to tell.

I could hardly wait.

If there had been any doubts in my mind beforehand, this trip banished them – I was going to be a speedway rider, and already was counting down the weeks before August, 1991 when I could get out there for real.

Phil and Carole and everyone else accepted after 1990 that he wasn't going to ride again in the UK and there was a general understanding that as soon as possible, I would!

In the meantime I was keen to soak up everything possible and also to be able to afford to buy more bits and pieces of equipment. When the Swedish touring team came to Mildura, I got a job to clean all their bikes. So my first contact with Tony Rickardsson was cleaning his bike! Darryl Nicol and Ian (Aggy) Taylor helped me and we earned a few dollars.

I also managed to score a frame from Jimmy Nilsen. He got Mick Poole to drop it over the fence at our place – I must have been at school at the time – and Mick still tells the story of how he was almost eaten by our blue heeler dog who came bounding round to check out what was going on.

Working on bikes wasn't unfamiliar, of course, because I got a great deal of my pocket money as a result of looking after my dad's equipment and maintaining it from meeting to meeting in the last few years he rode in Australia. They way I looked at it was that I wanted to do the right thing, and was earning and learning at the same time.

Latterly, I was also working almost every day on grandfather Bob Crump's fruit block. It was a journey of about 15 kilometres from our house and I didn't have a motorcycle licence, so I went by the back route to get there.

That meant a chilly start, working from about 6.30am until 5pm or so, and absolutely scorching temperatures during the day. It was hard work, but enjoyable.

My speciality from around the age of 11 was driving the tractor up and down the rows of fruit, waiting while the pickers filled their buckets and loaded them on to the trailer, and then taking them back to be laid out on drying racks. The fruit would be sprayed with drying oil and within a week they would be sultanas.

This was something I had done in most summer holidays, and on odd days when there was no school or any weekends when there was nothing doing with the junior speedway. It wasn't that unusual, because more than half of the kids in Mildura had some connection with the fruit-growing industry.

In the last summer or two I would turn my hand to anything, loading, unloading, whatever needed doing. It kept me fit and it helped my bank balance.

By now I had a 500 of my own after trading in my junior bike. I'd had a bit of a growth spurt and was getting too tall for the 125 anyway, and there was not much more to prove or achieve after winning the Aussie Under 16 title. Some of my former junior mates and rivals were now getting regular rides on the senior programme.

My parents were prepared to let me continue on the 125 or learn how to ride the big one, but not both. It seemed a bit harsh but in fact was perfect sense. In the overall scheme of things, it was much more important, career-wise, to spend as much time on the 500 as possible, even though my 16th birthday, and a licence to race with the seniors, was still almost a year in the future.

It meant I had to settle for rides before, during and after meetings. But that was good,. They let me go out at Olympic Park before the racing started and the track was perfect. I also got to go out after the solos had been on and then again later, following the sidecars.

By that stage of the proceedings, the track could be pretty rough and cut up, as I found out to my cost one time when I got caught up in a deep rut and crashed in a big way. It was the first major prang I'd had on a 500 and it took the wind out of my sails for a bit.

But by now nothing was going to deflect me from the fact that I wanted to go to England to race as soon as possible. When my birthday arrived at last I managed to talk my parents into letting me miss school for a few weeks to go over, stay with my grandparents in Exeter and get in a few rides before, hopefully, landing a team place in 1992.

Very soon I was on my way to England – arriving on the weekend of the World Final in Gothenburg which Jan O Pedersen won and Tony Rickardsson made his championship debut with 12 points and second place.

Just two days later I made my first official speedway appearance in the Crowncraft South West Junior Championship at Exeter and who should there be alongside me in my first race but Justin Elkins, who I'd got to know at Poole the previous year, and Steve Masters, who was to become a mate and team-mate at several tracks in years to come.

The record book shows that I won my first race, fell off in my next, won the third, was put out for a tapes infringement and then ran a third place to finish up on seven points.

Frank Smart won with a 15-point maximum and Justin Elkins beat Steve Leigh in a run-off for second after both had scored 13.

Then next night I rode for Poole in a junior match against Coventry, and that Monday-Tuesday arrangement was to be the pattern for the next few weeks.

I rode against, and then for Exeter in their junior team and pestered all the senior riders for their time and advice. Fortunately there were some good

THE hospitality and help provided by the Street family was big plus for Jason, who celebrated the arrival of his 16th birthday with a solo trip to England – supposedly for a month in the closing weeks of the 1991 speedway season.

Graham, the older boy, was 15 when Jason was born, and had already moved a couple of miles up the road. He was married with a couple of young children and into a blossoming career in property development.

He was and is a smart guy, and it was Graham who drove Jason to Poole and accompanied him to his first 'job interview' and helped negotiate his first deal with Pirates promoter Mervyn Stewkesbury.

Andy – officially Adrian, but Drew as Jason came to call him – is five years younger than Graham. He was single and at 26, quite happy to become a more or less full-time mechanic, chauffeur, and confidant.

The promised month came and went, and several times Jason telephoned home asking to stay on for 'just one more week'. As it turned out, he remained in England until the end of the season in October, riding two or three times a week, and being regularly reminded by his mother that on his return he was expected to achieve the required results for his Year 10 certificate.

"I told him that if he didn't pass his Grade 10 exams then no way was he going to England the next year," said Carole.

"Of course that meant I was, shall we say, persuaded to help him cram and catch up with his studies when he did get back from England.

"It was a lot of hard work as any parent who has ever found themselves in that situation would know. I particularly remember doing one assignment on Hitler for him."

When the results popped through the letter box, all the burning of midnight oil was rewarded. Jason's results were deemed satisfactory and the only hurdle to clear before setting off for another, this time full-on trip to England was impatience.

He went back to Mildura High at the end of January but he was doing no more than fill in time for a few weeks before he could board a plane once more.

blokes at both places – Mick Poole was riding for the Pirates that year and Steve Regeling was the top gun at Exeter and they couldn't do enough to help.

It was a terrific opportunity to see everything at first hand and then to have the chance to go out and try to do something similar in the second halves.

The big thing was that this was racing, real racing at last. I'd ridden around tracks in Australia and England but there's nothing like it when you actually sit at the starting gate and wait for the tapes to go up.

I even got the chance to line up in the Poole senior team at King's Lynn on September 14 – Marvyn Cox was missing and I went out in heat one with Pooley, Bo Brhel and Dennis Lofqvist.

More accurately, I went out for heat one and was thinking about dropping the clutch as the other three disappeared into the first corner.

I had one more ride and managed to stay on the same lap before predictably, and gratefully, being replaced.

I did manage to break my duck when included as reserve for the away match against Ipswich, which was a whole lot more encouraging. Realistically though it all emphasised how much of a journey it was to become a top-flight rider. It was a good lesson to learn.

The intention had been to spend a month in England but it turned out to be a couple of months running up to the end of that '91 season.

It was a brilliant experience, the first time I had been off on my own for any length of time – and a huge plus was the support of family members such as Bill Street, his wife Mary and my uncles Graham and Adrian or Drew as he's known to one and all.

Living in England was never going to be a drama for me because it was a second home, anyway. Drew was single and very keen to help me get organised, ferry me around, work on the bikes and generally show me the ropes.

Many Australian youngsters going overseas for the first time have it tough; as often as not they have never been out of the country, still less being required to live away from home in strange – sometimes quite ordinary – surroundings and having to fend for themselves.

Poole were very much into signing Australian riders at this time and with Bill the team manager there, it seemed a natural progression for me to sign up with them, with a view to going out on loan the following year.

When the season finished I came back to Australia, returned to school and completed Year 10, with a lot of catching up, many late nights and a great deal of help from my mum.

In between times I got to do a few senior meetings, not just at Mildura but at places like Murray Bridge, North Arm, Shepparton (always an enjoyable one) and anywhere there was a ride to be had.

My performances were very up and down. Funnily enough one of the places where it was tough was at Mildura where I battled to come to grips with the track quite a few times.

ROSTRUM ... Australian Under 21 championship at Mildura, 1992. Leigh Adams won the meeting with Jason Hawkes second, JC third and Cory Alderton fourth

The closest I came to winning anything of note was in the Australian Under 21 titles, in which I finished third behind Leigh Adams, who was in his last year. It gave me something to aim for the following season when I hoped to be able to do even better.

Officially I was still a school student and actually enrolled for the start of Year 11 at Mildura Tech – but there never was any intention of going on with it.

I couldn't wait to graduate to the next stage of my education ... on the speedway tracks of England.

DEBUT DREAM ... Peterborough, 1992. Back, left to right: Rod Colquhoun, Paul Hurry, Mick Poole, JC, Mark Blackbird, Stephen Davies, Neville Tatum. Middle: Kevin Hawkins, Jason Bunyan (mascot), James Easter, Peter Oakes. Front: Craig Swales (mascot)

CHEERS ...
Captain Davies, co-promoter Easter and cub Jason

The Start of Something

I GREW up riding bikes, junior speedway was an obvious natural progression and family connections meant I was always comfortable with the lifestyle – but it didn't automatically follow that I would go the same way. And there were no guarantees I would be successful if I did decide to go in to speedway.

For every son or daughter to follow in their parents' sporting or working footsteps there must be a dozen who go off in an entirely different direction.

Phil was racing, my grandfather was always doing bikes or managing teams. It could just as easily have turned me off the whole business.

But to tell the truth, I've always loved it.

And preparing for the real start of my senior career, that was a huge, exciting time. When you venture out into the big wide world after years of being protected by school and childhood boundaries, it can be scary. Instead, I just found it to be pretty much all that I had dreamed of for years, and then some.

I realised coming to ride in England in 1992 wasn't going to be easy but it had to be a thousand times easier for me than it was for Phil when he first came over in 1971.

He didn't ride a speedway bike until his late teens, he'd never really been anywhere, and within 18 months he was on a plane for the first time in his life and off up to Crewe.

Jason has been riding professionally since he was 16 and learning about life as you go along is not easy when you're always in the public eye. However I think he was much better equipped than many youngsters. He is intelligent, he'd had a good upbringing, and he has always had the ability to speak well, to thank and acknowledge people who have helped him.

– Jason Crump's grandfather Neil Street, OAM,
former Australian team manager

But he loved to race and if there is one thing I inherited from him it was that enthusiasm. Even into his forties he was keen, eager to try different things with bikes, and possibly he enjoyed himself more after he had given away riding in England than when he was doing it on a regular basis.

He had a terrific record in the UK and around Europe as well as in Australia when he was in his prime and of course as soon as I got involved I wanted him to do well.

Unfortunately I was just too young to have seen him when he had his first two World Finals (1975 and 1976) and have only vague recollections of being taken to the 1981 World Final at Wembley which imprinted itself so vividly on the minds of most who were there.

I barely recall him going to Los Angeles in 1982. What I do just remember is that he went to LA with a bike which was flying and in practice had looked the goods, but on the night was very disappointing – and he never again made a final.

By the time he won his fourth Aussie title in 1988, two years after giving away the British League, I was old enough to appreciate it, and of course by that time I was riding myself and very well aware that he had a load of knowledge and experience to pass on.

That's not to say that I found myself agreeing with a lot of the things he said – when you're 12 or 13 you don't do you? We had a fairly tetchy relationship for a long time and in many ways it was better for me to start my career in England without him being around.

What I knew I would have, and to this day it is impossible to over-state how much he has done for me, was the ever-present advice, encouragement and wisdom of Bill Street. It was 40 years since he first came to England and his knowledge is fantastic.

There was some speculation about having me to slot in as number seven in the Poole side in 1992. Young, inexperienced and immature I may have been, but I wasn't silly,. Teams then, as now, often put a kid in at the tail end to allow themselves to stack in more strength at the top of the order but I wasn't prepared to be that sort of sacrificial lamb.

There is a long list of riders who have been thrown in like that to sink or swim, and many sank without trace. Learning at an appropriate level was the way I wanted to go, and that meant riding in the second division to start off.

There was no way I was going to be riding first division. Those couple of meetings at the end of the previous season emphasised what any sane person should have known, which was that I wasn't remotely ready to mix it with the big boys. Fortunately Poole, and Bill, knew which end was up and so we had to figure out a suitable loan base for my first full season.

Exeter seemed to be the obvious one. I'd enjoyed a few good nights there at the end of the year before, was going to be living locally with my grandparents, my support team was there, and as I wasn't old enough to drive, the availability and willingness of my uncle Drew to ferry me around the place was a major consideration.

I didn't mind the track, big, fast and challenging but great fun and Colin Hill, the promoter, seemed to be a regular guy who usually had a kind word for me when I first rode in those junior and second half races there.

I was expecting him to get in touch but he never did and back in Australia, completing my Year 10 studies and enrolling for Year 11 – though without any intention of carrying on – it was a bit of an anxious wait to see what was going to happen.

Whether Colin Hill didn't fancy the fact I already was a Poole rider I don't know although there was no intention of them charging a loan fee or anything like that. It wasn't as if I was someone who was expected to be a big deal. Colin, though, just didn't seem bothered about having me there and as time went by I was getting a bit edgy.

I think Phil fielded a few calls from different promoters but I heard nothing until at last Peterborough got on the telephone to say that they had a place for me and painted a very attractive picture. They had just been taken over by ultra-keen new promoters, and it sounded great.

Peterborough had been going through some tough times when I was in England in 1990 and 1991, and they were ripe and ready for a change of fortune and promotion.

We knew Peter Oakes who was one of Wally Mawdsley's admin team at Swindon when Phil rode there, and as a keen reader of everything written about speedway I also acknowledged the fact that there probably was (and still is) no one better informed about the sport.

And we knew James Easter as a speedway nut who organised the travel and team managed Australia for a while and had been to our place in Mildura when he brought out a team of English fans for a speedway grand tour.

They had got together to form a new partnership at the East of England Showground and were full of bright ideas about how to revitalise the club and the team. The way it all started to shape up sounded great with Mick Poole recalled from loan, Stephen Davies as captain and Rod Colquhoun adding to the Aussie connection.

They also signed Paul Whittaker, Mark Blackbird and Paul Hurry, who, like me, was only just 16 and lining up for his first full season.

I'm sure that part of the attraction as far as Peter and James were concerned was that, as a British passport holder, I could ride on an ACU licence and come in at a two-point average. If I had been employed as an Australian, it would have been on a six-point average and as everyone knows, all those decimal points can make a massive difference when it comes to putting together teams for a new season.

No promoter building a team can resist the idea of smuggling in someone on an assessed average which is clearly lower than the rider is likely to produce

– and even allowing for my lack of experience, I always was going to be a lot better than a two-point man.

But it was all good as far as I was concerned. It meant that there was no great pressure on me, that anything I scored would be a bonus and if I could start picking up points on a regular basis it would be a result for all concerned.

My goal and intention was to achieve an eight-point average in my first full season and that was the target I set myself in the full knowledge that it would not be easy to do.

Once again I have to record that Bill and Mary Street made things so good for me. They are family of course and it wasn't like being away from home at all. My uncles, Graham and Drew, also went out of their way to be helpful and supportive.

I lived with them at St Leonards, near Exeter university, and got on great with all of them, including Graham's two kids Lucy and James who I often met from school round the corner.

The Street family were magnificent to me in that first year. I kidded myself that I was handling it all, being independent and responsible and all that, but thinking back, they must have worked overtime to prop me up, to keep me going and steer me in the right direction. I'll be grateful forever.

My uncle Graham and my grandfather bought a Talbot Express van for me which they allowed me to pay back week by week. It must have been like old times for Bill who had helped Phil such a great deal with his career. What he doesn't know about speedway bikes, riders and tracks isn't worth knowing.

Drew was always around, home and away. We spent many long hours travelling to and from meetings. He also had been around speedway all his life and loved it – though he never had any inclination to race. As chauffeur, mechanic, psychologist and mate he has been absolutely magnificent for me for years.

With a backroom set-up like that, I could not fail. But it was never a stroll. The money I earned all went back into my equipment. It was very tough. And the opposition was always a challenge. Every team had guys who you had hardly heard of who could come out and win races.

At first it was a good night if I got half a dozen points. It was much tougher, initially, than I expected. The guys at Peterborough were great. They really encouraged me, and helped me. Pooley was top-class and Stephen, Rod, and Neville Tatum when he came in quite early on, they all went out of their way to show me the ropes.

We opened up with a challenge match against Rospiggarna, and Mick Poole set the scene by beating Tony Rickardsson in the first heat in a new track record time. Stephen Davies beat him later on, and although Tony took 16 from six rides Peterborough won an exciting match 49-41.

My contribution was paid 11 from four rides, including a win in the reserves race, all highly encouraging. I came in for 5-1 wins with Stephen and

Rod and it was very tempting to imagine that it was all going to be easy although I was smart enough to realise it wasn't.

A trip to Eastbourne a couple of days later – for my first open booking – rubbed in the point. I was reserve for a team called the Anzacs, and it rained for most of the afternoon. I snuck a second place in the reserves race but didn't manage another point and my view of most of the proceedings was from the back. Welcome to England. It was a dirty, dishevilled and fairly detuned character who had plenty to think about on the drive home to Exeter.

The next meeting, at home to Stoke, was another testing one. After winning heat two, I then got rammed in the first turn by Ade Hoole and for a few minutes it looked as if I might have broken my arm. Fortunately it turned out to be much less dramatic than that, but it was another reminder that this was a tough, unyielding business. It was the first big crash in my career – that Peterborough fence doesn't move, however hard you hit it – and it slowed me down for two or three weeks.

A weekend trip to local rivals Mildenhall was another eye-opener. West Row was a bit like a mini-Showground but I couldn't get to grips with the place at all and hardly scored a point. Then the Fen Tigers came to Alwalton for the return and we were beaten at home, which meant that there were long faces all round, not just mine.

But I did try right from the off to make every experience a learning experience. There was no way I could afford to be discouraged by bad meetings because inevitably there were going to be a few.

Sure, I'd been on a number of the tracks to practice after meetings, but actually racing was totally different and trying to get to grips with places I had

LOOK out for the names of Poole and Davies to make an impact in Australia, and, possibly, in English speedway in the coming years.

Jason Crump had New South Welshmen Mick Poole and Stephen Davies as two of his colleagues in the Peterborough team in 1992.

Now Mick's son Taylor and Stephen's son Alex are going through the traditional route of junior speedway with support, albeit from a distance, from Jason.

He speaks with and exchanges emails with the two youngsters, both of whom have hopes of following in the well-trodden path to Europe, and from time to time he sends them items of equipment.

"I would like to do more but I spend so little time in Australia that it's difficult," he says.

"Encouraging them a little bit is the least I can do. Mick and Stephen were and still are two of my best mates in speedway and I will never forget the support they gave me when I was starting."

Poole recalls: "Jason used to come to my house at Turves to wind down from the drive from Exeter before a Peterborough meeting and would spend most of the time playing with Taylor.

"We had a joint birthday party for them when Taylor was two and Jason was 18."

never seen and opponents who all seemed to be going at a million miles an hour was a tough call.

It was after meetings like this that my grandfather was such a great person to come home to. He would never shout or criticise, just sit me down and ask what I thought had gone wrong. Was it the bike, were there problems with the track, did I feel right ... he wanted me to analyse what had happened and learn from the bad days as well as celebrating the good ones.

It also was important to get the idea that win or lose, there was life outside speedway. Of course, results and performances mattered but one ordinary meeting was not the end of the world even if it felt like it at the time.

Life goes on whether you've just scored two points or a maximum. The sun still comes up when you get out of bed next morning. It was a good lesson to absorb and it was something with which to remind myself ... I still do, in fact.

My grandmother, Mary, and Graham and Drew also helped keep things balanced. They kept my feet on the ground when required and were always there for me. Bill got to as many of my meetings as he could, but he was team manager of Poole and that came first. It was always good to have him along when he could make it, of course.

I didn't particularly appreciate being told off by Kevin Hawkins, the Peterborough team manager, who seemed to expect me to go out and be winning races all the time. That was my aim and intention and I did have a decent amount of success but at times he appeared to forget that I was a 16-year-old in my first season.

But my confidence came back and I started getting some good results. Even so, for the first half of the year I was unable to get out of the reserve position. Part of that was because we had a very strong top five, but I found it difficult to achieve any consistency. There were quite a few wins in heat two to get the ball rolling, and then just as many setbacks in tougher races.

Some of the experienced old soldiers in the league seemed to go the extra yard to put me to the test but that's what happens, I guess, when a new sprog starts winning a few races..

The incident which I remember most was in a Gold Cup match up at Stoke in June when Nigel Crabtree came charging underneath me at 100 miles an hour and carted me off. I ended up with a broken scaphoid and wasn't too thrilled.

Local legend was that this was one of Crabby's favourite ploys and if you were smart, you got out of the road. Nobody had told me what was supposed to happen and I didn't move over – not until he took me out, anyway.

It was the sort of thing you put down to experience. This is a tough business at any level, egos are on the line, and mine probably was running pretty rampant at the time. Going to places and beating a few of the guys was a rush.

Not so much fun was having Dave James cart me off to hospital for running repairs. That dreaded word 'scaphoid' had cast a shadow over the Crump household for years so I didn't know how this was going to play out but very fortunately, it turned out not to be a major injury.

That didn't prevent me from feeling pretty nervous about my first meeting back – so much so that Drew let me drive the last part of the journey up from Exeter to Peterborough. I wasn't even old enough to have a licence but he thought I needed something to take my mind off the meeting – and it worked!

Traditionally, one of the highlights of the year at Peterborough was the staging of the Four Team Tournament. It was the biggest meeting of the season at the track, and rated second only to the league riders' championship.

The Panthers had a pretty good record in it, too, prompting regular cries from opposition supporters that home track advantage played too big a part in deciding the outcome ... although when you are assembling the best riders in the competition, that's not too much of a factor to be honest.

Disappointingly for me though, I couldn't score a place in the Peterborough team and although they picked up the title, the first of what turned out to be a trio of major prizes, I didn't have any part of it. That preyed on my mind for a while.

The Showground was a good track on which to build your confidence though, and importantly I started to get some scores away too, including my first maximum, 11 paid 12 at Long Eaton where they had a few good, experienced riders. Then I had another big night at Edinburgh, loved the place in fact, and this was real progress.

My results started to show some serious improvement. when I got hold of an engine from Otto Lantenhammer, The motor arrived courtesy of Otto Schroeck, a big speedway and long track enthusiast in Germany.

He'd been involved with people like Egon Muller for years, and his elder son Peter rode. I became friendly with Otto's other son Alex who came over to Australia in 1990-91 and talked himself into a job as a mechanic with the Russian and Polish touring team which Trevor Harding had brought out.

One thing led to another and after this new engine arrived, speedway suddenly seemed a whole lot easier. It also coincided with my parents coming over to see how things were going. My confidence started to soar sky-high and in the last two or three months of the year the decent scores began to flow.

I was at that stage of life where I was prepared to be who I felt like being – like going to Newcastle with beads in my hair just after Gary Havelock (who favoured that fashion at the time) won the 1992 world title, His dad, Brian, was the Newcastle team manager and I have to tell you he looked at me very strangely.

By the time October rolled around I had hauled my average above eight points, and was starting to feel pretty confident in my ability against all opponents, home and away.

At a glance the record suggests that this first year had been one long run of success for me, but it wasn't. Of course it was pleasing when things started to fall into place, it was sensational when I went to two or three meetings and went through the card. I wasn't getting carried away, though.

From a team point of view, it just got better and better as we won the league championship and the Knockout Cup. The confidence in the side, much like my own, simply went from strength to strength.

When Neville Tatum came in he gave us an added ingredient which was reflected by the fact we finished up with something to spare over Berwick, who had the league's top man in Richard Knight – a World Finalist only two years earlier.

It certainly wasn't that easy a league to win, or ride in, either. Knight, Jan Staechmann, Neil Evitts, Robert Nagy, Les and Neil Collins, David Bargh ... these were just a handful of the star names sprinkled around. Then you had the likes of Martin Goodwin, Peter Carr, Alan Grahame and Nigel Crabtree to contend with, not to mention an Aussie presence which, in addition to our own boys, included Tony Langdon, Shane Bowes and Steve Regeling all of whom finished in the top 10 of the averages.

On an individual front Peterborough were led by Stephen Davies (16th) Mick Poole (20th) and myself (22nd) but what we had was a tremendous togetherness, a great fighting spirit and solidarity all through the order which meant that if someone didn't perform, you could depend on somebody else stepping up.

The same sort of qualities saw us through to the KO Cup as well, a big home win over Rye House making the return leg at Hoddesdon, while no formality, a match we were never going to lose.

As it turned out, rain washed out the scheduled second leg. Rye didn't have lights in those days and to fit the final into October as the regulations required they had to forego home advantage and take us on at Arena Essex.

It made no difference, and although the Rockets had the consolation of winning on the night, it was mission accomplished for the Panthers who matched the feat of the great Newcastle teams of 1976 and 1982 by completing a clean sweep of the three big prizes on offer.

The promoters were rapt, the fans were ecstatic – the place was buzzing and I couldn't have asked for a better set-up in which to take my first steps in the sport.

Viewed overall, of course, it was good, as good as I could reasonably have hoped for. But I learned a lot of valuable lessons without knowing it, just by going to the races and having fun.. I learned that you don't take any opponent or any occasion for granted. And there could have been no better example of the fact that good teamwork and a happy environment makes a huge difference to performance.

One of the first details which needed to be sorted out when I headed home was to establish that after flying the flag of convenience for a couple of years, it was time to reassure everyone of my allegiance to Australia – and I promptly applied for and received an international licence.

Its immediate effect was to entitle me to contest the world championship rounds, starting with the Victorian championship which was to be held at Myrtleford, and the Australian Under 21 title at Mildura the following night.

My lead-up schedule included racing at Ivan Mauger's long track at Parklands Showground on the Gold Coast, and a first ride at Brisbane's Ekka, the famous Exhibition Ground speedway both of which were a lot of fun.

I very nearly missed the Parklands meeting because Mark Carlson and I, flying to Brisbane together via Gatwick and then America, were stranded at Denver airport for 14 hours after a couple of flights had been canned. They decided to put everyone on one aeroplane and we were standing in a queue with what seemed like about 500 people in front of us.

Fortunately David Bargh, a much more experienced global traveller, turned up and casually walked to the front of the line and after a few moments came back with three boarding passes in his hand.

Preparations for the big Myrtleford-Mildura weekend were not helped when I crashed and broke a collarbone at Gosford where Terry Poole had invited me to top the bill on Boxing Day.

It left me with a week to piece myself together and something had to give, so I opted out of the state title (which Mark Lemon won) and decided to go for the Under 21 at Olympic Park.

A decent win in the first ride was accomplished without major drama, but next time out there was a terrific bingle with Ryan Sullivan. I was excluded from the re-run and, feeling pretty sorry for myself, didn't ride again. Ryan went on to win the title

I was very keen to go back to Peterborough the following season. People were so welcoming and helpful, it was a thoroughly enjoyable introduction to full-time racing, and I liked the place. It also suited me very well, with a Friday race night, ideal as I was planning to do a lot of continental long track and grass track meetings in 1993 to broaden my experience and earning capacity.

Otto Schroeck had extended his involvement and came up with two long track bikes and a full programme of meetings. Otto did all the arrangements, just faxed me the details of each event, his son Alex collected me from the airport and off we went to the races. Alex is a highly intelligent guy and we had hit it off from the start.

He's out of it now, and doing well as a technician for one of the world's leading laser eyesight machine firms; we are still mates.

At first it looked as if the plan for the year might have a spanner in the works when I wasn't allowed to go back to Peterborough. Out of the blue Swindon became the first team to be compulsorily relegated after ADT Auctions, the stadium owners, pulled out.

They had had a few difficult years there – changes of ownership and promotion were among the reasons which persuaded Phil that he'd had enough of British speedway. But Mervyn Stewkesbury and Pete Ansell (who owned my contract at Poole) came breezing in, determined to make a go of it again.

They restored the traditional Saturday race night, appointed former rider Martin Yeates as team manager, and told Peterborough they couldn't have me back for a second year because they were going to put me at Swindon.

The first of a number of moves I've made in my career was nothing to do with me, but fortunately it did work out well. Importantly, Merv and Pete had experience of dealing with riders who had overseas commitments, and understood how necessary it was for me to be able to fit in everything without any hassle.

I was nervous about what people at Swindon would expect of me. Phil had been a legend there for years, and could do no wrong, so I was on a bit of a hiding to nothing. It was weird to start with, riding at the place where I spent so many of my earlier years.

But I need not have worried. People were really good, they were prepared to treat me on my own merits and recognise that this was Jason Crump, not Phil Crump the second. Fortunately they took to me and any doubts about whether the atmosphere and the support would be there were quickly blown away.

Swindon had to settle for fourth in the league, and were runners-up in the Cup, but probably I enjoyed it as much as I had the Peterborough experience of the year before. Blundson always had been my favourite track and I had a great time.

Before the season started I talked to Bill Street, who was of the opinion that I should do just a couple of seasons in the lower division before moving up. I remember telling him that whatever happened, I didn't want to go in with the top guys until I had achieved a 10.5 average.

As it turned out, we won all our home matches and I averaged 10.92 with seven full maximums and two paid. I also had seven full scores (six full, one paid) away from Blunsdon and a 10.18 average.

It was a season in which I first started to win races consistently and for a 17-year-old it was pretty exciting stuff. Looking back, I probably got over-excited, over-full of my own importance, and did and said some things which would make me cringe today.

But hey, when you are just at that stage of your career and beating guys and pretty much everything you try turns out well, it is so easy to think you are better than you are. It's easy too, with the best will in the world, to rub people up the wrong way.

I had every respect for the riders in the Second Division though, let's be clear about that. There were plenty of good riders who had been there, done that, and their record spoke volumes. It was hard racing, with some terrific battles. But I just had a dream run.

There was one point just after I'd turned 18 when I couldn't seem to put a foot wrong. Starting with 18 from six rides at Edinburgh on August 27 through to September 18, for nine matches in a row I went unbeaten in 46 starts.

SUPER EIGHT ... That's eight maximums in a row for Swindon, 1993, beating the record held by Barry Briggs

Barry Briggs had set the Swindon club record with seven successive maximums way back in 1967, so it was a hell of a thrill and quite an achievement although of course, his was in the top flight.

I would have extended the run, too, but for a dodgy refereeing decision at Rye House.

You learn at an early stage that when things are going well, your next disappointment might be only a moment away.

One of my big targets for the year was to do well in the World Under 21 final in Pardubice. I'd finished second in a quarter-final, third in the semi final, but didn't really rate my chances of winning it because guys like Joe Screen and Mikael Karlsson were much stronger and better credentialled.

Nevertheless this was an event I'd set my sights on winning at some stage and I fancied my chances of maybe making it to the rostrum. With Drew we drove over to collect some engines in Germany and then carried on to Czecho.

But I was laid low by a viral infection and couldn't do the meeting. It was stinking hot, I felt absolutely shocking, and it was a long way to go for absolutely nothing. At practice I had started to feel pretty crook and after it I was really bad, throwing up everywhere.

RACING FATHERS AND SONS ... 1993 Under 21 Final in Pardubice. Jiri Jirout with Mario, Phil Crump with Jason, Ole Olsen with Jacob, Antonin Svab with Toni

There was no way I was going to be fit to ride so we simply loaded up the day before the meeting, hightailed it back to England and the doctors told me I had picked up some bug. They stuck a load of needles in me and assured me I would be fine in three or four days, and I was.

Pretty soon I was back in the routine and we kept up our momentum until the KO Cup Final. The first leg was good and bad. I got 18 points but Glasgow held us to a 54-all draw and all the odds looked to be stacked in their favour.

Sure enough, they blew us out of the water 64-44 in Scotland and after one controversial exclusion, I had a run-in with a reporter who caught me at the wrong moment. It was stupid behaviour, witnessed by quite a few people, and it didn't do me any favours.

The one big prize which was still on offer was the National League Riders Championship and in my mind there was only ever going to be one winner – me.

I went to King's Lynn convinced it was going to be my night. I was top of the averages, I'd beaten all of the contenders and press, public, just about everyone seemed sure that the title was mine for the taking.

In the middle of all that hype and build-up it is very easy to forget that you still have to get on the bike, make sure everything comes together, and win races.

I ran a second first up, then got a win but completely cocked up my third ride, bringing down Mark Simmonds and copping an exclusion. That was it all over, red rover. To say I was disappointed is a big understatement.

Meanwhile Gary Allan, my team-mate at Swindon, was consistently putting together all the right results and with one race to go he was in the box seat, especially if I beat my big mate Mick Poole, another major contender, in our final race.

Martin Yeates, who was Swindon team manager, came up to me and said: 'If you can beat Pooley, Gary will win the meeting.'

Now team mate or not, Gary Allan was not my best buddy. We had a reasonable relationship but one that included a fair bit of rivalry as we traded big scores through the season. He was the ultra-professional former first division rider who had stepped down and I was the young punk who was collaring a lot of the headlines.

DOWNER ... National League Riders Final at King's Lynn 1993. Swindon team manager Martin Yeates stops by for a chat, but his timing's not great

I didn't have anything against Gary but there was no way I was going to try to deny Pooley his shot at the title. Mick and Michelle were and still are two of the most loyal friends I have known in or out of speedway. If I couldn't win the meeting there was nobody, repeat nobody, I would rather have seen the title go to.

I told Martin as much and I don't think he or Gary appreciated it, but that was it. Mick did win the race but he didn't win the meeting. Gary Allan did, after which he packed up, went back to Brisbane and as far as I'm aware, he's hardly been near a speedway since then.

I also had a pretty good first year on the continent, doing about 14 meetings, qualifying for the world long track final as a reserve, and learning so

AN EARLY ally and still a fast friend to Jason is Alex Schroeck, son of German speedway identity Otto and brother of Peter, one of the first foreign riders to appear in Britain's second division.

Alex met Jason at Barry Briggs' Golden Greats meeting at Swindon in 1990 and the friendship developed when the teenager came out to Australia later that year. He readily recalls when Jason boosted his savings by arranging to clean the bikes of the Swedish touring team members, contracted out most of the dirty work to his schoolmates, and turned a neat profit which also included being paid in kind with a couple of rolling chassis.

Otto Schroeck sponsored Jason in his early racing adventures in Germany and Alex acted as mechanic. Years later it can be revealed that the new kid was very nervous before his debut on long track at Plattling – so much so that the night before the meeting, Jason dragged his bed into Alex's room and the pair talked deep into the night before sleep eventually took over.

Neil Street helped address the nerves at later meetings, encouraging the youngsters to spend some time in the beer tent to relax on the night before the racing.

"It was also very hard for him in his first couple of seasons in Australia on a Queensland licence," says Alex.

"No matter where we went it always ended up in a big pile-up in the pits. I was quite good after the first season in fighting with officials. If he went to Townsville there were people who didn't like it because he was from Victoria and if we went to Mildura there were those who didn't like it because he had moved to Queensland – and wherever he went, plenty of the locals gave him a hard time because he was Phil's son."

To all outward appearances Jason was born confident but Alex recognised that a rider needs to be able to translate everything on to the race track.

"I think he knew before he really first rode in England that you can't talk your way to a race win," he says.

"But I helped a lot of riders and no one knew so much about speedway and what it takes to win races."

"I have great respect for him as a rider and as a friend. He's had a lot of people who helped him during his career but it was always him and his will to become what or where he is now."

much from racing alongside blokes like Wiggy, Karl Maier, Gerd Riss, Kelvin Tatum, Egon Muller, Klaus Lausch and Marcel Gerhart. You couldn't help but improve, racing in such company.

One important international occasion which did turn out pretty well was when I was called into the Australian side for the World Team Cup A final in Slangerup. The Danes were always favourites to go through but to finish on top of the pile for the Aussies was a big buzz, especially as most of the other riders in the meeting were established internationals and British League first division regulars.

It was a pretty special feeling to be on parade in this sort of company and flying the flag.

I beat Tomasz Gollob a couple of times and handling myself in this sort of meeting gave my confidence a real boost. It's not that I was unhappy with my achievements in the domestic racing, but this was something else.

One way and another I was itching to get into the top flight to race guys like this on a permanent basis. There wasn't much chance that I could do any better or progress further with another year at Swindon.

I even got the opportunity to mix it with the big boys when Gary Havelock pulled out injured from the Division One Riders' Championship at Poole. I had no business to be there but decided to enjoy the experience and collected five points in some pretty distinguished company.

The occasion told me that my step up into the top division the following year was not going to be easy. But I was up for it, and in my heart, felt confident I was up to it.

I had it in my mind that I would like to go to Reading when I moved up – just because of my respect for Per Jonsson.

I didn't have anything against Poole, who owned my contract, but when Per and Jimmy Nilsen lived down the road from us in Swindon, we used to see a great deal of them.

Nothing seemed more obvious than to want to go to ride with Per who had been a good friend of ours for several years, and, more than that, was a sensational rider.

His technique on the bike was just brilliant. He could do unbelievable things. From a watching point of view, seeing his 1990 World Final victory at Bradford was a huge highlight. If not before, from that moment on I wanted to be like Per.

Poole, however, were not about to let me go somewhere else after keeping a watchful eye on me during my second division years and it was never a big drama about going there. I'd had a couple of good years in the second division, there wasn't much else left for me to do in it, and I felt ready for the bigger stage.

Phil thought so, Bill thought so, and if there were any doubts about it, a good season in Australia pretty much blew them away.

In four Test matches against the British Lions I scored a paid 48 points, with 14 and a bonus in the final match at Wayville, always one of my favourite Aussie tracks. Then I scored 11 and won a run-off with Craig Boyce to take third place in the Australian Final at Mildura, a couple of points behind Leigh Adams and Jason Lyons.

There were some decent results elsewhere, including second place behind Simon Wigg in a Brisbane Ekka meeting billed as Phil's farewell, and trips to Claremont in Perth and over to Hamilton for the New Zealand long track final. More importantly, I was rubbing shoulders with, racing with and – as often as not – beating some of the best blokes going around.

It was a different kind of homecoming because Phil and Carole had sold up in Mildura and moved to the Gold Coast – to a new development called Forest Hills, in Oxenford. It was just down the road from the theme parks and maybe a quarter of an hour to the best beaches in the world.

Brisbane was only about 40 minutes away and my parents were both given a job by Trevor Harding who ran his Kwiksnax catering company there.

South-east Queensland was, and still is, the fastest-growing area in Austral;ia and there was a big buzz about the area. Quite a contrast to country Victoria for sure.

My first outing as a Queenslander, mind you, was not exactly a local affair. A small matter of nine months out from the World Final, the world championship trail began with the Queensland titles up in Townsville, which is as far from the Gold Coast as Mildura is in the opposite direction.

The real test for the next European season turned out to be multi-dimensional and the end result almost unbelievable. I ended up qualifying for three world finals.

There was so much to be pleased with, and yet missing out again in the Under 21 championship – which I made my main individual focus for the year – was a bitter disappointment. It was a long time before I was able to get over that, and to view the year from a less emotional perspective.

Going to Poole always was going to be a challenge, but Bill Street being there as team manager was a major consideration and having Alun Rossiter move back from Swindon with me was good, too. The down side was that instead of having as a home track one which rightly rated among the best, Poole, at that time, was one of the worst. It was narrow and rough, and while the football club were playing there, the corners were tight to say the least.

It's fair to say that not everyone thought much of the team Mervyn Stewkesbury and Pete Ansell put together for the 1994 season. Boycey had a bit of a spat with them towards the end of the previous season before they agreed to kiss and make up – and among the others there was no obvious heat leader, even allowing for people like Lars Gunnestad and Steve Schofield to improve.

A lot of the vibes locally were not that positive, coming on the back of a 1993 season when the Pirates had stuggled badly. There was a fair amount of

SUPER PIRATES ... the outstanding Poole team of 1994, Back: Steve Masters, Alun Rossiter, Jorgen Johansson, John Tarr (JT Commercials). Front: Pete Ansell, JC, Craig Boyce, Mervyn Stewkesbury, Steve Schofield

criticism because Marvyn Cox had not been re-signed. A lot of the locals tipped us to be down at the bottom of the table.

Well, you can listen to what people say and believe what you read, or you can do the other thing. When someone has given you a serve like that, though, it usually strengthens the resolve to prove those opinions wrong, and that, the record books show, is something we did very successfully in the next few months.

Craig Boyce was determined to do well after an ordinary 1993. And we all responded to his lead. Boycey is a true blue Aussie, he calls a spade a spade, puts in 100 per cent and expects the same of everybody else. I'm happy to call him a mate and the impact he made that year was out of this world.

Our other secret weapon was Bill Street as team manager, another factor which made things especial for me. I didn't get any favours – just the same sound, sensible, wise advice he dishes out to any rider who is prepared to listen and learn.

We led the table virtually all season, and finished up winning the title with a record 77 points from 40 matches. We won all 20 at home and lost only nine away, had a 15-point margin over Eastbourne, and Mervyn Stewkesbury said he had 'never known a team work so hard for each other'.

In the opening weeks, there were a few frustrations. Our first couple of meetings at Wimborne Road were washed out, before we finally got on track at Cradley Heath and I won my first race. Even then the meeting was rained off after 12 heats.

Then we started winning a few. We got our first away victory at Belle Vue where I went through the card and a month or so into the season, the same people who had been predicting gloom and doom were talking about us as possible championship contenders.

It was a baptism of fire for a newcomer to the top division and this was when I first got on the wrong end of Sam Ermolenko. No stickers, goggles or freebies from Sam this time. We had two or three colourful clashes which left me on my backside at Wolverhampton where, as the reigning world champion, he was a protected species.

POOLE'S fortunes, and those of Jason Crump, underwent a dramatic 'before' and 'after' change over the course of the 1994 season.

The Pirates had a poor year in 1993, lost Marvyn Cox in the off-season, and were widely expected to struggle again.

Dickie Howard, who rode for the club in 1949-50, told the *Speedway Star* how disenchanted he was with the line-up.

"The fans deserve better," said Dickie, who helped his son David run Scorpio, a firm in Ringwood Road which produced speedway gear.

"There isn't a star rider amongst them and where are the heat leaders?

"No one is going to enthuse about this line-up and Jason Crump has yet to prove himself in the First Division.

"Fans at Poole want a team that can win things. I can't see them winning anything."

By the end of the season Jason had achieved a nine-plus average, the Pirates were runaway winners of the British League title and their critics had been sent packing.

Of course it was a team effort but Alun Rossiter, who like Jason had moved across from Swindon, had no doubt who deserved the greatest credit.

"It goes without saying that the signing of Crumpy was a turning point in the club's fortunes," he told Neil Evans of *Speedway Star*.

"His enthusiasm is endless and his passion, determination and willingness to learn has rubbed off on us all. He's won some unbelievable races this year, beating top-class riders he should never get near when one considers his age and experience – but that's the way he is."

I learned fast that it's dog it dog. When he came to Poole it was Sam's turn to bite the dust. It was nothing personal. I just didn't want anyone thinking that the new kid was going to be a soft touch.

My form was pretty decent, especially away from home, and things just kept getting better. A favourite memory was winning at Coventry where I beat Hans Nielsen twice, and Scoie and I rode together in four 5-1 heat wins which silenced the Brandon fans.

It was pretty sweet for all of us, not least Rosco who had been in the 1989 and 1990 National League-winning teams before going to Swindon, and as usual, wasn't short of an opinion.

We clinched the title on a grey night at Arena Essex, needing not to win, but to score at least 32 points. We got to the magic moment when I beat Leigh Adams in Heat 12 and the noise our travelling fans made was unreal.

Unfortunately we never got to ride as a team in front of our home supporters because our final home meeting was an England v USA Test match ... but the crowd gave us a huge reception when the trophy and awards were presented beforehand.

Seven guys who got on great all responded to the challenge, everyone upped their average, the doubters were put to flight and it was a memorable year. We all helped one another and nobody helped me more than Alun Rossiter.

He was a constant source of encouragement and he and his wife Julie also allowed me to use their place in Swindon as a second home. I was spending half my time charging up and down from Exeter to Heathrow for an increasing number of continental meetings, and having the opportunity to use the Rossiter pad as a base was invaluable.

Most teams that have had Rosco on board have clicked. He's a chirpy, energetic character with a lively mind and people respond to him.

Boycey was the supreme inspiration. He had been around for a few years, promising a lot and then suffering from inconsistency. This was a stellar season for him. His leadership was special, and the way everybody pulled together owed a lot to his example.

In addition to the British League there were a few meetings in Sweden, some in Poland, long track and grass track to fit into a very crowded schedule. Increasingly I had to work to ensure that all my arrangements slotted in with one another and as far as that went, uncle Drew was brilliant. From my first year in England he has never been anything less than enthusiastic and willing to go the extra mile.

But if there was one person who kept things on track and was always there for advice, encouragement, or a gee-up if one was needed, it was his dad, my grandfather Bill Street who as team manager enjoyed the team's success as much as any of us – and contributed to us as much as any rider or official.

My first year end of term report showed 463 points, a 9.35 average, and, pleasingly, I did almost as well on the road as at home. Although quite a few of the tracks were new to me I averaged 9.12 away, and only Henka Gustafsson (who had a few matches late on for Belle Vue), Hans Nielsen, Tony Rickardsson and Leigh Adams did better than that.

But if the league scene was great, it was even more remarkable on the international front. I ended up qualifying for three world championship finals – the individual, Under 21 and long track.

I grew up in the era when the world championship still was conducted over a series of qualifying rounds with a one-off final. Even now, 12 years on, people still argue about the merits of the Grand Prix system and a lot of the old-timers get a bit misty-eyed about the passing of the old-style World Final.

The elation I felt when reaching the World Final at Vojens in 1994 remains one of my best memories. And anyone who figures that the Grand Prix series is a much more demanding test might like to be reminded of the nine-month route I took to the last of the one-off finals.

First up there was the Queensland championship, followed by the Australian title – at Mildura, which was good – and then the Commonwealth, Overseas and a semi-final in Prague.

I didn't go in with any huge expectations ... I had the Under 21 championship uppermost in my mind, and the long track to think about as well. The individual speedway one was the real bonus.

The longer it went, the more optimistic I became. I had Bill, Phil, and, usually, Mick Poole, to help me through the European rounds.

I was pretty relaxed about the Commonwealth Final at King's Lynn, just went along to enjoy things and soak up the atmosphere. The thing was I kept scoring points and got through without any huge drama; then in the Overseas Final at Coventry a good win in my last ride took me to the next stage.

The Prague semi was tough, but I drew no.1, which ensured an even spacing of rides, and seven points in my first three set me up. There was a bit of drama in my second race when Billy Hamill brought me down in the first corner but referee Frank Ebdon ordered a re-start with all four. As luck would have it, my nine points proved sufficient to clinch my spot in the final while Greg Hancock, on eight, had to beat his mate Hamill and Tomas Topinka in a run-off for the last position.

By then, the celebrations in our corner had already begun and the only shame of it was that Mick Poole couldn't be there – he was riding for Oxford that weekend.

There was no time to get carried away with the fact that I had qualified as I still had the Under 21 and the long track finals to think about before Vojens.

I'd been determined to make a big effort in the Under 21, after the disappointment of the previous year. I won my qualifier in Randers, Denmark, and the semi-final in Gyula, Hungary and probably was the favourite for the title in Elgane, Norway.

But the plan didn't come quite together. I beat Rune Holta in Heat 13 and needed to win against Mikael Karlsson in Heat 17 to have the chance of a run-off, and even that hinged on Holta dropping another point in his last ride.

But it seemed like it wasn't my time. Probably I went there feeling too confident, and ended up putting too much pressure on myself. Karlsson was too quick for me, Holta won his final outing and then the two of them had a run-off for the title which Mikael won. I had to settle for a run-off for third with Tomas Topinka, which I won.

It didn't seem like it at the time but it was a good learning experience. The long track final at Marianske Lazne was another big occasion but one I could soak up without any realistic expectation of doing more than make up the numbers. Which is pretty much what happened, though it was good to join in the fun when Simon Wigg clinched his fifth title.

From a personal angle though it was another very ordinary meeting. I broke a chain when lying second in my first race and that really detuned me. I was pretty hopeless after that.

Sampling the atmosphere of so many important occasions didn't do me any harm in the run-up to the World Final, though. It was a dream start too when I jumped out of the box and beat Tony Rickardsson, Sam Ermolenko and Mark Loram in my first race but unfortunately I went missing after that and only scored another couple of points.

Again, my head wasn't in the right place. After a start like that I should have been able to rustle up enough points to get in the top half which was critical as the FIM announced that the leading 10 riders in the meeting would be automatic qualifiers for the first year of the Grand Prix in 1995. A lot of the pleasure in reaching Vojens went out of the window when I didn't do the business.

The drama of a three-man run-off, in which Tony Rickardsson beat Hans Nielsen and Craig Boyce after they had all scored 12 points, ensured an exciting finish to the old-style finals but it was a bit lost on me.

At a stroke my chances, and those of riders like Leigh Adams (who made his World Final debut in 1993 but missed out

HELLO WORLD ... Waiting for the start of the 1994 World Final in Vojens

this time) and Joe Screen (who had been injured), were put on hold for a year. Instead of starting a season on level terms, knowing that you're in with a chance of becoming world champion and progressing through the various rounds of the competition, we were on the outer with no prospect of looking in.

I have to say what should have been an entirely joyful memory was one of the most disappointing moments of my career. It was a tough time. I'm an optimist by nature, life should have been great after all the achievements I'd managed during the year, but this was a kick in the teeth, big time.

There was so much controversy over the changeover from the old system to the new, and many of the initial proposals by the FIM left a lot to be desired. Still, there's a saying about what doesn't kill you can only make you stronger. If nothing else, it convinced me that I didn't want to be left in the same position again.

My other taste of world championship action was bitter-sweet too. In the World Team Cup qualifier in Wroclaw I scored 12 points and helped Australia win the meeting – but Bill Street gave the nod to Craig Boyce for the final in Brokstedt a fortnight later.

Boycey had just been within a whisker of winning the world title so it was a fair call but not one I was thrilled about at the time. And we finished fourth behind Sweden, Poland and Denmark.

There are plenty of things worse than losing a few races, though, and easily the worst moment of this year was hearing that Per Jonsson had been left paralysed after a crash in Poland. When something like that happens, it puts everything else into perspective.

The first I knew of Per's accident was the following day. I had been racing in a long track in Germany and both of us were due back into Heathrow at about the same time. We arranged to meet up at his place in Swindon on the Monday afternoon because I needed to get back an engine I had loaned him at Poole a few days earlier.

It was only after going round to Jimmy Nilsen's place that I heard what had happened.

It was a bit weird when Pat Bliss rang me up and asked me to guest in his place at Reading the following week, and a few times after that.

My own baptism in Polish League was one to forget, with the aid of a bout of concussion which landed me in hospital for an overnight stay. I had been signed up by Stal Gorzow as cover for Billy Hamill, and on the Easter weekend started off with a couple of wins in the away match against Torun. Then in my next ride I was trying to go round Tomas Bajerski, collected his back wheel, and crashed big time.

Fortunately Bill Street had made the trip with me and was able to check things out and ensure that I got home safely. His presence saved me from freaking out about the whole Polish thing. These days we all nip in and out of there without a second thought but back then, I couldn't communicate with anyone, no one could understand what I was talking about and frankly, it was scary.

I had quite a phobia about going back to Poland for a while after that and for one reason and another, did only one other match for Gorzow that season – at Wroclaw.

It was a similar story in Sweden, where I was the third foreigner, behind Greg Hancock and Joe Screen in a Getingarna team which somehow managed to finish bottom of the league.

The regulations allowed only two of us to ride at any given time, and all I managed was a home match against Valsarna which we won by eight despite 17 points from Tony Rickardsson, and one away, a narrow defeat at Visby against Bysarna.

Winning the Queensland championship in Brisbane – the first time I rode a GM with a laydown engine – then the Australian title, and performing strongly in David Tapp's new 500 Series, all helped set me up for a decent start to 1995.

In the busiest Aussie season I've had before or since, it was good to be battling it out with guys like Tony Rickardsson, Sam Ermolenko, Simon Wigg and Greg Hancock on a regular basis. David Tapp, son of Johnny Tapp, one of Austrralia's best-known horse racing commentators, had become involved in motorsport and his idea of putting together a nationwide grand prix-style series was a big shot in the arm.

It was good, too, to have some great support from Trevor Harding, who has always cared passionately about the state of the sport and the welfare of riders. He paid special attention to Mick Poole, Stephen Davies and myself and we had the use of a big van for the series which meant we could please ourselves and not be reliant on the group transport.

One of the toughest things about the series was the travelling. We all covered vast distances over a period of a couple of months, but the meetings were all very competitive and the boys were pretty happy to be making a real effort to sell speedway in the big centres and a few country venues as well.

There were 11 rounds with meetings in Sydney, Melbourne, Brisbane, Adelaide, Canberra and elsewhere. I was pretty consistent and scored well in most of the rounds without ever quite getting up alongside Wiggy, Tony and Sam who set the standard. We're talking here about a five-time world longtrack champion, the reigning speedway world champion and the guy who had the title the previous year.

Simon led the series more or less from start to finish but was pipped right at the end: Rickardsson 197 points, Wigg 193, Ermolenko 189. That's how tight it was. Craig Boyce was the best-performed of the home riders on 178, I had 158, Leigh Adams 141, followed by Hancock on 135 and Jan Staechmann with 129.

Ensuring we stayed in touch with those guys meant I was reasonably organised, machine-wise and mentally, for a pop at the Australian title which my dad had won four times – in 1975, 1979, 1984 and 1988. Even so, it probably was a timely stroke of luck when the scheduled first staging at Gosford was washed out on January 20.

It gave us the opportunity to get back home to the Gold Coast, to have a week of solid preparation, working on bikes which had been given a tough going-over for several weeks, and taking a bit of time out. There's no doubt everything was in better shape by the time the re-run came around.

And on the night, it all went like clockwork. Some critics reckoned the odds were against Leigh Adams winning a third successive Aussie title. If anyone was fancied it would have been Boycey who'd had such a stellar year in England, was the best-credentialled Aussie rider in the Tapp series and lining up on his favoured home track.

But I managed to beat both of them, broke the track record second time out, and arrived at my last ride on 12 and needing just a second place to be sure. Jason Lyons made the start and I was so busy trying to make certain I got my safe second that I rode my worst race of the night ... but it was enough.

To have my name on the trophy along with the likes of Aub Lawson, Vic Duggan, Bluey Wilkinson, Jim Airey, Billy Sanders, that was something special. Seven years after my dad's last Australian championship success, I had one too. He was there, so was Bill Street, and my mum and sisters. It was great for everyone to be able to share the occasion.

It also provided the top five with a place in the Overseas Final and a world championship lifeline. Not that it mattered, but I wasn't the youngest to win it. Troy Butler was only 18, a year younger than me, when he took the title in Ayr in 1986. That's a statistic he's reminded me about a few times since then.

So it was in a very upbeat frame of mind that I headed back to the UK, ready for a few changes and lot of challenges.

One obvious focus was to set the ledger straight in world championship events. I was hopeful of getting one or two wild cards in the inaugural Grand Prix, and determined to do whatever it took to earn myself an automatic place for the following year.

One route would be to qualify via the Grand Prix challenge in Lonigo, Italy, towards the end of the season – assuming I could negotiate the Overseas Final at Coventry and the Inter-Continental Final in Elgane, both sure to be cut-throat meetings.

Another was on offer if I could put behind me the frustrations of two successive Under 21 campaigns which ended badly and win the newly-named World Junior Championship. Victory in that would guarantee the Grand Prix berth I desperately wanted.

I was keen to do better on the continent as well, and to make a worthwhile impact in the world long track championship.

There was the added task of trying to help Poole stay in the honours in a revamped British Premier League. The two divisions had been merged into one

WIZARD OF OZ ... Australian champion, Gosford, 1995, flanked by Craig Boyce, Leigh Adams and Jason Lyons

big league of 22 clubs and like all the senior tracks, the Pirates had to lose someone from the top end of the '94 title-winning side.

According to the rumour mill, there was a strong push for me to go back to Swindon (which was still under the Mervyn Stewkesbury banner at that stage) but there was no way that could happen. With my continental commitments increasing – I was looking to do a full club stint in Sweden for the first time – a Saturday night track was out of the question.

I had enjoyed myself at Poole, had developed some good support there, and in any case, I didn't want to keep switching tracks every year. In the end Craig Boyce went to Swindon – where shortly after the start of the season Peter Toogood and Martin Yeates were unveiled as the new promoters – and I stayed put.

It was a pity to see Craig go, after he had been so influential as captain, but we were determined to get on with life. Most of the other lads from '94 were still at Wimborne Road, we figured there were plenty of points to be had from Lars Gunnestad and Steve Schofield, in his testimonial year, and we quite fancied our chances of doing well in the new set-up.

I had the added prospect of being much more centrally based – lodging with Alun Rossiter and his wife Julie in Stratton St Margaret, just a couple of minutes down the road from the Swindon track.

The travel to and from Exeter was getting to be too much, especially as my continental diary was getting busier all the time. The Rossiters made everything just great for me, a huge gesture considering that they hadn't been married for more than a year or so and did not need to have a hyperactive lodger around the place.

Julie was terrific – she cooked, washed my clothes and, like grandmother Mary Street had done, always kept a pack of frozen peas in the freezer just in case any knocks or bruises needed attention!

Poole got off to a poor start, losing home and away to Eastbourne in the Premiership, and I piled up at Arlington, although fortunately without major damage. But then we won our first league match at Coventry after being eight points down with four races to go and I got paid 15; we again came from behind and won at King's Lynn where I had another maximum, and in between times drew at Reading.

Then it all started to go wrong. Reading came to our place and won by two on a night in which I should have had another five-ride maximum but punctured and fell in Heat 13. Gunnestad was out injured, then Scoie. Suddenly we had slid from being early pacemakers to the bottom three, our supposedly impregnable home form became extremely vulnerable and there were continuing concerns over the future of the stadium.

For a couple of months we seriously under-achieved and after being associated with highly successful teams – and not losing a home match in three years – I found it a bit unsettling. It was new territory for me.

The Overseas Final at Coventry was another nervous night. We had bike problems throughout, mostly with a dodgy carburetter, and although five

JULIE Rossiter (wife of Alun) who acted almost as a surrogate mum when Jason lodged at Swindon, believes that his youthful hyperactivity and punishing programme helped his career development.

"He was very driven and he wanted to be racing and taking on new challenges all the time. He always had the determination and those meetings in so many different leagues in various countries were just what he needed.

"It was all about the experience and not the money. He'd gone off to race somewhere, Sweden I think, and when I was checking the pockets of his jeans before doing the weekly wash I found a wad of notes, probably about £1500.

"When Jason came back I asked him if he had mislaid anything and he was sure he hadn't. So I said 'you won't be needing this, then".

"I'm not suggesting he was being irresponsible, but he just wasn't too organised then, and it said something about his priorities.

"In a lot of ways he was very grown-up, quite mature and level-headed compared to a lot of riders of that age. He just knew what he wanted, what his goals where and where he wanted to be.

"I don't think what he has achieved has changed him, either. He's so normal and down to earth.

"We've still got his World Under 21 trophy on a table at home. I mention to him from time to time that perhaps he might take it away, but it hasn't happened so far."

Aussies made it through and kept alive their world championship dream, I was probably the least convincing and most highly stressed of the lot. Ryan Sullivan signalled that he was going to be a rising force by winning the meeting in a run-off against Leigh Adams after both had scored 14 points.

But August 5, 1995 was the occasion on which I finally thought I was getting my career and my life in the sort of position I wanted and needed it to be. The World Junior Championship Final in Tampere, Finland, a day before my 20th birthday, will remain one of my personal highlights long after I've given the business away.

Second place behind Paul Hurry in the first qualifier at Arena Essex had been followed by a maximum and victory over Sullivan in the semi-final in Olching. It was an important one, that, because Sully had just won the Overseas, and I needed to make a statement.

The bike problems from Coventry seemed to have been sorted out when I scored a maximum at Poole's next home meeting. I got the opening I wanted in Olching when Ryan and I both arrived at Heat 17 unbeaten, – and didn't miss the chance.

It meant I was able to go to Finland with a bit of peace of mind. The lessons of the past disappointments were in the corner of my mind and fortunately they stayed there for the most part.

Equalling Hans Nielsen's six-year-old track record confirmed that the set-up was good although Sullivan gave me a wake-up call, riding a super race to beat me. Then Sweden's Dalle Andersson got the run on me from the inside and that meant he and I ended up on 13 points apiece and needing a run-off to determine the title.

All you ask for in these situations is to have the opportunity and I was determined to make the most of it. I won the run to the first corner and tried to make sure Andersson was not going to go round me. But he read my intentions, cut back underneath and grabbed the lead.

By now I was building up a head of steam and we both went charging for the third corner. It was all or nothing and there was no way I was going to back off. Dalle, though, couldn't make it and came off so for three and a bit laps I had the track to myself before that welcome chequered flag was shown.

Perhaps it wasn't the greatest way to win but hey, who cares? The race was for a world title and I rode as hard as I could without being unfair. We were racing for a massive prize and at that level there can't be any quarter asked or given. I was a bit more savvy than before. The experience of those various finals the previous year had rubbed off on me. Perhaps it was a bit like the old soldiers who knew more than I did when I was starting to make my way in second division.

Dalle Andersson to this day probably reckons I knocked him off and of course people can argue about these things until the cows come home. The bottom line is that I did what I had to do and won the event, collected the plaudits and booked my GP spot.

The next day we were on the boat coming back to England. Not only was it my birthday, but Ronni and Nicki Pedersen's dad was having his birthday too. We joined forces and had quite a lively combined celebration.

To be on top of the world, at this level at least, was a thrill but more than anything it was also a relief. A relief to win a title I'd set my sights on for a couple of years, and a massive boost to know that with it came the ticket to the Grand Prix.

It meant I had a victory which assured me of a place in the record books, and it also meant I didn't have to go through the drama of the Inter-Continental or the Grand Prix challenge rounds.

Maybe it was coincidence, perhaps it was just a whole new sense of self-confidence, but my year kept getting better after that. Not only did we start winning again at Poole, I had a couple of big ones away – the first visiting rider to score a maximum at Exeter where I also collected the track record, and another full house at Oxford. We won at both places, too.

In the Premier League Riders' Championship at Swindon I shared the top spot in the qualifiers with Leigh Adams, although we finished behind Gary Havelock and Greg Hancock in the decider. Importantly I felt I was back on the pace with the guys.

WEEKEND TREAT ... Riding in long track meetings in Germany was an important learning experience for Jason

The world long track championship was a lot better for me this time round, as well. I didn't end up doing as many German meetings as had been hoped after Oto Schroeck had to cut back his involvement. But my self-belief was given a big kick along when I did really well against a lot of the top guns at Nandlestadt, winning the meeting. Otto Lantenhammer was providing me with really quick motors and Phil was over for this stage of the year.

Scheesel, where the long track final was being held, is huge, really deep and grippy and throws up stones. If you want sheer speed, this a place tailor-made for it. In the end I missed out on a final place and to this day I reckon I was dudded out of it.

I had 13 points, the same number as Marvyn Cox, and was told that I was in the six-man final. The method of separating riders who are level was supposedly that the one who finished in a higher position in the semi-final would go through. I came third in mine, Cocker fourth in his – and he was given the nod. Go figure.

We argued for ages but to no avail. It was, how can I put it, extremely frustrating, and the hassle took the gloss of what had been a more than reasonable effort. But at least there was poetic justice for Kelvin Tatum who beat Wiggy in a run-off for the title after both had scored 20 points. Kelvin had been winning everything but stopped in his third qualifying ride whereas Simon, by his own standards, had been hit and miss all day.

In one important respect, though, I did add to my record of overseas success – as a member of the Rospiggarna team which won the Swedish First Division in the first year after being promoted.

In the first couple of rounds we were struggling but Per Jonsson was great to me all year. The Hallstavik club was his last Swedish team and he made it his business to help and encourage me at every turn. When we were building up a bike early in the piece, he insisted on giving me a load of new bits although I had convinced myself that all the equipment I had lined up to use was perfectly serviceable.

He also was very hospitable whenever I was over there, and the atmosphere at the club was good. Toby Harrysson, who had been such a good rider in his day, was the team manager. I enjoyed the company of Erik Stenlund, Einar Kyllingstad and Greg Hancock who was good value as the other foreigner. And of course we all enjoyed winning.

A 49-47 home victory over Valsarna in July was a key result – I beat Tony Rickardsson in the last heat – and there was a huge crowd when we saw off Ornarna in August and went top for the first time. We finally clinched the title by beating Bysarna, Mark Loram's team at that stage.

I was a league winner in Germany and Poland too. Following on from my long track meetings I had an invitation to ride for Brokstedt and enjoyed helping them to a few good wins. My contribution to Wroclaw's title was not exactly significant as I only did one away match!

There were Danish League commitments as well – with many of the same riders as in Germany, including Wiggy, Kelvin Tatum, Gerd Riss and Roberth Barth plus of course the best Danes such as Hans Nielsen and Tommy Knudsen.

I rode for Fredericia and used to stay over with Brian Karger. One night he introduced me to one of his sponsors, a car dealer who had a mobile telephone, which was quite an unusual status symbol way back then. When I showed some interest, he promised to get one for me if I beat Hans in the match at Randers the following night – which I did.

Brian had been a friend since way back when he rode at Swindon. I spent a bit of time with him and Leigh Adams when we were in England in 1990 and then, as now, he was a top bloke.

On the international front I played a decent role for Australia in a 2-1 series win over England. We lost by eight at Poole, had a big win at Sheffield and then finally took out the series by winning 59-49 at King's Lynn. I say finally because the decider was originally scheduled shortly after the Danish Grand Prix at Vojens, but was put off to October because so many of the riders would have had problems getting back.

That was a night when laydown engines were used with spectacular effect, and it was the ultimate reality check because there never was going to be any going back to the old uprights after that. The GP had already opted to go that way and just as the four-valvers replaced the old two-valves, this was technical revolution which couldn't be resisted.

I spent a lot of time during 1995 trying not to think about the Grand Prix, and failing. It had been suggested (by Jacob Olsen among others) that I'd probably get some wild cards after a couple of rounds although as things turned out, I got just one ... for the final round in England at the end of August.

Mind you, I got close – being hired by Sky TV as a guest when they showed the Vojens round. Truthfully, it was frustrating seeing a lot of quite mediocre riders getting a start in different rounds but after clinching my '96 spot, I was good and ready to make the most of my one appearance of the year.

There was a big campaign for Joe Screen to be given the wild card for the meeting after injury had ruled him out of the series. He was going like a train, the most consistent rider in the British Premier League – but the FIM chose me. Whatever their reasons, I thought it was a good call, at least.

The British Grand Prix was a bit like a magical mystery tour for months. The previous year, when the diehards were still hoping the old one-off World Final system would be retained, there had been plenty of publicity about a possible return to Wembley.

When that evaporated, Coventry was allocated the first British Grand Prix, a decision not greeted with universal enthusiasm by supporters or riders. That was nothing to the storm which blew up when it was announced that Brandon wouldn't host it after all ... and Arena Essex would be given the event.

Eventually, Terry Russell pulled one out of the hat by announcing that London Stadium, formerly the home of Hackney, was being redeveloped and it would host the British Grand Prix. There was a lot of work to be done, the end result wasn't perfect, but that's where it all happened.

Probably 80 per cent of the public didn't want me in it for one reason or another. Apart from that, though, I went there under no pressure at all. I had nothing to do with the decision-making, so all I had to do was go along, see how I would go against the big boys, and enjoy myself.

Hackney was a blast. I loved it. The rain was tipping down, it was a tough night for everyone – especially all the people who had put in such a mountain of work to get the place ready at all – but for me it was entirely positive.

The world title had all but been decided, the series was almost over, and I was not burdened by a great deal of expectation, or downcast by earlier disappointments. Three wins, then a second place and last-race duck gave me a total of 11 points.

I missed out on a place in the A final because Mark Loram, who had the same total, had the higher GP placing, and then I fell in the B final. But the night demonstrated – much more so than at Vojens the previous year – I could handle myself in that sort of company on a big occasion.

The second place I ran in Heat 14 was behind Hans Nielsen, in the race which clinched the championship for him. I had the opportunity to be the first to congratulate him on his latest success.

How cool is that, I thought as he reached across to shake hands. I told myself that I'd love to be in that position one day.

> ‘Winning the British Grand Prix at Hackney on Saturday, August 31, 1996, was the best and worst thing to happen to me in the first few years of my career as a GP rider.’

CELEBRATION ... At the age of 21 years 23 days Jason Crump becomes the youngest Grand Prix winner, Hackney, 1996

Win some, lose some: an unfolding story of Frustration

HAVING a taste of what might be can be inspiring. On the other hand, it can be frustrating as hell, as the next two Grand Prix seasons proved.

On the strength of my Under 21 title win, I was in the 1996 GP series from the start but was awful in the opening round in Poland, missed the next one in Italy, and did nothing in Germany or Sweden. Then I got it right for once at Hackney and won the British Grand Prix. A half-decent performance in Vojens could have got me into the top eight and a place for the next year but I had another poor meeting and didn't make the cut.

Even then there was an opportunity to snatch one of two places in the first round on offer at the Grand Prix Challenge in Prague, or, at the worst way, there also were a couple of reserve spots up for grabs. Again I hit the stress button and narrowly missed out.

That left me kicking my heels for most of the 1997 series, with just one wild card call-up for Sweden, and nothing else. It's not a good feeling seeing riders I was regularly beating in league matches not only nipping off for their championship rounds, but getting a few decent results as well.

It was not until 1998 that I got back in and started to consolidate. Until then I'd had to listen to people telling me it was just a matter of time, my domestic form was so good that things had to come together eventually, that I shouldn't be impatient.

But nobody wins things if they're not impatient to some extent and in any case, the apprenticeship period seemed to be stretching out far too long for my liking. Sure, I was 'only' 22 going on 23 at the start of the '98 season, but guys like Peter Collins, Barry Briggs, Ove Fundin, Erik Gundersen, they were all world champions by that age.

Winning the British Grand Prix at Hackney on Saturday, August 31, 1996, was the best and worst thing to happen to me in the first few years of my career as a GP rider.

The best, obviously, because to win any major world championship event is a tremendous morale-booster, and to do so against the odds and contrary to most people's expectations carries an extra sweet taste.

The worst of it was that even at this stage of my life – three weeks past my 21st birthday – I had hoped and pretty much expected to have established myself as a serious contender for world honours. And come up short, well short in fact.

If at that moment I believed that at last this was the result that cracked open the door, and revealed the trick to consistently being up there with the guys, there were to be many more rude awakenings to come.

After reaching a World Final in Vojens in 1994, and apparently cementing my position as one of the most successful riders in domestic competition, this should have been my time. But it wasn't.

I had spent most of 1995 on the outer looking in, made very little headway in the next year's world championship (apart from that one victory) and was pretty much back to square one as an outsider in 1997.

I grew up confident, I'm optimistic by nature, and genuinely believed I possessed all the tools and all the support necessary to be right up there. The speed with which things came my way in England, in particular, suggested that it was all on track.

I knew enough speedway history to recognise that there have been plenty of top riders who served a long apprenticeship and went through a lengthy learning curve. There also have been riders who got to be very good very quickly and then faded. Then there were those who got to be good very quickly and just went on from there.

I guess I always put myself in that last category, so it was a big reality check and a long-winded test of character when world championship success didn't come my way quite as expected.

In recent times people have said to me that the three years of finishing as runner-up, as I did in 2001, 2002 and 2003, would have be tough to bear. They must have overlooked the fact that I was twice as long just getting myself into a position in which I could have a realistic shot at the world title.

For three of those early seasons I was flat out simply getting into the Grand Prix, never mind doing anything of consequence. When they expanded the format and 24 riders started each meeting instead of 16, it was the first time I had felt anything remotely close to belonging. Even then, it took two full series to embrace the enormity of it all.

Perhaps it was all down to the pressure I put on myself, maybe it was fuelled by the hopes and expectations other people placed on me, but I must have been very difficult company for a long while.

Nobody goes into professional sport without being fiercely competitive and that's the way I have always been. When you set targets, you tend to set them for tomorrow rather than some time in the dim and distant future. When I went into speedway I was a young man in a big hurry and while people did tell me to slow down, to let things take the course, I rarely wanted to hear that sort of advice.

In the old days, riders placed a lot of importance on the world championship and their ability to negotiate half a dozen qualifying meetings was a key thread running through their season. If they missed out, there was plenty of other stuff going on, and there was always next time.

It is difficult to imagine that it could have been quite so cut-throat, quite so intense as it seemed to be in the first few Grand Prix years, although the old timers probably will insist that it was.

What has defined the GP era is that every fortnight or so, the caravan moves from Poland to Sweden or Czecho or wherever the next big show hits the road. Very compelling if you are a part of it, nerve-wracking if you are trying to make your mark, and scary if you are falling short for whatever reason.

And if, as I did in its first three seasons, you happen to believe you should be a significant part of it, and all your life has been geared towards this time, it is very tough indeed to discover that dreams and realisation are such a way apart.

There's this saying about sometimes having to take a step back before you can take two steps forward. All I seemed to be doing was taking two steps back and none forward.

Some of the more experienced riders going around gave the impression that they were quietly pleased to see me struggling. They wouldn't want anybody to think it was all too easy, would they?

And other riders who were in the same sort of position, battling to get into the championship or trying every which way to stay in there, well, they couldn't be expected to wish me a ride that was any easier than their own.

Some people think I'm quick to anger and easy to rile but I don't believe I am quite as transparent as that. From day one I recognised, without being told, that you have to work long and hard to succeed at elite sport and nothing's for nothing. The frustration comes when after all the effort, all the build-up and preparation, things still go wrong.

You can't win races without having decent equipment. But even if you're on board a rocket machine you can't win unless your head is right, your body is right, and, quite often, you can't win unless Lady Luck has decided she's going to make this a good day.

Every rider will tell you that he's been to meetings in which – as far as possible – every little detail has been attended to, everything is just so, conditions are perfect, the script is waiting to be played out. Then, suddenly, for no obvious reason, it all falls to pieces.

Many's the time when the stage appears set for a successful night and fate deals out a dodgy hand. A rough refereeing decision, a misbehaving bike, an unpredictable track, a touch of the flu, a nagging injury, a decision off or on track taken in haste and regretted later. During those frustrating early years, I almost felt I had written the book on the subject.

Maybe there was only one person to blame, but I blamed plenty more.

Yet when you go right back to Vojens and that first World Final, with a bit more brain I could have saved myself a lot of the frustration which accompanied my absence from all but one of the 1995 Grand Prix meetings.

And if I had been more balanced and composed during 1996 then Hackney might have been the icing on the cake instead of the only worthwhile item on the menu.

But the GP series, with the notable exception of that British round in London, was a real bummer. It was the start of a couple of years which kept dishing up reminders that nothing can be taken for granted. You think everything's dropping into place and then, bang, something goes wrong.

Winning the junior world title in Finland really was a back door route into the big time. On reflection it had been a bit of an anti-climax in some ways. It was a world title, and nobody knocks them back, but there were only a couple of thousand people there, there was no real atmosphere and it could have been just another meeting anywhere.

AUSTRALIAN youngsters are not alone in being fairly casual when it comes to the social graces – especially at the age of 20.

Adviser and sponsor-getter Neil Bird smiles when he recalls a trip to the FIM Congress in Las Vegas to attend the gold medal ceremony at which the year's world champions are acknowledged.

As the Under 21 champion it was all new territory for Jason and reassuring for him to be with Bird who knew Kevin Schwantz, Max Biaggi and a number of other world champions because of his road racing connections. But Bird could not have anticipated the sartorial problems which lay in wait.

"We went to a suit hire company to get fitted out for tuxedos for the presentations but there was a delay and two hours before the dinner we still did not have them. Finally the suits arrived. I made a dash back to the hotel and we got ready as quickly as possible as the press conference was on prior to the presentations." said Bird.

"Our only problem was they hadn't supplied the shoes so here's Jason and me walking through the casino dressed to the nines in tuxedos ... and Nike trainers. We did manage to get shoes in time for the ceremony, fortunately.

"After the presentations were over we all headed to the bar for celebratory drinks. It was the who's who of motorcycle racing and we were all having a good time and spending lots of money.

"The drinking age in the USA is 21 and Jason and 125cc world champion Haruchika Aoki were under age. Aoki had been checked earlier by security and was given the all-clear as he had used his older brother's

The Grand Prix, I felt sure, would be something else, with thousands packing into the big stadiums and the sort of atmosphere to inspire anybody to great things.

Meanwhile back in Australia, for a second year there was a David Tapp series and initially I was not too bothered to do it. Trevor Harding was involved with Tappy the previous year and gave me a couple of good reasons why I should do the first one, but this time it was a one-man show.

It was a fair assumption that David wanted me as I was now the World Under 21 and Australian champion, but I only found out how much after quoting him a silly amount of money as my terms for the tour. To my surprise, he agreed to pay and so I was in, like it or not.

As is usually the way when you're not fully committed, it is not realistic to expect the results to keep coming your way. That's all the more likely to be the case when the standard of competition is pretty high. There were a few good nights and several others where I should have done better.

Craig Boyce rode out of his skin to top the scoring with 162 points, and there was a lot of competition for the next few places. Sam Ermolenko (138) and Tony Rickardsson (136) just edged me out of third spot overall. I got 134, seven ahead of Simon Wigg with Leigh Adams next on 125.

ID and they placed a green wristband on him to show that he had been checked.

"But the staff asked Jason to leave the bar. With that, Kevin Schwantz casually stood up and addressed the 30-plus other world champions and said that if Jason Crump could not drink in the bar, then they would all leave and everyone got up and left the bar in support of Jason. You could see Jason's head swelling and he was as proud as punch for the support.

"Aoki then took Jason in the men's rooms, slipped the wristband off and placed it on Jason and said in his broken English 'Okay Jason, I have brother ID. They check me again. No problem', and so the party continued for the rest of the night.

"For the trip home, I managed to get us upgraded to business class.

"We were in Los Angeles airport ready to board the flight for the 12-hour flight home and Jason, not being fussed about airline food, bought two pizzas to take on the flight.

"As we boarded the flight I asked to see the chief steward.

"I asked the chief steward if so-and-so (another Qantas chief steward) was on the flight tonight and it turned out he was a very good friend of my contact so quietly he advised that once the flight took off he would come and get us and take us up to business class. So I told Jason to 'look the part' when he came back.

"The chief steward, to his word, came down to us and we were escorted up to Business Class and here's Jason with two pizzas under his arm.

"Not a good look ..."

The travelling ensured it was a tough few weeks but the Gold Coast was a great base for a young, single bloke. I had palled up with several of the locals, including Jeff Hardwick who manufactured a few pieces of speedway equipment and did some work for Shell – his dad was one of their top guys in Australia.

He had grown up with people like Mick Doohan and his brother Scott, Mark Carlson and Troy Butler and we got on well from the start. The pair of us got up to some mischief, as you do, and I still laugh about one escapade which happened when he was trying a wheelstand on his motocross bike outside the factory unit he had in Brisbane Road, Labrador – just round the corner from the speedway.

CLAP HANS ... A dazzling display at
included two wins over Hans Nielse

The two of us liked to go out bush on our bikes but pulling a wheelie alongside one of the busiest roads on the Coast was not recommended behaviour. Jeff lost control, but clung on for dear life – ripping skin off his knees, chest and various other parts of his anatomy – because he didn't want to crash into the nearby unit where they made expensive AC Cobra cars in kit form.

When he finally crashed in a heap with dirt and blood everywhere he was the only one who couldn't see the funny side of it. I had to take him to the doctor for some treatment and he was bandaged up like a mummy. He was game, though. We were due to drive down to Gosford for a meeting and then on to Adelaide for another one. The plan was to put our motocrossers in the trailer as well so we could have a ride in the Adelaide Hills in between the meetings.

Although he was not in much of a state Jeff insisted that he was still coming on the trip. We stuck with the original schedule but it was not the end of the drama. After we had been out riding with Mark Gilbert and one of his mates, we parked up at a motel overnight – and woke next morning to find that some jokers had unloaded our motocross bikes and made off with them and some of our riding gear.

They left my two speedway machines by the side of the road!

We were pretty unhappy about this turn of events, and set off across country to spend some time in Mildura. Three days after we arrived, there was a telephone call from police saying that they had waylaid some characters and found a few motorcycles, and could we come back to Adelaide? So off we went again and at least the story had a happy ending – they recovered our bikes.

The season more or less finished with the Australian Final at Newcastle in February and it would have been good to successfully defend the title. Craig Boyce, however, had other ideas. He was still at the top of his game as a 15-point maximum confirmed, and I had to be satisfied with second place, beating Tony Langdon in a run-off after we had both scored 13 points.

After that, it was on to the plane and back to Europe for the start of what was looming as a huge season.

For the first time Poland was an important part of my programme in 1996 and quite early in the piece I beat Hans Nielsen a couple of times for Gorzow in a league match at Pila. Suddenly everyone in Poland and Denmark went crazy. The telephone was ringing non stop and everyone was telling me I was going to be world champion.

Expectations on going into the Grand Prix were high, unrealistically so as it turned out. I was very confident. At 20 or 21 you think you know a whole lot more than you actually do. I was averaging 10 points a meeting in league competition, there were articles in the press saying what a great prospect I was and how I could surprise a lot of the established riders, and maybe this was the start of a new era, all that sort of stuff.

But I was out of my depth. Too often I was crashing or riding out of control.. I couldn't understand how I could regularly beat Hans Nielsen, Tony Rickardsson, Greg Hancock, Billy Hamill and those guys in league racing but couldn't get near them at the Grands Prix.

Racing-wise I wasn't too bad but as far as the mental side of it went, I was not on the same lap. They were prepared, they were ready and they were able to treat each race, each meeting on its merits. That's the sort of stuff you have to learn.

Winning the British Grand Prix at Hackney was the one meeting in which I did well enough to reassure the doubters that I wasn't there under false pretences.

It didn't dawn on me until later that I had treated it like just another meeting, an hour and a half down the road to Hackney, instead of all the drama and organisation and travel involved with shooting off to Poland, Germany, Sweden, or wherever.

Looking back, I was very naïve, not remotely prepared for what it was all about. Hackney '95 probably lulled me into a false sense of security.

The first round of 1996 was in Wroclaw, which turned out to be a disaster. I was in the wrong frame of mind, did not have enough plans and no safety nets. I had only two bikes, one of which blew up on the line in my first ride, and I ended up bottom of the pile after crashing with Leigh Adams in the D final and injuring an ankle.

The system meant that I was only reserve for the next round, in Lonigo. I hated it, being there but not part of it. The only thing to do was watch and learn.

Another wrist injury when I came off at Wolverhampton threatened to put even more of a damper on proceedings but microwave treatment with Don Gatherer, the England rugby physio, got me going again in time for an England-Australian Test match at Poole where I won my first three races, and then it was off to Pocking for another GP round.

It was another meeting which summed up the sort of problems of the time. My clutch burned out in the first heat, but five points from my next two rides improved my mood. However, I fell trying to challenge Hans Nielsen in my next race, and went from first to third last time out – which meant that yet again I was due to be missing from the Linkoping round.

None of this was doing much for my confidence in the big events but injuries to Tommy Knudsen and Gary Havelock gave me a reprieve and I got into the Swedish meeting after all. No fairytale there either, though, as I kept getting myself in all the wrong positions and fell off in the C final.

It looked as if my hopes of qualifying for the following season were shot to ribbons and I was reconciled to the fact that I wasn't going to be in the British Grand Prix at Hackney. Maybe I relaxed a bit in my own mind because

HANS Nielsen, defending champion, series leader and still the man to beat, was quick to salute Jason on his maiden GP win at Hackney. It was almost a reverse image of the previous year when the youngster was first to congratulate Nielsen on a win which earned him the 1995 world title.

Little did he know that three weeks later Billy Hamill would jump him and snatch the title by a two-point margin, the closest finish in GP history.

"Jason deserved to win," said Nielsen.

"I hope he makes the top eight and gains automatic entry to next year's world championship Grand Prix, because we need new faces."

In the midst of the euphoria which enveloped the Crump camp, Neil Street – in his usual understated and possibly prophetic manner – put a finger on the mindset which allowed his grandson to signal his pending arrival among the big boys.

"Jason has ridden really sensibly tonight," he said.

"He plodded through the meeting consistently and has not done anything rash."

A proud Phil, on a brief visit from Australia, shared in the moment.

"I don't think Jason was really set up for the GP series at the start of the season," he said.

"It is completely different to anything else in the sport. But he's worked hard to catch up and got the reward."

I went to Belle Vue with Peterborough and fired off a 21-point maximum which would have to be one of my best league meetings.

Then came the bonus of a call to go to Hackney after all, and the first GP victory of my career. I just got my head down and rode sensibly through the qualifiers, and then got it right when it mattered most in the final. Simple, really. The emotions it unlocked were unbelievable, indescribable.

What made it even more special was to have my dad there. He had flown in from Australia the previous day and he and Bill were as excited about it all as I was.

So how come I got it so right at Hackney and so wrong almost everywhere else over that period? Don't ask.

Looking back, I certainly went to that British Grand Prix in a relatively relaxed frame of mind. I thought (and was proved right) that I'd done my dash in the series, and was grateful to get the opportunity to be in the meeting at all, reprieved only after Tommy Knudsen and Gary Havelock were ruled out because of injury. But going to Hackney was one of those occasions which always excited me.

The previous year had been such a buzz, and I loved racing at the place. Several visits for domestic fixtures went really well, and on a night when everybody was beating everybody, I strung together some quite consistent form to qualify for the A final – no heroics, nothing spectacular, but always comfortably in touch. I went into my last qualifying heat needing to win and when Mikael Karlsson touched the tapes it made it that much easier.

Hans Nielsen, Billy Hamill and Greg Hancock were the three front runners in the championship and it was shaping as a huge final for all of them. I had third choice of gate and wanted two. Hans chose one and Greg four so someone must have been looking after me. Once I dropped the clutch, I was gone and left them to it. It was a huge feeling.

Jim Lynch of Central Engineering made a bit of a killing with the bookmakers. He put £50 on me at 20-1 and generously agreed to split his winnings with me afterwards.

When you have sampled exhilaration like that, anything short of it is a disappointment. Little did I know at this moment that for the best part of the next two years, I wouldn't be remotely close to anything like it.

The British GP victory showed not only that I could win, but meant a decent result in the final round in Vojens would still give me a shot at being among the top eight and an automatic qualifier for 1997.

But three weeks later I was back from penthouse to outhouse when half a dozen points in the final round of the year left me down in 12th spot overall and outside the automatic qualifying positions. It was a pressure cooker situation and I didn't handle it.

It was disappointing but at the end of the day, there was still the Grand Prix challenge to come, an opportunity for a reprieve I was optimistic I could grab with both hands. While Billy Hamill was celebrating his come-from-behind world championship win and Hans Nielsen wondering how he had let slip another title, my more immediate concern was Prague – definitely a last chance saloon if I was going to feature in the next year's series.

What none of us reckoned on was the controversy over solid block tyres which the FIM were trying to introduce for use in the championship. Of all meetings, they chose this one to make their use compulsory and it was a farce. What was already one of the most nerve-wracking meetings imaginable turned into a big drama which helped blindside a few people who should have been concentrating on other things.

Nobody was comfortable with the tyres and this was no occasion to try to learn how to handle them. Tommy Knudsen crashed while leading the first race and damaged his shoulder, and I was in front in the next one and also encountered trouble when the bike just took off after I hit a hole.

After 20 heats Simon Wigg and Leigh Adams had made their spot secure for the next year's opening GP by scoring 12 points apiece and four of us – Mikael Karlsson, Andy Smith, Sam Ermolenko and myself – had cobbled together 11 to slug it out for the remaining two reserve places.

I again got off the start from the inside but couldn't maintain it as the bike lost power. Karlsson was taking no prisoners and the other two followed him past me. First to last in no time, and out of the world championship. Not just for 1997, but with no guarantee I would be able to force my way back in for '98. It was a not a good feeling.

JIM LYNCH, who as boss of Central Engineering was involved as a sponsor at Alwalton, notably helping Danish rider Ronni Pedersen (elder brother of Nicki), stepped forward to play a pivotal role in bringing Jason to Peterborough.

"As silly as it seems now, but the only thing that appeared to be holding up his move from Poole was a van. I said to Peter Oakes 'if that's the show-stopper, I'll sort him out'."

And sort him out he did, with a Ford Transit van and a fuel card thrown in for good measure.

It was the start of a relationship which has extended into further personal contact with Lynch's daughter Sarah, a longtime fan from 1992 and latterly friend of Melody, often stepping in to house-sit for the Crumps on Grand Prix weekends.

Jim first met Jason on a trip to see the 1995 World Under 21 Final and for a few years the Lynch family were closely allied with Jason's blossoming career. His first Grand Prix victory at Hackney brought a bonus, with Jim – unbeknown to his wife Janice – investing £50 on Crump at 20-1 and collecting £1000 when he won.

"It was supposed to be hush-hush but Jason went on television and mentioned that I'd had a win ... and that he wanted half of it. We didn't mind too much, though."

In an instant my short to medium-term GP hopes had disappeared, and it was one of the most demoralising moments in my career to that point. Little did I know that there would be several more to come in the next few years. It was a long, quiet ride home from Prague, let me tell you.

They say everything happens for a reason, and no doubt this and other experiences toughened me up for the future, but it's difficult to see it at the time. At that stage I wanted everything yesterday and the prospect of sitting out the world championship was a massive disappointment to cope with. Certainly I wanted to learn from the moment and avoid putting myself in a similar situation again.

From the world championship angle, then, it wasn't the best time, but at least in domestic terms there were indications that things were ready to move on to a new level.

Peterborough showed just how they rated my capabilities and potential by forking out £35,000 to buy me from Poole in a British record transfer deal. I'll always be grateful to the Pirates for the part they played in my first few years in speedway, but it was time to move on. As a club, they were not the force back then that they have become in recent years, and going to Peterborough was an important step up at the time.

They were still in the first flush of excitement after doing well in their debut year alongside the traditional big clubs, and seemed to be going places. The faith they were prepared to place in me suggested that they were really ambitious.

In a lot of ways beyond speedway, this was a major year in my life, a growing year. I had moved out of the protected environment in which first my grandparents, then the Rossiters housed and looked after me. As a home owner for the first time, there were new responsibilities and commitments to meet.

Troy Butler had been a leading Australian rider for several years but he was finished with Brtitish speedway and he had his house in Duston, near Northampton, up for sale. It suited me perfectly, both from a geographical point of view and also because everything was set up with a workshop and the various necessities.

Troy rode in England from 1985, won the Australian championship as an 18-year-old in 1986 and the National League Riders' championship in 1988. He probably was rated more highly in Aussie than in England – especially at the Brisbane Ekka where he was a match for almost anybody.

But he'd had enough of it and went back to earn a living and live a 'normal' life, renting out the house for a while until he decided he may as well dispose of it. My parents back on the Gold Coast happened to hear from Troy's mum Doris that he was wanting to sell. We worked out a quite unusual deal. I agreed to buy the house as soon as I was 21 – I couldn't get a mortgage before that – and in the meantime was able to live there and also have Troy along as my mechanic for the season.

Troy was a great help, very supportive. He always backed me. It could have been a shambles of a bachelor existence because I had never been the tidiest or most domesticated person, but it was pretty good. Everything was pretty orderly. We might disappear for a couple of weeks of racing non-stop and come back to find the grass had grown a bit long but there were no mountains of washing or stuff piled in the sink. That sort of lifestyle definitely isn't for me.

In that first year at Peterborough, I couldn't complain about the move or the new surroundings. I averaged double figures at home and away, and the Panthers finished as Premier League and Speedway Star KO Cup runners-up, losing out to Wolverhampton in both competitions.

There was no shame in that as Wolves, with the Karlsson brothers and Ronnie Correy all in great form, were the team of the year, winning the league by a mile. We were good enough to win all our home matches and a respectable five away.

Going back to Peterborough and joining up again with Peter Oakes was just great. The Panthers took the chance on me when I was 16 and nobody knew whether I was going to be any good. A lot of people who supported me then were still around, and there were plenty of new ones coming in to make me feel welcome.

It was important that Oakesy knew how much the Grand Prix and other commitments also meant to me in the overall scheme of things, and he kept me up to date with everything that was going on. He always has his ear to the ground.

On an individual note I topped the scorers in the Dunlop Premier League Riders Championship at Bradford, won my semi-final but then had to watch as Sam Ermolenko won the final. I wasn't the only unlucky one though as Chris Louis was leading when his motor seized and Sudden Sam was quick to capitalise.

It was always a buzz to do well against the established riders and the schedule was pretty busy, even though I didn't get a run in Sweden. They had decided to restrict each team to one overseas rider and I missed out.

But I was racing in the Polish and Danish leagues. Troy and Andy Street were driving out after Friday night meetings, so I could do Poland on the Sunday and Denmark on Wednesdays, staying over at Brian Karger's place.

He helped me a lot, as did Peter Johns with engines. Troy gave me heaps of advice on starting techniques and bikes. There was a great deal of experimentation, and we were all learning on the run.

My first full season in the Polish league was a real eye-opener. We lost the first fixture 49-41 but apart from my wins over Hans, I had a really good meeting, collecting paid 17 from six rides.

The team lifted after that and we won six of our next seven matches including victories at Rzeszow, Torun and Tarnow and a draw at Wroclaw. But Pila completed the double over us and Torun won at Gorzow which pushed us down to fourth place going into the play-offs.

Pila continued to have the wood on us as they won 59-31 at their place to more than cancel out our 49-40 win in the first leg at home. All the same, it was a pretty satisfying first full season there for me – a 9.19 average and a couple of maximums.

Zenon Plech was the trainer and team manager and he always made it fun for the guys, a real cool guy.I didn't see anything of him when he was riding but people tell me he was something special, especially when he first qualified for a World Final at 20 and with a bit of luck might even have won the thing.

I was still doing long track as well, and made it through to the world final in Herxheim, but didn't have much to write home about from there. Gerd Riss won a meeting in which Germans took the first three places.

Away from racing, big things were happening on the personal front. Meeting Melody Johnston not only made an instant impression, it was without exaggeration the luckiest day of my life.

As these things often are, it came about through pure chance. For two or three years Neil Bird helped me get organised with a few sponsorships but I also managed to score some myself, including one from Hot Tuna, an Australian surfwear company who made a lot of very cool gear.

This came about when Drew and Alex Schroeck were staying on the Gold Coast, and we spent a lot of time hanging out at shop called Summer Breeze at Runaway Bay Shopping Centre – just down the road from where Ivan Mauger lives.

Eventually Darren McCormick, who owned the shop, asked what we were up to. It turned out he was quite a motorcycle enthusiast and one thing led to another. He helped organise backing for me which continued even after he sold up and got himself another shop south of Newcastle. Later on his brother Wayne ran that shop and so the connection continued.

That's how I happened to call into Out Of Control at Swansea, on my way to a meeting down south, and Mel was there, helping out during the holidays.

NEIL Bird – nicknamed Roy because of his love of corduroy trousers – witnessed the spell Melody Johnston wove on Jason when they met in Newcastle.

"She was 19 years old and stunningly beautiful." he said.

"I suddenly saw a side of Jason Crump I had never seen before. He was always mature for his age and quietly confident but this day he was like a 15-year-old meeting a girl for the first time. He was shy, didn't know what to say and totally besotted.

"When we left Newcastle the next day all Jason could talk about was Melody. He couldn't stop thinking of her. So we rang her up to say hi about 10 times between Newcastle and the Gold Coast.

"Melody too must have been excited as she did not discourage us from telephoning her."

Talk about sparks across a crowded room – there was an instant attraction. She was drop-dead gorgeous. I'd never seen anyone so beautiful.

There was not much chance to develop the relationship when I came back to England, but in the following Australian summer we got together and started to see a lot more of each other. It didn't take me long to realise that this was one special person and I did all I could to persuade her to come over with me in 1997.

There was a bit more time available as this time round I opted out of the Tapp series. The only meetings I did in the competition were at two of my favourite tracks, Wayville and Brisbane. It was at the Ekka that I finished as runner-up to Leigh who put the seal on the series that night.

Boycey was again the man when he collected the Australian title – also in Brisbane – with a maximum. My runner-up spot came after beating Ryan Sullivan and Adams in a run-off. It meant the four of us were through to the Overseas Final with the prospect of battling into the '98 GP series through that route.

I still think my biggest win that summer was persuading Melody to come over to join me in England. Mel already was a very confident young woman – she had plenty to be confident about – but she hadn't travelled or even been away from her family for any length of time, so it was a big call.

Fortunately, I eventually convinced her it was a great idea for her to come across, live at Duston and see what Europe was all about. I had to play down my racing activity a bit, because I didn't want her to think I was playing at being a big star.

It was all a bit of a culture shock for her when she did arrive. But she soon adapted and straight away brought an order and meaning to my personal life which I had never experienced. It was brilliant, just the best time. I thought I had won the lottery.

From the GP angle, 1997 was a nothing year. I got a wild card into the Linkoping Grand Prix – I was riding for Vargarna and the organisers figured I would be an added attraction – but there's nothing like being in the competition proper. The occasion was stuffed for me when I was excluded for supposedly knocking off world champion Billy Hamill, which a lot of people felt was an outrageous decision,

While I hadn't fully absorbed all of the lessons of the previous season, it was obvious that when you are in the Grand Prix proper, there is a requirement to get everything sorted, your equipment, your back-up, your schedule, the whole deal.

That British round wild card a couple of years earlier had been a bonus and, as it turned out, that was a great night. But after having been in the series in '96, for all its ups and downs, one meeting wasn't ever going to do much for me.

Mel, though, was an immediate, tremendous help, providing the sort of support, encouragement and stability which gave everything an added spark and purpose.

I certainly needed all the organisation I could get because I signed up to ride in England, Denmark, Poland and Sweden, determined to get as many meetings and as much experience as I could possibly pack in to one year. I figured it would keep me sharp and get me up to the mark for the bid to qualify for another shot at the world championship.

Uppermost in my mind was to get the business out of the way as early as possible, and the Overseas Final at Bradford looked to provide the perfect opportunity to become the first qualifier for the following season. I'd had a lot of good meetings at Odsal, and enjoyed going there. Great stadium, great track, the best facilities. I was winning races everywhere at this stage and was looking forward to it.

So many people told me that this was the meeting to win. But any position in the top eight was almost as good as a win. Certainly I wanted to avoid the tensions of the previous year's last-ditch failed attempt.

But I was just lousy. It was a rainy, miserable day, and I never produced any sort of form. Kelvin Tatum and Joe Screen, grass trackers who would handle anything, tied with 14 points apiece (Kelvin won the run-off) and Craig Boyce and Ryan Sullivan qualified for the next round.

I managed only eight points, which left me in ninth position and, to all intents and purposes, out of the championship. It was an awful feeling. I'd approached Bradford feeling so confident, only to quickly get the idea that it was not my day.

DOLEFUL ... Jason looks as if he fears the worst at the Overseas Final at Bradford, 1997

Bottom line, once more I was not able to handle the pressure. Too many people were telling me things, and I wasn't mature enough to sort the good from the bad and get myself organised. At the time I just could not believe it had happened.. It meant facing the prospect of yet another year on the outer.

Fortunately Mel was there to put a consoling arm around me and to tell me that it wasn't the end of the world. I was not in a receptive frame of mind – but as it happened, she was dead right. A month later Dean Barker, who had been the last qualifier, crashed and hurt himself.

Bad timing and bad luck for him, but a tremendous reprieve for me. It meant that the Inter-Continental Final at Vastervik offered another opportunity.

DELIGHT ... A happy face this time after Jason negotiated the 1997 Inter-Continental Final at Vastervik to regain a GP place

This time there were two guaranteed 1998 places on offer and, for the next five finishers, a spot in the end-of-year GP challenge.

The meeting didn't start too brightly with an engine failure in my first ride. On another day, I might have spat the dummy. But by now I'd had so many knocks I was starting to learn to live with it. To achieve you must be prepared to scrap. Instead of throwing in the towel, I just got my head down, got on with things, and won my next four races.

The fact that Ryan Sullivan finished on top of the points with 13 and was through was neither here or there for me – now it was all on the line in a race with Craig Boyce to secure the other automatic spot. I'd had some great battles with Boycey down the years but this was the most important of the lot ... and I won it.

The realisation that victory had secured a spot for the start of the following season's Grand Prix series was everything. To have that security ... after a fairly ordinary first year, followed by a year out, and then thinking I had blown my chance in Bradford ... was a tremendous relief and a great boost.

It was as big a moment as any up to that point, made so much sweeter by the fact that Mel, already my greatest supporter, was there to share it. I remember the celebrations – just – including taking the decision to have my hair dyed jet black. The welcome back to Peterborough was spectacular, made all the more special when we won the Four Team Final a few days later.

As far as league racing went, though, the best part of the year for me was in Sweden. It was good to be back after missing the previous season. Peter Nahlin, a good mate, teed it up for me to go to Vargarna and that was a move which turned out to be a good one for a number of years.

I was the first big-name foreigner they'd had for a few years – since Erik Gundersen was injured in 1989 – and they were only just back into the top flight, so it was quite a challenge. This, remember, is one of Sweden's oldest-

FOUR TEAM CHAMPS ...
Peterborough, 1997. Back: Ryan Sullivan, JC, Rene Madsen. Middle: Mario Jirout, Sam Tesar, Front: Jamie Smith (mascot)

established and most famous clubs, having been outstanding when the sport took off there just after the war.

There was a great deal of interest with crowds at Norrkoping being the best in the country. The team finished a respectable fourth, and my average of 9.13 was quite reasonable.

We were competitive everywhere and one of the highlights was when I went back to my former club Rospiggarna and scored 18, my first full maximum in Sweden.

It wasn't such a smooth ride at Peterborough, who had done so well in the two years of everybody being in the one big league but struggled in the first year of the new Elite League.

Richard Knight, who had helped out around the place the previous season, replaced Kevin Hawkins as the team manager and had a hint of what we were in for when we lost first up at Ipswich and then went down by eight points at home to King's Lynn – the last people on earth Showground fans want to lose to.

DESPITE the young Australian's continuing stellar contribution, all was not well at Peterborough in 1997, with results disappointing and Peter Oakes quite pre-occupied with his new involvement at Skegness, a venture which eventually cost him thousands.

"I don't think we got any satisfaction whatsoever out of Peterborough's Elite League team (last year)," he told *Speedway Star* after the Panthers had finished ninth in the 10-team league, largely as a result of losing an unthinkable eight home matches out of 18.

"The results overall were very, very disappointing.

"Even the Fours victory was not the euphoric occasion it should have been. We were already under so much pressure then and you looked at it it and thought 'if they can produce it on the Sunday, why can't they produce it in an Elite League match?'"

It impacted greatly upon Peterborough's ability to fund their 1998 campaign, so much so that the directors – of whom Jim Lynch was now one – opting to take a year out so that they could re-group in the less rareified atmosphere of the Premier League.

"Had it not been for Jim's growing influence towards the end of the season, I don't think we would have been running Peterborough speedway this year (1998)," said Oakes.

"I have never heard of any speedway promoter who has become rich out of speedway. A lot have got very poor out of it."

Even Lynch, with his newcomer's enthusiasm, had to accept the switch.

"It was a move we had to make to ensure the viability of the club and it meant Jason, Ryan Sullivan and others went out on loan for the year," he said.

"But after we had won everything in the Premier League, it seemed logical to call back our assets and go again in the Elite in 1999."

Jason's

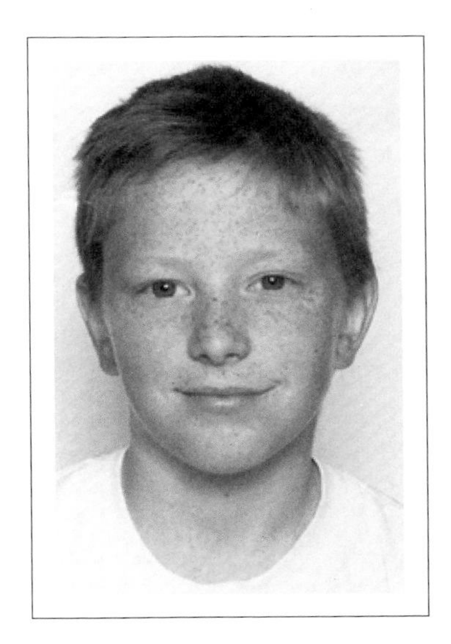

PHOTO ALBUM

1 x world title

1 x world U21 title

3 x world team champion

1 x Australian champion

1 x Aus U16 title

2 x British ELRC winner

... in pictures

Tips for Speedway riders

THE START

CONCENTRATION . . . no matter what distractions are present (see back page of this section for the preferred outcome)

KING OF THE KIDS ... Australian Under 16 champion at Bibra Lake, WA, 1990, flanked by runner-up Ryan Sullivan, Brett Woodifield and Nathan Hawkes

A KID LEADING KINGS ... a first (and last) World Final at Vojens, 1994. Jason heads for an opening-race win over eventual champion Tony Rickardsson, defending champion Sam Ermolenko and British champion Mark Loram

AUSTRALIAN CHAMPION ... Jason celebrates his title win with mum Carole, sisters Gabi and Justine, Gosford, 1995

WORLD UNDER 21 CHAMPION ... Jason Crump, 1995

GRAND PRIX DEBUT ... Jason making an instant impact at Hackney, 1995

GP No.1 ... Jason celebrates his 1996 British Grand Prix win at Hackney, with placegetters Hans Nielsen and Billy Hamill

BEST OF BRITISH ... Another British Grand Prix win, this time at Coventry, 1998, with Melody on hand to enjoy the moment

CHAMPION ... British Elite League Riders title-winner as a Peterborough rider, 1999

MISSING LINK ... Pardubice, 1999 and Jason Lyons, Leigh Adams, Todd Wiltshire, Ryan Sullivan and team manager Neil Street celebrate Australia's first World Team Cup success since 1976. Jason was already on his way home in anticipation of the birth of daughter Mia

HOW SWEDE IT IS ... Celebrating a third GP title in the Swedish Grand Prix at Linkoping, 2000

WALKING ON AIR ... Team Crump enjoy victory in Bydgoszcz, 2001

STOCKHOLM SLING ... A second win for the 2001 season, just three weeks later in the Olympic Stadium

HI HO SILVER ... Jason (second), Tony Rickardsson (world champion 2001), Tomasz Gollob (third)

WORLD BEATERS ... Wroclaw, 2001 Australia have won the inaugural Speedway World Cup, JC leads the chorus and the great Ove Fundin joins the party

CHAMP AGAIN... British Elite League Riders title-winner as a King's Lynn rider, 2001

CLOSE QUARTERS ... Jason (2) withstands the heat from Billy Hamill (6) and Lukas Dryml (14) on his way to victory in the 2002 Czech Republic GP in Prague

No.2 No.2 ... 2002 series runner-up Jason, Tony and third placegetter Ryan Sullivan

THREE-PEAT ... Neil Street takes centre stage and Australia are world team champions once more, Peterborough, 2002

HOW ABOUT THIS ... Jason surveys the scene at the Parken stadium before the first GP to be held in Copenhagen, 2003, which he won

KRRRR ... Krsko, 2003. Jason coasts back to the pits after his fuel ran out on the last lap of a Slovenian GP semi-final race

TWO IN A ROW ... Jason heads for a second successive victory in Prague, 2003

SAY NOTHING ... BSI boss John Postlethwaite offers consolation after Jason's 2003 world title bid disintegrated at Hamar

THE ONE THAT GOT AWAY ... 2003 series 1-2-3 Nicki Pedersen with Jason and TR

ALL OVER ... Jason struggles to deal with the disappointment of Hamar, 2003

SPLASH HIT ... JC charges to victory over Leigh Adams in a Marketa Stadium mudbath, 2004 - this was his third Czech Republic GP win in a row

DANE GAME ... Back to back in Copenhagen, 2004, as Jason leads Andreas Jonsson and Greg Hancock in the final

DELIGHT ... Hamar, 2004, Heat 19 - Phil Crump and deposed champion Nicki Pedersen are first to salute the new world No.1

NOBODY DOES IT BETTER ... Melody, the champion behind the champion, delivers her congratulations

A FAVOURITE PICTURE ... Jason Crump, world champion 2004, with runner-up TR and third-placed Greg Hancock

HAPPY FAMILY ... Mia and Seth join in the title celebrations in Norway

HAPPY DAY ... Always a thrill to win in Sweden. This was the Scandinavian Grand Prix of 2005 at Eskilstuna

BEST OF RIVALS ... Swedish GP winner Jason congratulated by Tony Rickardsson, Malilla, 2005

SILVER ONCE MORE ... the 2005 Grand Prix medallists: Tony, Jason and Leigh Adams on the rostrum after the Italian GP in Lonigo

Tips for Speedway riders

THE WIN

SEE YA . . . if you followed the advice on the front of this section, this is the view you will be able to show your opposition

Colour section picture credits:
Front (Peter White, Carole Crump)
2 - (Dave Schooling, Jason Crump)
3 - (PW, JC, PW)
4 - (JC, PW, JC, Mike Patrick)
5 - (all MP)
6 - (MP, MP, Lynn News)
7-15 - (all MP)
16 - (Dave Fairbrother, CC)

Rökning förbjuden
KEYNE EXPRESS DELIVERIES
BICESTER
JAWA
LNB
HAGON
CRUMP
SCHROECK

Kelvin Tatum was quickly added to the side and he and an improving Ryan Sullivan both were good value, but we just didn't have the depth of the previous season. We beat Wolverhampton 55-35 at Alwalton in the first leg of the Premiership and couldn't defend it at Monmore Green, losing 58-32.

My results were reasonable, including eight maximums at home but only one, at Swindon, on the road. Winning the fours again, with all the hoopla and atmosphere that goes with that occasion, was a big day for everyone.

But Peter Oakes was having problems with his involvement in opening Skegness, and the atmosphere around the place wasn't the same as it had been the previous year. When the promoter is having a tough time, it is bound to have a flow-on effect. Riders notice, supporters notice. The increasing involvement of Jim Lynch, one of my sponsors, was responsible for helping to weather the storm.

It was not easy going in Poland, either. I moved to Gorzow's local rivals Zielona Gora but they struggled a bit and finished in sixth spot, out of play-off contention.

My average slipped back a tad from the previous year although there were some good meetings, including a paid 17 at Gniezno. It was all part of the learning curve, dealing with the expectations and conditions which make speedway such a big deal to the Poles.

By now this was becoming the place to be on a Sunday, at the expense of Germany.

I was able to fit in a few speedway meetings there and collected another league championship award when Brokstedt again took out the German title. But there was not much room left on the calendar after that.

The 'traditional' continental scene had been a big part of my racing education. I was never going to be world champion on long track but it was terrific, unbeatable experience. Lining up alongside Simon Wigg, Kelvin Tatum, Robert Barth, Karl Maier and the like provided a very swift lesson in learning how to handle yourself.

Taking a couple of facefuls of dirt from those guys half way round the first corner and realising in a flash that you don't know if you're going left or right soon wises you up.

You also have to quickly take on board the fact that over there, whether it's on the 1000 metre circuits or grass tracks, the show goes on rain or shine, and it doesn't matter if conditions are swimming in mud and flood. Everybody gets stuck in and makes the best of it. Dealing with those situations toughened me up, for sure.

I didn't have the equipment to shine on the big, super-fast circuits such as Herxheim, Scheesel or Marianske Lazne. I had my moments though, especially on some of the smaller tracks. One of the last long tracks I did was at Parchim right at the end of that 1997 season.

I'd been in the Elite Riders' Final at Odsal on the Saturday and then we did the overnight trip to Germany. The meeting was a big one, billed as a long track world final revenge with all the gun riders on parade.

Most of them were laughing as we set up in the pits area with just two speedway bikes – one dirty from Bradford, the other one clean – and a long track chassis at our disposal. Even Martin Hagon, who had travelled with me, probably thought the trip was a waste of time although he didn't let on.

So here are all these superstars with their super-tuned flying machines and I'm debating which engine to pull out of which speedway bike to put in the long track frame. The track was deep and it's a tight one. The almost unanimous opinion was that I need not have bothered – until the action started. I won every race and then left them all behind in the final to claim one of my most satisfying wins on the continent.

I've done only a few meetings over there since being involved in the Grand Prix – the whole scene has lost something since the GP series came in – and as things stand, won't be doing many more in the short to medium term. That's not to say that I wouldn't fancy another go in a few years' time. It would still be a big challenge.

I signed up for another stint in the 1997-98 Tapp series in Australia. It was part-business, part holiday as Mel came with me and saw parts of Australia she had never seen before. The series was a close-run affair, with Leigh shading it from Ryan and Todd. I was 16 points adrift at the end, close but no cigar.

The real surprise packet of the competition was Mark Lemon, my old buddy from Mildura, who scored 122 points, finished fifth overall, and probably had never ridden better in his life.

Leigh also collected another Australian title at Murray Bridge, beating Jason Lyons and myself in a run-off after we had all scored 13 points.

One of the most significant features of the summer was seeing Todd Wiltshire firing again after several years out of the sport. He had done some meetings in Germany and Bradford wanted to sign him, but were knocked back. Todd, who finished third in the World Final in 1990, was a man on a mission to show everyone, himself included, that he could still cut it.

Back in England, Peterborough were doing it tough and eventually they opted out of the Elite League because of financial concerns. It meant another enforced move and I just went out of the frying pan and into the fire, on loan at Oxford.

They were taking the reverse route, with Steve and Vanessa Purchase buying out Dave Pavitt and deciding to run in the top league instead of the lower division.

The Cowley track had never been one of my favourites, I'd not been one of the crowd's favourites either, and it looked as if we were going to struggle with a team which didn't have any other really established top riders.

BIG SPLASH ... Jason ploughs through less than favourable conditions for Oxford against Swindon, 1998

There were plenty of good old boys, guys like Steve Johnston and Steve Schofield who I've always had a lot of time for, and Paul Hurry with whom I was a Peterborough reserve back in 1992.

But after an opening challenge match win at King's Lynn where I went through the card, we then didn't get a competition win until the eighth match and were rock bottom for the first three months. I missed a handful of meetings after breaking ribs on long track and then crashing again on an overwatered track at home to Poole.

Then Todd Wiltshire was given the go-ahead to race again in the UK and Oxford were quick to sign him. Todd was under an enormous amount of pressure to do well. He'd had a shocking injury and for a few years didn't ride at all. Everybody was disappointed that what looked like a hugely promising career was not going to happen.

It must have been a heck of a time for him and when the permission finally did come through, he was straight into a side which was at the bottom of the league and looking for some sort of white knight to provide instant salvation. It was asking way too much of anyone, never mind a guy who'd been out for so long.

On his home Elite League debut, a local derby clash against Swindon, we were paired together – and he ran over my foot, which caused a nasty crash and left me with torn ligaments and an extremely bad temper. When I got back to the pit gate I just couldn't help myself and took a swing at him, which was stupid, not an action to proud of, but summed up much of my frustration at the time.

I saw red, reacted in the heat of the moment, and was immediately branded as speedway's David Beckham – he'd just been sent off in a World Cup match against Argentina a day or two earlier.

Team manager Martin Goodwin read us the riot act the following day and, good to relate, we sorted it out. At least things did start to improve in the later stages of the season. Wiltshire settled down, we made up and the team started to get some results which lifted us away from the foot of the table and for a while, gave us a fighting chance of making the play-offs.

One of our best wins was 47-43 at home to Ipswich, when Steve Johnston and I got the team home with a last heat 5-1 over Tony Rickardsson and Tomasz Gollob.

I finished off with a good performance in the Elite League Riders Championship at Swindon and topped the qualifying scorers but lost out to Rickardsson in the final.

Sweden was tough as well that year. Vargarna didn't look like repeating their effort of the previous season and some of my absences through injury probably did not help. I managed to edge my average up to 9.33, though.

STEVE Purchase and his wife Vanessa found out the hard way that promoting speedway at Oxford is no guarantee of commercial success.

The Purchases reportedly lost £50,000 on the 1998 operation but Steve was unstinting in his praise for Jason's efforts – even though the rider and the record books suggest it was one of his most disappointing domestic seasons in England.

"I would like to pay tribute to Jason," said Purchase at the end of the season.

"He has been a credit to Oxford Speedway and he has always given his best for the club.

"He is a very naturally talented rider and in my opinion he will be world champion one day, he has time on his side and I can see him winning the title eventually.

"He has been a pleasure to deal with. I know people will point to one or two controversial incidents with Jason, but he is such a determined character that he can go over the top at times.

"But he is also getting more mature and he is not far away from being the world number one. I really do wish him all the best."

Not much joy in Poland, however – Zielona Gora were going through some financial problems and only called me over to ride for them three times, all away meetings. They were relegated at the end of the season.

For a while, it appeared that my return to the Grand Prix was not going to be that crash hot. Bunged up with the flu, I went out early on in the first round in Prague after breaking a rocker arm in the first race. Pocking was no better and it seemed as if it was all going to be more of the same.

I should have learned from my first full year in the competition that to succeed you have to bring a different mindset to everything, but initially I didn't. I hadn't been good enough to stay in, and yet here I was making the same kind of mistakes.

Mind you, the knockout system was a killer. It's easy to go to a meeting and take a couple of races to sort out everything. There is never a limit to the things you might try – but if you didn't get it right straight away it was two strikes and you're out.

It's important, too, to be on top of your game as far as domestic form and fitness are concerned. This year I had neither of those going for me. It was probably my least effective year in England, and there were knocks and bangs all the time. I had broken ribs, torn tendons in my ankle, concussion, just one niggling problem after another.

But then things started looking up. In the Danish Grand Prix at Vojens I qualified for the A final for the first time in two years ... and although I placed fourth overall behind Nielsen, Chris Louis and Rickardsson, it was encouraging. It also was the first time in the year I had gone to a GP feeling healthy, although that was not to last.

The British GP at Coventry, on August 7 – a day after my 23rd birthday – was even better. I won the event for the second time, and Phil, my lucky mascot, was there again. He had come over for the Under 21 final in 1995, and again just before I won at Hackney the following year. Who knows whether it was coincidence but as ever it was good to share the celebration.

I had to wear a special brace on my ankle as the ligament injury was still a problem and Daytona made me a tremendous carbon fibre boot. Don Gatherer, my physio in Aylesbury, also did a great job to get me halfway fit.

It was another special moment, after the meeting began badly. I copped a first race exclusion for taking Henka Gustafsson's front wheel on the pit turn. I thought it was a tough decision – you have to go for these openings – but the referee wouldn't listen to my point of view.

As Vastervik the previous year had shown, you have to get on with it. I did so in a manner which gave me a lot of satisfaction because I felt I was maturing as a person as well as a rider. The guys in my crew were good, they helped me cope and settle to the task. At the end of the day though, it's still down to the rider to make things happen on track.

Consistency was what I was after and this was a performance which indicated I was getting closer all the time to the speed and level needed to match the top guys on a regular basis.

The British GP was a case of being in the right place at the right time. I had a good night when Oxford were at Coventry a week earlier, so I knew in the back of my mind which bike I wanted to use. There was also a paid maximum for Australia against England at King's Lynn and that exciting win over Ipswich to keep my spirits up. Driving half an hour down the road to Brandon seemed like just another day at the office.

Bill Street reckoned that the enforced holiday because of injury and illness has actually done me some good. He figured that a few of the other GP riders were beginning to show signs of wear and tear as the season moved into its most hectic phase. I wasn't in the mood to over-analyse things. But I did feel that the result showed I could learn from those earlier setbacks.

However Sweden and Poland, the last two GPs, were nothing to write home about. I crashed out in Linkoping, and then in Bydgoscz dislocated my shoulder in in a big coming-together in with Billy Hamill, who crushed a verterbra in his lower back.

OH NO ... More disappointment as Jason reflects on an early exit from the Swedish GP at Linkoping, 1998

Leigh Adams performed some on-the-spot repairs on the track and popped my shoulder back and I battled through to Heat 20 only to miss out on the semis once more.

It was just enough to secure eighth place overall and with it a guaranteed spot for the following year. This was progress. I was starting to feel much more comfortable with the demands of the series, much more part of the whole thing. Call it experience, confidence, organisation, whatever you will.

One of my major moves in getting more organised was to take on Klaus Lausch. He was an Oxford asset, a handy speedway rider, very good on long track and a tuner who had successfully worked with Hans Nielsen, Tony Rickardsson and Tommy Dunker and helped all of them to win world titles.

Engine tuners do not just tune engines, they play a priceless role in keeping the rider confident and content with what he is riding. Klaus was excellent to work with. It is hard to explain but he gave me a lot more than just fast bikes and the GP is so much a mental challenge.

He gave me a lot of attention, we talked endlessly about set-ups and tracks and I immediately felt more comfortable about my chances of making an impact in the series.

But if there was one person to whom I felt especially grateful it was Mel, who from very early on has played a tremendous role in supporting me. She had the ability to keep my head straight, my feet on the ground and give me a life away from racing.

Mel was very much a calming influence and no matter what drama was going on in speedway, she gave me the benefits of a strong relationship and a steady home life. It wasn't easy as we were pretty much on our own. Mel has no family in the UK and while I had my folks in Exeter my immediate family were all in Australia so we had to fend for ourselves.

It was good to be able to catch up with everyone at the end of that season, and especially to see my new niece, Milla, born to Justine and Nick during that year.

Back on the Gold Coast, I spent a bit of time with Daryl Beattie, who had been one of Mick Doohan's closest rivals on the 500cc road racing scene for a while. Darryl fancied having a skid and we went along to the Mike Hatcher track at Labrador on several occasions. He picked things up quickly but, at 27, probably was a bit late to start taking speedway seriously.

The big plus of the season there was winning the International Masters series which I decided to contest again. While the depth of standard wasn't comparable with the Grand Prix, there were a few parallels to be drawn and lessons learned. Up to this point I had won a couple of GPs but other than that only once had so much as qualified for a B final. It was always all or nothing.

OH YES ... Winner of the International Masters 500 Series in Australia, 1998-99

What I deliberately tried to rehearse in that Australian summer was the sort of consistency and physical and mental preparation which would give me the best possible chance. Mark Loram, Joe Screen, Rune Holta, John Jorgensen and Toni Kasper were the international visitors and you knew there would always be a battle on with guys like Leigh Adams, Todd Wiltshire and Craig Boyce in the mix.

For the record I finished 44 points clear on 212 from 11 rounds in which there were 20 points up grabs for each meeting winner, and a premium 30 on the last round at Wayville. I won that one to go with victories at Brisbane, Gosford, Warrnambool and Mildura and four second places so this was just the sort of consistency I was looking for.

In the wash-up it gave me a lot of satisfaction to win the series. Leigh's challenge faded after he hurt himself when a chain snapped and he crashed leading the A final in the sixth round, but I managed to stay clear of trouble and kept making finals and scoring points. It was a good, encouraging sensation.

Back in Europe, I had to settle for eighth place again in the 1999 Grand Prix but all told I was starting to give more constructive thought to what was going on and what was needed.

It didn't get any better than a rostrum place in Prague in the opening round, won by Tomasz Gollob, but the way began to seem a lot clearer. No doubt it was still too early to think of making an impact on the top two or three

AFTER Peterborough had done everything and won everything in the Premier League in 1998, Jim Lynch wanted to take them back in to the Elite League – but Peter Oakes was not convinced.

Ian Jarvis and his partner Sue Crowley of sponsors Contraband liked the idea, though, and bought out Oakes to join Lynch in the promotion.

Central to their thinking was the recall of club assets such as Jason, who had spent the previous year on loan to Oxford, and Ryan Sullivan, who rode on loan at Poole.

Initially Crump was only too happy to return to a track he always had regarded as one of his favourites, and headed up a team which carried all before it. His rivalry with Sullivan was mostly positive for the Panthers, just as were various other elements of a side which, motivated as much by competitive edge as genuine togetherness, just kept winning.

"We had some interesting characters but it turned out to be the right mix," says Lynch.

"Jason had a great year and he was magic with the fans, especially the youngsters. He and Ryan bounced off one another, but it was all fairly easy to manage."

Jason, though, was of the opinion that Jarvis was much more of a Sullivan fan and his unease was crystallised when the new promoter – extensively quoted in the *Evening Telegraph* – was critical of his contribution in a tight match at Oxford which the Panthers narrowly lost.

An argument broke out in the pits when Jason refused to take a ride as a tactical substitute, which Jarvis saw as a public betrayal of trust. What

places but what did seem obvious was that I was moving towards a better mechanical set-up.

Tony Rickardsson won the title, coming up on the rails to pip Gollob who after being third in each of the two previous years, led going into the final round but hurt himself a week before Vojens and missed his chance.

There was a bit of a sense of change, however. Hans Nielsen signed off his fantastic career with third place but a few of us were beginning to knock on the door. After missing the first round, Mark Loram announced himself by winning the second in Sweden. Joe Screen and Leigh Adams were more consistent than before and while I didn't win a GP, I still mustered a few more points than the previous season.

Winning the B Final in the British GP at Coventry was my next-best result, and even if the score charts did not always reflect as much, I felt more at home, a bit less pressured and a step or two closer to the level of preparation and performance required. Yet there still was a lot to be done to make the jump.

Martin Hagon had sponsored me for two or three years and his support was awesome, just what was needed at the time. The trouble was that Hagon Shocks still owned virtually all the equipment and at the end of each year I really didn't own anything apart from a few engines lying around the workshop. No frames, no wheels, no sprockets, nothing – they all went back.

was never made public was that at the time Jason had been waiting in vain for some promised bonuses to come his way and decided it was time to take a stand. The kerfuffle blew over but the relationship did not recover even though the rider's double-figure contributions continued week in, week out.

In this mood of disaffection, he was ripe for the blandishments of Nigel Wagstaff, one of his sometime sponsors and a longtime Simon Wigg backer, who in the winter of 1999 bought into the King's Lynn promotion.

Wagstaff, coming in to partner Brian Griffin after Tony Rickardsson moved on and Mike Western moved out, wanted a marquee star and a team capable of improving on the previous year's third place. The £36,000 fee didn't faze King's Lynn, nor the prospect of paying an additional £4,000 were Jason to win the world title within two years of making the transfer.

Peterborough, never among the best-supported of clubs, could only be pragmatic about the situation. They didn't want to lose their top attraction, least of all to their closest neighbours, but economics dictated that someone was going to have to go – and Jason made his move by submitting an official transfer request.

"He's the sort of guy who doesn't move once he has made up his mind – and he had made up his mind," says Lynch.

"It was a pity but nobody could fault what Jason had given to Peterborough. In that last season he was absolutely awesome. It has to be one of his best years in the sport."

I was starting to use Brian Karger as a tuner and Klaus Lausch, by now a Jawa main agent in Germany, was very keen to get me to switch from GM, which I had ridden since I came to England

It meant that even as the 1999 season continued I was starting to think and plan ahead for the next year. To be honest, my mind wasn't entirely on racing in the later stages of the season, anyway, as Mel was expecting and as the big moment came closer, that was uppermost in our thoughts.

Of course you keep on going to the races and doing your best, but it's such a huge time in anyone's life, waiting for the birth of your first child, that everything else fades into insignificance for a while.

We had decided that this was our time, private and personal, and we wanted to do it on our own. Our parents were in Australia, we were growing as a couple and we felt really pleased and proud of ourselves and how we handled it all.

Our attention to detail in family planning worked out to the extent that the GPs were finished before she was due – but there were still plenty of meetings going on, with one of the most significant the World Team Cup Final in Pardubice.

With our strongest squad for a number of years, we fancied our chances, especially after a convincing win over Poland, Sweden and Russia in the semi-final in Leszno.

We had a six-week wait to the final but the fires were still burning and it all came together for us on the day. In one of the most emphatic performances in the history of the competition Australia scored 51 with Leigh, Ryan, Jason Lyons and myself all in double figures.

The Czechs, Americans and Brits had no answer to our fire power and it was clear from early in the piece that we were going to be unstoppable that day. Victory was a big deal, not least for Phil, who rode in the only previous Aussie win, at White City in London in 1976, and for Bill Street who since becoming the team manager had given a new sense of purpose and direction to our efforts.

The only thing missing on a memorable afternoon was a souvenir picture of the complete team. As soon as the last race was over, I was packed and gone, out of there, and hurrying back to be with Mel who was expected to give birth at any moment.

As it turned out, I could have stayed for the presentation ... Mia didn't arrive until four days later ... but we were not to know that at the time!

On the domestic speedway front, it was a very busy, exciting and eventful season. Going back to Peterborough was always something I hoped might happen, and when Jim Lynch – by now co-promoter at the Showground – started to put together his plans for 1999, he was very keen to return the Panthers to the Elite League.

Peter Oakes, on the other hand, felt that they were better suited to the less demanding financial waters of the Premier League. Peter probably had had enough by the time the previous year finished but persuaded himself to keep going. However his well-intentioned project at Skegness brought him nothing but heartache and by all accounts he was ready to call it a day.

Jim, though, had enjoyed his first year as a half-owner of Peterborough. They won the Premier League, the fours and the pairs and had the likes of Simon Stead and Oliver Allen showing terrific promise so there was no shortage of success on the track. He also had a new partner waiting in the wings in the shape of Ian Jarvis, whose company Contraband sponsored the team.

When all that went through, the club's return to the Elite League was always going to happen, and the recall of assets including myself and Ryan Sullivan meant there already was a strong spearhead around which to build. I was delighted to have the opportunity because to that point Peterborough was where I had been happiest and always hoped the chance to go back would come about.

Little did we know that the Panthers would celebrate their return to the top flight by taking out the league, the Speedway Star Cup and the Craven Shield.

It was a good, but not quite so productive year in Sweden where Vargarna were one of a number of clubs whose support levels increased quite dramatically. Masarna, with Tony Rickardsson leading the way with an incredible 11.14 average, and Smederna, drew crowds of over 5,000 for their home meetings.

I had my best season on track and averaged 10.40, the second-highest in the league. We had Jimmy Nilsen and Peter Nahlin on board and began the campaign with a terrific 56-39 home win over defending champions Valsarna, but lacked consistency and ended up sixth out of 11 teams.

Riding on the same team as Jimmy for the first time was a buzz. And he tried to look out for me.

Valsarna had Sam Ermolenko and not for the first time, we clashed with both us hitting the deck at the first corner in Heat 9. Jimmy encouraged me to get across a bit quicker in the re-run and I took his advice but the end result was much the same. At the third attempt, after Jimmy had again urged me to be even harder into the corner, Sam and I tangled once more – and this time I was excluded.

I complained to Krister Gardell, the referee, that he was being unduly harsh, because I'd made the start each time and in my book, if anyone was going to be out I thought it should be Sam. The ref said "Look Jason, if I don't exclude somebody and get this race run we will never finish the meeting" so I had to cop it and limped back to the pits to nurse my bruises

It was back to Wroclaw in the Polish League and I scored quite well – although they used me only twice at home and called me in for away meetings. There was tremendous pressure to deliver. They had Greg Hancock and myself as the two foreigners and Greg started off with a string of big scores. He had just one indifferent meeting so they roped me in and I was going all right until I too had a dodgy one and they promptly called him back.

After finishing fourth in the regular season, in the play-off semi-finals Wroclaw beat Bydgoszcz and then lost just by two points in the two-legged final against Pila.

Of course there was no end to the success at Peterborough and it was a shame that my return did not work out quite as hoped. As far as results went, both personally and teamwise, it was a huge season. Not so pleasant was tension with Sue Crowley, who was Ian Jarvis's girlfriend, and an uneasy relationship with Ryan Sullivan, who by now was less than thrilled with the idea of being number two to anybody, and especially not me.

After my ordinary year at Oxford where I had a 9.10 average, this time I finished top of the Elite League averages, top in every other team competition, and won the Elite League Riders Championship at Coventry. I scored 14 maximums in 42 meetings and posted a 10.69 average.

Peterborough had three losses and a draw in the first four league matches, all away, but we really fired up midway through, and thoughts of title success began to ignite in the last couple of months of the campaign.

We lost only one of the last 14 matches – including seven successive wins to finish. It could not have been a more exciting finale. It all came down to the last Thursday in September, with Peterborough needing to not only beat Belle Vue at the Showground but pull back 16 points to claim the bonus.

And 38 miles along the A47, longtime leaders Poole had to win at King's Lynn to clinch the title. Sky Television, for the first time, were covering the matches simultaneously and had sent their number one crew to Lynn obviously expecting to see Poole crowned as champions.

But after being four points up with three races to go, the Pirates couldn't hold on, going down 48-44 and we made sure of it in the end by beating the Aces 60-30.

The last few weeks of the season, I have to say, were absolutely exhausting. I had to miss the Speedway Star Cup semi-final trip to Poole because I was just so knackered, but the boys fought a great rearguard action and we got up in the home leg.

In between times I won the Elite Riders title at Coventry, a nice little personal bonus. Mark Loram and I tied on 12 points in the qualifying heats and both went straight through to the final.

We were joined there by Todd Wiltshire and Jason Lyons and with Mark pulling up in the decider it was an Australian 1-2-3.

That left the Craven Shield in which I was a virtual passenger in the first leg at Coventry, suffering from flu. Fortunately I managed an all-important second place in the last race of the return leg at Alwalton to secure a 55-35 home win and a 92-90 aggregate victory.

It's still a matter of pride that the very last race I had for the club helped bring home another trophy.

So much of my times at The Showground had been good – that exciting first year, then going back there in 1996 and again, after the year away at

HUNGRY PANTHERS ... Peterborough's 1999 treble-winners, left to right: Mario Jirout, Sam Tesar, Nigel Sadler, Jan Andersen, JC. Front: Ryan Sullivan, David Howe

Oxford. The people are genuine, they supported me from the time I was a kid struggling to get on the pace and both from a team and individual point of view, on balance it was a great place to be.

Unfortunately, in the time I have been riding speedway there very often seems to be a limited shelf life in a rider's relationship with his club. There isn't the sort of continuity in speedway that there is in some other sports. You tend to get constant changes of personnel, frequent changes in the promotion, and far less emphasis on staying with one club for years than used to be the case.

Maybe the points limits have had a fair bit to do with that, but that's just a convenient excuse for some promoters to use when they are making changes Ipswich had decided that even Tony Rickardsson was surplus to requirements the previous year, which underlined the fact that nobody can ever consider themselves 100 per cent secure.

It can be such a hugely unsettling time for riders, such an upheaval, and I was determined not to get caught up in a situation like that if it could be avoided. While being in the GP required focus in one direction and league racing demands something else, you always hope things will be going along smoothly on the home front. That wasn't the case at the Showground in 1999.

After the success we had as a team it was obvious that Peterborough would be moving on one or other of the top men. Apart from anything else, the averages dictated it, and the vibe was that Ryan Sullivan was the first rider they wanted to keep.

Of course they made all the usual noises about me being in their plans and if I had been convinced they meant it, no doubt it would have influenced my thinking. But sometimes you can sense when the mood shifts.

For me, it changed when Peter Oakes went and Ian Jarvis came in. I think Jarvis – and his partner Sue – were much more in tune with Sullivan than they were with me. And when I was slagged off in the press after we'd lost a match at Oxford it definitely didn't encourage me.

I'm not saying promoters are not entitled to have their say and I'm the first person to understand that sometimes in the heat of the moment it is easy to sound off and then later to think that some things might have been better left unsaid.

But riders are only human, they don't go out to lose races and they rarely appreciate being criticised in public. It's a betrayal of the relationship and usually means you just harden your attitude.

That's how I felt with Peterborough when it came to the end of the year. I'm not sure that Jim Lynch was committed to keeping me for the following season and I was convinced that Ian Jarvis wasn't bothered. He went public – again – and this time accused me of not negotiating properly.

This wasn't the way I wanted my Peterborough career to end. Their idea of negotiating was to offer me a deal before I went back to Australia and it was a case of 'that's it, take it or leave it'.

I'd returned there on what was far from being the most expensive deal, partly because of my respect for Jim Lynch, and partly, too, because I didn't have a great record in '98 to bring to any bargaining. But for the most part, it wasn't about money. I'm no different to the next guy inasmuch as I want to do the very best I can for myself, my family, our future, and for my professional set-up. Most of all, I want to be treated with respect.

A year on I was the top man, and I was aware the sort of deals other Grand Prix riders were getting at their clubs. Riders talk, and even allowing for a bit of exaggeration from some of them, it was clear to me that what I was looking for was some distance from what Peterborough were prepared to do for me. So that was a problem.

What bothered me was that it was impossible to escape the impression they were either looking to back me into a corner or perhaps that they already had decided that I would be out of their calculations. Mel knew how I felt – she had copped a lot of the backlash during the year in any case – and as always was there to support me whatever happened.

So I put in a transfer request. It was a gamble because you never can be sure how things will work out but we saw it as the only way to get things out into the open and give myself the best chance of having something happen.

There are always some clubs you like and others where you would never choose to ride. I really wanted to ride at King's Lynn. It's the sort of track where you have to have your set-up spot on to consistently win races and there's a lot more to it than Peterborough. I saw it as a move which would help me towards the goal of winning the world championship.

I had known Brian Griffin and Nigel Wagstaff as longtime supporters and sponsors and now they were teaming up with the intention of taking King's Lynn forward. Fortunately they were full of enthusiasm and went out of their way to try to sign me. I didn't have any prior arrangement but I was comfortable about putting it on trust that they would do the right thing by me if their transfer bid was successful.

I knew just how desperately keen they were to make a real success of things at King's Lynn. They both had a reputation as being generous and supportive as sponsors and now they were putting their money where their mouth was as promoters.

Because they had experience and a track record in other areas, I was confident that they could bring to King's Lynn a professional approach and give it a high profile and all of that appealed to me provided the clubs could work out a deal.

After all that had happened during the year, we were happy enough to let them sort things out. A break in Australia, showing off Mia, catching up with everybody, was how we wanted to see out the year.

I didn't want to do too many meetings but as the holder, felt some obligation to do a few rounds in the International Masters. I did four of the early ones, at the Ekka, Newcastle, Parramatta and Wayville, and went pretty well, trying out the Jawas and enjoying the racing.

Apart from that I limited myself to a couple of meetings for Ivan Mauger, at Archerfield and the Gold Coast, and won both of them.

I did plan to do the Australian Final at Gosford that season, but was taken ill on the morning of the meeting and was lying in hospital as Leigh Adams raced to the title in the evening.

There was a gala function put on by Motorcycling Australia at the leagues club the previous night to recognise the World Team Cup success and whether I ate something which disagreed with me I don't know. It was not the way I would have chosen to spend the next day.

There was nothing wrong with my appetite as far as the year 2000 was concerned, though. In a personal sense, both with the Grand Prix and as far as league racing was concerned, I was as hungry as I had ever been, if not more so.

LNB
POLAND
2
LNB
POLAND
POLAND
POLAND
JCB
CANAL+
Hamar

So near and yet so far

> ‘For a while there I honestly didn’t care if I never sat on a bike again – I was just too stunned to blow up’

THERE are several stages involved in getting to be a world champion, as the first few years of the new millennium were to prove.

I’d made the transition from beginner to feeling that I belonged in the Grand Prix series. The next step was to find the ingredients that would make me a contender.

You don’t get to be a winner without believing and it’s naïve to believe until you have some experience, a good support team, and the ability to prepare properly.

It was during 2000 that for the first time I felt I was getting to grips with the demands of the Grand Prix, and confident of being able to have a fair crack at it. As events worked out, the world championship, which at this stage was still being decided over six rounds, went to the wire and I was in the mix right up to the last one.

It would have taken quite a turnaround to have won it, although Tony Rickardsson had come up on the rails to pip an unlucky Tomasz Gollob the year before.

In the end I was not unhappy to finish up with fourth place, only 14 points behind Mark Loram who won the title despite not winning a round, the only time that’s happened.

Nobody begrudged him the championship, though – he was the best rider going around that year. Mark also is one of the most popular riders on the circuit. You would have to go a long way to find anybody who ever has a bad word to say about him.

He had the consistency over the series which one or two of us just lacked, and that’s the key ingredient. He totalled 102 points, Billy Hamill had 98, Rickardsson 94 and I was back on 88.

For Benfield Sports, who had taken over the rights to the series and boosted its profile, especially on the television, as well as the ground-breaking introduction of air fences at all venues, it was an encouraging introduction,.

There was a good distribution of talent, the series seemed to be settling down after a few years of uncertainty over its long-term future, and it was a good time to be stepping up my act.

I had a nightmare first round in Prague, eliminated after a couple of rides, and paid a big price for it in the final reckoning. But I was pretty happy with my performances overall. I won in Sweden, and then in the last two rounds got second in Vojens and fourth in Bydgoszcz.

You couldn't be too disappointed with that. It added up to a heck of an improvement and it was good to get to grips with some of the tracks which hadn't been too kind in the past.

The win in Linkoping was a highlight. It provided another example of how it's possible to put misfortune behind you and still come up with the right result. It was a bit like Vastervik '97 and Coventry '98, only more so.

In the first race of the night I copped an exclusion for a tapes offence, but I buckled down and won my next two to move into the main event. The wins kept coming and everything was going well until Tomasz Gollob ran into the back of me in the semi-final.

We were both grateful for the air fence but I was feeling pretty average.

I felt a whole lot better after winning the re-run and was flying in the final but unbeknown to me there was some drama being played out in the minor placings. The race was stopped and there was a lengthy delay as Tony Rickardsson was excluded, then reinstated and finally excluded again!

The locals were not too thrilled but I had to put all that out of my mind and get myself together for another re-start. Once again I had the edge and saw off any thoughts Mark Loram may have had about doing one of his famous dashes from the back.

This result encouraged me to think that things were starting to fall into place. Not so. It was back down to earth with a semi-final exit in Wroclaw and at Coventry (where wild card Martin Dugard popped out to win) it was more of the same. I hit the deck in the semi and was not best pleased.

Denmark shaped up promisingly and at least I qualified for the final but didn't quite get it right despite making a decent start. It had been a rainy, greasy night and Greg Hancock was a bit too cute, going round the outside of me.

I had a last chance of making a name for myself in the European GP in Bydgoszcz but, off gate four in the final, missed the jump and got squeezed out when Hamill and Greg Hancock went 1-2 and Tony clinched his third spot on the night and overall.

Missing out on a top three place really didn't bother me hugely. I wasn't keen for my first rostrum appearance to be in third place, don't ask me why but it was something I was happy to avoid. Phil got a third in 1976 but never went further. I had it in my mind that there were a few other riders who'd had a

PAINFUL ... Jason is helped off after crashing in the Swedish GP, Linkoping, 2000. He recovered and won the final

similar experience (I don't know whether history bears me out on that) so to be thereabouts without actually being on the rostrum wasn't a drama for me.

The difference was that psychologically, I felt good about myself, good about my chances. You could detect a new respect from other riders, too. Some of them were looking at what was going on and starting to recognise that instead of the hit and miss merchant of previous years, capable of winning the odd meeting but unable to sustain a challenge, things were starting to be different with me now.

I took some confidence out of the way the Jawas had gone for me in Australia but knew the real test was to come. The changeover in machinery was a big deal and took some getting used to. People like Martin Hagon, Guiseppe Marzotto, Trevor and Pam Hedge and Dave Perry had looked after me for years.

Martin and the Hagon family didn't have a specific alliance with GM and he has continued to help me in various ways but it was tough telling the others

I was changing camp. However, when the opportunity came to go with Jawa it represented the best chance so far to get the sort of back-up support necessary to have a real crack at the world championship.

Of course it wasn't all going to come together at once, but we took a deep breath midway through the year and decided that a new engine tuner could make a significant difference.

Basically we just put a lot of faith in Otto Weiss to get the best out of the new Jawa engines, and now I really felt I was at the races. We were learning all the time. Michael Blixt also helped me with some tuning towards the latter part of the year and it was all part of the learning process.

There were changes on the league front, too. When I began to suspect that Peterborough was not the best place for me to be if my world championship plans and ambitions were to continue to move forward, it didn't take much to realise that getting a move down the road to King's Lynn would raise a few eyebrows.

There was a terrific rivalry between the two clubs at this stage. King's Lynn had been in the top division from way back, coming in just a year after the

KING'S Lynn and their promoting duo of Brian Griffin and Nigel Wagstaff went into the 2000 season buoyed by the capture of Jason Crump for a record-equalling transfer fee.

"We were determined right from the start to cover for the loss of Tony Rickardsson and to do that we had to go for the top rider available – Jason Crump," is how Griffin described the motivation behind their move.

"Because we have such a superb track at the Norfolk Arena and other teams relish coming here to race against us, we must have a powerful combination to counter that.

"Neil and I have bitten the bullet, we have spent a considerable amount of money and that has come from our own pockets. I hope this will show our commitment to the club and to the future of speedway at King's Lynn, and that the club will be recognised as a major player in the Elite League."

Wagstaff, who came on board at the end of 1999 in time to help steer through the Jason move, was similarly enthusiastic.

"I have known Jason for quite some time and he is really is something special in the world of speedway. He is never beaten; and if he has a weakness, that is it. I have seen Jason in some Grand Prix events where he may have missed the gate and he could have settled for second place to go through to the next round, but he has still been battling in there for the lead.

"But what you see is what you get with Jason. He is an out and out

British League started, and being there ever since – apart from one year when Buster Chapman was negotiating to buy the stadium. Peterborough had ruffled their feathers a few times, especially when they were in direct opposition for the first time and started winning.

Not everyone at Peterborough was too thrilled at the idea of me going but when it came down to it, King's Lynn were prepared to do a deal – I believe it cost them the £36,000 which took me to the Showground from Poole, plus a clause which would add a further £4,000 if I won the world championship in the next couple of years.

It wasn't all about me, though. Brian Griffin and Nigel Wagstaff were putting together a team which was looking really good. Leigh Adams was there, and Craig Boyce, Shane Parker and Travis McGowan were on board so we started off with a remarkable five Australians in the side including three (Adams, McGowan and myself) from Mildura.

There was a good feeling about the whole set-up. It was a team capable of anything, and a promotion trying to take domestic speedway to another level. And we very nearly won everything.

racer and he has so much talent. He will be a tremendous asset for King's Lynn.

"I think the world of Jason, he's a lovely boy. He is not the easiest person to get to know because he respects his privacy and not a lot of people get to know him. But once you have gained that friendship, you couldn't have a better friend.

"Making a transfer request was a big step for him. It was a very big step and only then did we make our intentions known, but I never, ever asked Jason to do anything so he could come to King's Lynn. We have bought him for the future. We want to build a team around him for years to come. It's not short-term.

"When it came to Jason's deal I thought 'this guy is not screwing us at all'. He said 'that's what I want' and I agreed. He wanted what he felt was a good deal and we have given him that."

Griffin described the signing as 'so obvious'.

"It made business sense to sign one of the best riders in the world. He is still young. I can see him taking the world title, so there has to be a price paid.

"He is a charismatic speedway rider who sends shivers down your spine every time he gets out on the track. He reminds me of some of my boyhood heroes in that respect."

CUP THAT CHEERS ... King's Lynn, 2000 KO Cup winners. Back row, left to right: Steve Masters, John Cook, Leigh Adams, Craig Boyce, Travis McGowan. Front: Tom Madsen, promoters Brian Griffin and Nigel Wagstaff, and JC

In the final analysis, we were pipped for the championship by Eastbourne and had to settle for the Speedway Star KO Cup by way of consolation – the first silverware the club had won in ages.

Riding with Leigh was great. We'd been rivals since we were growing up and a lot of people said that it wouldn't work with the two of us in the same team. But there was no nonsense, no jealousy, no division of promoters or fans into separate corners. I pushed him, he pushed me, and when we rode together in a lot of Heat 13 and Heat 15 races we were always confident riding within inches of one another. It was a great partnership.

Leigh actually finished a fraction ahead of me in the averages but with a 10.15 to my name I wasn't disgraced. I knew it would be tough to match the previous year's stats because King's Lynn is the sort of track where even the visitors love to race. There wasn't the same degree of home advantage as you get at most other places

But it was a great circuit to have as your home base. It's one of the best in the world and going there every week was a pleasure. The way the team fired up made it all the more so, as we won 11 and drew one of our first 14 league matches.

Then we had a bit of a hiccup and much to his disappointment, Shane Parker was released and Peter Nahlin brought in. He only lasted a couple of matches before being injured and John Cook took over for the later stages of the year as we went flat out for the double.

In the end it was down to the last couple of matches, both away from home and on successive nights. We went to Poole and won 49-41and moved along the south coast to Eastbourne hoping to do the same.

We needed to win at Arlington, which is never easy, but we were up for it. Unfortunately it was a night when almost everything went wrong. The turning point for me was being excluded after a crash with Joe Screen and we ended up losing 50-42.

Waggy and Brian Griffin tried to put a brave face on things and complimented us on our efforts but it was a huge disappointment to everyone.

We did re-group and got our act together in the KO Cup Final, beating Coventry on aggregate. King's Lynn had developed quite a reputation as a cup side in the past as the locals were quick to remind us. Most of the hard work was done at home where we won 58-32 but you never can take anything for granted and we still had to do the business at Brandon.

At the first time of asking, the second leg was washed out, and we all had to go back the following week. This time there were no mistakes and although we lost by six on the night a 100-80 aggregate score was pretty emphatic. It was a very happy bunch who celebrated the club's first major trophy for 20 years.

One of the most bizarre things during the year happened to Darren Groves, a young rider from the Gold Coast who came to England in 1999 to try his luck. His career was over almost before it had begun after he broke his neck. It's a frightening story.

He started at King's Lynn, and then was signed by Workington. We hooked up before the start of the 2000 season, and he came to stay with us at Duston to help me as a mechanic in between his own riding commitments. He crashed in a meeting at Sheffield, and Ian Thomas called me from there to say Darren had been taken to hospital.

Somehow he made his way to a friend's place at Grantham, and came on to Peterborough the following night. Alun Rossiter picked him up from there and dropped him back at our place, where he promptly took over the sofa and stayed there for a couple of days looking decidedly unwell.

When he didn't respond to our good-natured ribbing, Melody took him to the accident and emergency department at Northampton where he was x-rayed twice and told to rest up for a couple of weeks.

He still looked terrible and two days later a letter came from the hospital, telling him to get back in there. As soon as Mel dropped him off there were white coats all over him. Within five minutes they had put him in a full head collar and strapped him to a bed.

Unbelievably, it seemed that two doctors had failed to identify the fact he had a broken neck. I went absolutely mad with the medical staff.

Probably the key to Darren's recovery was the massive feed of Kentucky Fried Chicken which I managed to smuggle in to his hospital bed. It must have kept him going for a couple of days.

Eventually they moved him to a special hospital in London where he had the first of several operations. He's back on the Gold Coast now and walking around, very grateful and very lucky that he lived to tell the tale after this brush with near-disaster.

It was an up and down season in Sweden. Vargarna started off like a train but faded and did not even qualify for the play-offs which had been introduced for the first time.

Just like the previous year, Vargarna made a superb season start, outclassing Smederna at Eskilstuna by 59-37 and then taking the bonus point (another innovation) by winning the return 53-42.

The third match looked like being the most difficult of the season, away to 1998 and 1999 champions Valsarna. But after winning 49-46 there, Vargarna were sky-high favourites for the title.

It all changed when Valsarna won at Norrkoping by 52-44. And the biggest knock to our confidence came when we were thrashed 65-31 at Avesta by Masarna, who, with Tony Rickardsson an inspiration, were to go on to win the

CHRISTER Gustavsson was chairman of Vargarna for five of the seasons in which Jason rode for the Norrkoping club, and architect of a contract designed to tie him to the Wolves for 10 years.

They had what Gustavsson describes as 'a very fine partnership' before problems caused him to step down and, later, Jason decided to cut back on his Swedish Elite League commitments. But fans still regard him as a big favourite and he was named as 'Best Sportsmen Of The City'.

He and Jimmy Nilsen formed a formidable combination, leading by example and encouraging other members of the team to greater efforts.

"It was a big experience to look at Jason Crump and Jimmy Nilsen riding in the last heat. Almost every time it ended up with 5-1 to Vargarna," said Gustavssson.

"I have had the privilege to follow Jason from being a young boy to growing up to an adult with his own family. It has been exiting to see how he has matured both on and beside the track.

"Jason is a very earnest sportsman, a perfectionist and a good team companion who always helps everyone in the team.

"When sometimes there was a party after a match or when the league had finished, Jason always was the one who went to bed first ... every time except one.

"After celebrating a match in Norrkoping he woke up next morning bald-headed, after he had shaved off all his hair.

"We are still wondering what Melody said when he came home."

THE WOLVES ... Vargarna, 2000. Back row, left to right: Bo Jansson, Jason Crump, Tomas Olsson, Emil Lindqvist, Jimmy Nilsen, Ake Bergstrom Front: Shaun Tacey, Jimmy Jansson, Niklas Karlsson, Jesper B Jensen, Jason Lyons

title. We were never the same force after that although there was a revival which left the Wolves in a reasonable fifth place.

There was plenty of interest though with crowd figures up everywhere. Masarna had 12,242 spectators for the title-decider against Rospiggarna. I finished fourth in the Elite League rankings on 9.60, behind Tony Rickardsson, Leigh Adams and Peter Karlsson.

Poland was much better after my switch to Gorzow. We collected third after the play-off series and my form there was pretty solid, the highlights being a couple of very good meetings at Torun which was fast becoming one of my favourite tracks.

Australia's World Team Cup defence was well short of expectations. Sweden pipped Great Britain in the decider at Coventry with the USA third and we were an ordinary fourth.

It was a quiet time in Australia for a change. David Tapp decided that he'd had enough of running a series each year and I wasn't desperate to go far afield chasing meetings.

I rode three times at the Gold Coast which, as always, was fun. It's a good little racing track and it was always a pleasure to have a blast round there.

Bob Cowley, who ran a motorcycle shop in Nerang, was the driving force at the club for a number of years. I got on with him from the moment I landed in the area and that friendship has stood the test of time.

Bob's one of the most reasonable and understanding officials you could imagine and you couldn't put a price on the amount of unpaid labour he put in. He has helped riders from Mick Doohan, Troy Butler, Mark Carlson, Vic Martin and Bob Hill who were the Australian sidecar champions, and plenty more.

He always has been very supportive towards me, lending me a moto cross bike and doing various kindnesses so it was my way of saying thanks to go there and do a few meetings – mostly for nothing – to help out.

Before the start of the 2001 season, I felt thoroughly refreshed, and really confident of my ability to win the world championship. After the previous year, I figured I was ready.

I'd learned and absorbed a lot of lessons, my temperament was improving, my equipment set-up good, and I felt comfortable to be bracketed alongside the top three or four guys who already had made a habit of finishing at or near the top of the pile.

All I had to do was avoid the sort of first round disaster which had got things off to such a bad start in three of the four years I'd been a regular on the series. So what happened? We went to Berlin for the opener, it rained and rained and everything was a total lottery. I lost out, having two outings on a rain-soaked track and bombing out.

Tomasz Gollob won from Henka Gustafsson, who hadn't even made a final for the past four years, with Nicki Pedersen on the rostrum for the first time and Tony Rickardsson fourth.

Over nine or 10 rounds, which was soon to become the norm, most times it would be possible to have the odd bad meeting without wrecking the entire season. With only half a dozen GPs, to crash and burn in the very first one was the not the rocket-propelled start I was looking for.

But things got a whole lot better in the British Grand Prix, staged for the first time at Cardiff. This was a huge occasion, with a noisy, excited crowd packed in to the new Millennium Stadium, and an unbelievable atmosphere which lifted the whole dimension of the championship into new territory.

I made it to second behind Rickardsson, which moved me up to fourth in the overall standings Maybe that German result wouldn't prove so damaging after all..

This was the first world championship meeting at which I'd had my dad involved since he came over from Australia, initially for just a couple of months, but in the event it turned out to be much longer, and the start of a permanent role in the team.

Phil always has been pretty cluey with engines. My grandfather taught him much of what he knows but he's got his own ideas and methods and very quickly was making his presence felt after we set him up with a workshop down the road from our place.

We set off for Denmark in good shape and the outcome in Vojens was similar to Cardiff, a 1-2 result which pushed me up to third in the rankings. What I really needed to do was steal a march on Tony, but even when Billy Hamill got up to take the Prague round, he still finished second to my third. And Gollob, who had taken the fourth spot in three meetings, was clinging on to second overall.

If I could just turn those rostrum placings into victories ...

Well, I did. A win in Bydgoszcz – taking Rickardsson from the back – with Gollob, unusually, missing out, put me into second spot. But TR collected 20 points and it meant something had to go seriously wrong to prevent him from reclaiming the title.

All I could do was to head to the final round, in Stockholm, looking for nothing less than another victory and hoping Tony had a rare off night. Feeling very confident about my form, I did my part but by winning the B final Rickardsson did enough to collect the crown in front of his delighted countrymen. He signed off with 121 points to my 113 with Gollob by now a distant third on 89.

Honestly, I wasn't discouraged. Second was terrific, given the handicap I placed myself under from the start. Qualifying for every final after Berlin, and winning the last two, suggested it was all coming together nicely.

As well as winning in Poland and Sweden I capped off a really great end to the year by winning the Elite Riders Championship at Sheffield. In those three big meetings I think the only race I lost was to Ryan Sullivan in Heat 18 at Owlerton – and I got the verdict over Scott Nicholls, Nicki Pedersen and Mikael Karlsson in the final.

Things were going well in other ways, too, with a move to a new home at West Hunsbury, which is on the opposite side of Northampton from Duston and equally central and convenient for everything.

We actually moved in on the day of that ELRC meeting but it wasn't one of those moves in which we had to shift everything in one go – we kept on the other house and Phil and Ben Powell, my mechanic at that time, stayed on there until the end of that year.

This also was the first year in which the Speedway World Cup was staged under its revised format, with Benfield Sports including the competition under the same umbrella as the world championship.

Poland were strong favourites to win the revamped tournament which was being staged on their own tracks, but Australia helped themselves to another slice of history by winning the event.

I got a 15-point maximum in the semi-final at Gdansk – and it got even better four days later when we took out the final in Wroclaw, scoring 68 points, three ahead of the Poles with Sweden, Denmark and the United States some way adrift.

MAGIC MOMENT ... Maximum man Jason laps up Australia's 2001 Speedway World Cup victory in Poland

It was a great team effort with Leigh Adams (16), Ryan Sullivan (13), Todd Wiltshire (10) and Craig Boyce (9) all on song. It was pretty memorable from a personal angle too as I racked up 20 points, still the only full score in a final.

This was one of the few decent meetings I've had at the Olympic Stadium, although the venue does have massive atmosphere and great history. When the city was called Breslau and was part of Germany, it hosted events in the 1936 Olympic Games and when I rode for Wroclaw in '99 I had a tour round the whole place, including the old athletes' village and various facilities.

My thoughts about the venue can never quite shake off the memory of 1996, my first GP there, which was a nightmare. It is a big, wide typical Polish track where it's easy to feel you are never quite on the pace. Hopefully it will be better in 2006, because Wroclaw will once again be my home base in the Extra League.

Fortunately, everything went right on this day and this time I was able to take part in a typically enthusiastic Aussie celebration after we had won.

By contrast, the domestic season at King's Lynn was one of the most frustrating I have experienced. The team was much changed from the previous year, the most notable absence being that of Leigh Adams who had gone to Oxford.

Nicki Pedersen came in from Wolves, a very lively, determined newcomer with a truckload of ambition but not yet the world-class rider he was to become within a year or so. And we didn't have anything like the strength in depth which had taken us so close to winning the lot.

Brian Griffin also faded out of the promotion during the year, the fans sensed that all was not well, and a lot of the optimism of the previous season was replaced by one struggle and drama after another.

Two matches involving Eastbourne within a few days of each other summed up the extent to which things had turned. Our home match against the Eagles was abandoned after three riders were injured. Then we went there and were denied the use of Danny Bird at reserve despite the fact that Waggy insisted we had the necessary BSPA permission.

He pulled the team out of the meeting leaving the Eagles to ride round for a 5-0 in every race for a ludicrous 75-0 win. In principle he may well have been within his rights but it was a dire day and later cost the club a £7500 fine as well as a lot of credibility.

I had known Waggy since I moved to Northampton. He had helped Simon Wigg and Troy Butler and was supportive of me – and a friend – for three or four years before he moved into promotion.

But it was obvious he was struggling, and the place was not doing well enough to justify the sort of money I felt my status now warranted. Realistically, it wasn't up to scratch as an Elite League venue at the time. I didn't want to fall out with him, but from a business point of view it just couldn't last.

It was disappointing that King's Lynn later went out of the Elite League when Waggy decided in 2003 that he couldn't make the sums work, though it was not a huge surprise.

It's a great race track, very possibly the best in the world. Buster Chapman and his family have ploughed in so much there in the past two or three years so maybe they will be back in the top flight.

I got the chance to ride there again in the first meeting of their 40th anniversary season and you could not fail to be impressed by the amount of work which has been going on. If everything adds up and they find a way to run in the top division again, I'll be the first to applaud it.

If the way it went at Lynn was a downer, 2001 wasn't the best year in Sweden, either. Crowds continued to be good in most places but from a Vargarna point of view, things didn't happen. We had basically the same team, with Jason Lyons in for Peter Nahlin as the only change. But we dropped another couple of places in the league.

There was the usual decent start, but a really ordinary finish in which we lost six of the last eight matches. I was seventh in the averages, as usual topped by Tony Rickardsson.

By contrast the end of season in Poland was really full-on with Gorzow placing third in the Extra League but then losing out in the third and fourth-place play-offs.

It was a strong finish though as I produced some of my best form in the last four meetings – 15 at Torun, paid 14 at home followed by 15 at Wroclaw and 17 in the return match – and had four maximum scores over the season.

Back in England, matters came to a head at King's Lynn and it was clearly time for me to move on. I wanted my next move to be one which would provide some continuity and going to Belle Vue offered that possibility.

The Aces have been the longest-running club in speedway, going back to the year dot. Their tradition and history is second to none. I'd had quite a number of good meetings there, and John Perrin, their promoter, always seemed to be a straight shooter. He had hinted that he would be pleased to have me there and when it came down to it, he was good to deal with and keen enough to work out a deal with Nigel Wagstaff.

We came back to Australia while all this was going on. I believe they spent some time arguing over a transfer fee without reaching agreement, and eventually came up with a loan arrangement for the 2002 season and the understanding that there would be further talks after we had all seen how things went.

Again the plan was to do no more than a handful of meetings in Oz and spend most of the time winding down, taking some serious relaxation, and then gearing up for the next campaign.

The Australian Final was one meeting I was happy to put back on my list when it was allocated to Wayville, one of my favourite tracks. There was a lot of expectation about this event. It was the first time in a while that virtually all the leading riders were on parade – some of them probably influenced by the hope of putting their hand up for a Sydney Grand Prix wild card – and there were six riders in a race.

It didn't go entirely according to plan as once again I had to settle for second place. Leigh Adams took out the final and Ryan Sullivan, Todd Wiltshire, Mick Poole and Steve Johnston occupied the next places.

I crashed in my second ride but qualified for the final without further drama. Leigh was a bit quick for us in the deciding race, adding yet another title to his belt. It's almost his special event and he's built a sequence which probably won't be matched for ages. Good luck to him, he has a fantastic record and I wouldn't knock it. I just haven't made the Oz titles one of my priorities.

In fact this was to be the last year in which I rode in anything more than the odd meeting in Australia. An eight-month season is long enough for almost anybody, certainly for me since the family came along. You need time to wind down, to chill out, and then some breathing space in which to get together all the necessary arrangements for another full GP year and domestic speedway commitments.

Being comfortable with all your league arrangements definitely plays its part in creating the right mindset for everything. In addition to my change of track in England, I was on the move in Poland – again to a club which seemed to be making all the right moves. Pila came on with a tempting offer and it looked to be a smart move.

Increasingly, getting my act together and the build-up right has been the main reason for braving those European winters. And for me, it is so important to have a promoter who understands where a rider is coming from and where he's aiming. Finding yourself at the right club is a much more detailed business in England than it is elsewhere.

In the early years of the Grand Prix you would forever be seeing stories about John Perrin being opposed to the GP and complaining about its impact on British speedway. But my new boss assured me that he was right behind me and supportive of my title ambitions.

So after the steady progress of 2000 and the predominantly encouraging performances of 2001, I definitely felt ready to win the world championship in 2002 Another runners-up spot was not what I was looking for, yet that's how it turned out. Not as thrilling as the first one had been, but set against the events which happened in the lead-up to the series, a pretty good effort..

For the first time the championship had gone from six rounds to 10. The final one was scheduled for Australia, at the same stadium where the Sydney

MANY northerners regarded Belle Vue's Hyde Road as the spiritual home of British speedway, and there were claims that the first speedway meeting in the UK took place at nearby Droylesden in 1927, rather than at High Beech in February 1928 as popularly held.

Whatever the merits of that historical argument, the current Belle Vue has its place in the record books – it staged the first greyhound race around an oval track in Britain on July 24, 1926. Furthermore, the Kirkmanshulme Lane stadium was home to the first Belle Vue speedway team in 1928 before the team relocated to 'the Zoo' the following year.

The 'zoo' nickname derived from the Zoological Gardens which from 1837-1977 was part of Manchester's social and entertainment history with its theme park, fairground rides, circus and exhibition halls, function rooms and ballrooms.

The speedway stadium was built on the site for the 1929 season, and ran throughout the second World War, but had to go in the wake of health and safety findings prompted by the 1985 Bradford football fire.

When the Aces moved out and took residence at the greyhound stadium, they were going back to their origins, and bringing back speedway rather than introducing it to the venue.

Olympics had been so successfully and spectacularly staged a couple of years before.

All the signs seemed promising. Jimmy Nilsen had packed up riding and asked me to be the first signing for his new GP team. The deal was that he would arrange and co-ordinate all the sponsorship and various other details. All I had to do was race.

Guys like Tony Rickardsson, Billy Hamill and Greg Hancock had shown the way with their organisation and arrangements and the idea of linking up with someone such as Jimmy, who had been around for so long and knew how everything worked, could only be a positive.

He also signed up Krystof Cegielski, and told us about various back-up deals he had going for the new team. It sounded ideal. Racing all the time, there is a limit to the amount of time and energy you can devote to planning, sponsorship and all those other details which go together to form the big picture.

I was comfortable with myself, confident about my form, very happy with the engines which Phil, Peter Johns and Michael Blixt were looking after. Riding-wise, I figured I was very close.

You can only do so much to prepare. Sometimes things are taken out of your hands. In my case, that happened big time when I crashed in the last race of a Polish league match in Gdansk on April 14. It left me with a broken left elbow and three busted ribs.

There were 27 days before the first GP in the Viking Ship indoor stadium in Hamar, built when Norway hosted the 1994 winter Olympics..

Team-mate Rafal Dobrucki and I were on a 5-1 which would have forced a 45-45 draw. Then I got speared from behind by Marek Cieslewicz and was slammed into the fence. It was pretty obvious that there was some serious damage[1].

The headache which came with the territory was not improved when they carted me off to hospital and after a lot of fussing about, announced that they would operate on the elbow.

Call me a wimp if you like but from the first time I went there, I never have been a huge fan of Polish hospitals – well, hospitals anywhere, to be truthful. You used to hear some horror stories and while I am sure there are plenty of great surgeons and some terrific facilities in Poland, I much preferred the idea of getting treatment back in England where at least nothing would get lost in the translation.

So I booked myself out of the hospital, holed up overnight in the Holiday Inn, and had Mel meet me at Heathrow when I got back in there on the Monday morning.

[1]Crump was replaced by Tomasz Gapinski who partnered Dobrucki to a 5-1 in the re-run.

I have a physiotherapist in Harley Street who had treated me before, and he was our first port of call. He phoned a top surgeon in Nottingham whose speciality was repairing broken elbows, who told him that he was going on holiday the next day and if I wanted to see him, I'd best not hang around.

He also added that I should not eat or drink anything because, depending upon what he found when he examined me, he would do the operation that afternoon. When we got there he pronounced himself satisfied with what he saw, confident he could repair the damage, with the one reservation that it would be eight weeks before I could race again.

"Hang on," I said. "The first GP is in less than four weeks, that's no good."

The only way of possibly accelerating the recovery was for me to spend rehabilitation sessions in a hyperbaric chamber. They are best known as a decompression chamber to help deep-sea divers avoid suffering from the bends when they surface after a long time under water. More recently, they have become a sophisticated aid to treating injuries.

To cut the story short, that was the route I chose to go. I didn't have the operation and spent the next few weeks making a daily rail trip from Northampton to Euston, followed by an underground trip to St John's Wood. Then I walked across the Beatles' famous Abbey Road zebra crossing but, initially at least, not with too much of a song in my heart.

At the St John and St Elizabeth Hospital, I put on a gas mask and sat in that chamber breathing pure oxygen for up to an hour at a time. A lot of football clubs and other sporting organisations have used these chambers. It's pretty scientific stuff.

They work, but there are a few side effects. One is weight loss and diminished appetite, another dehydration, and, if you don't mind me mentioning it, constipation, But the big plus was that the injury mended in double-quick time. I followed every second session with physio treatment, and with just five days to go before the opening GP was able to get back on a bike at Belle Vue on the Monday night.

Come the Hamar meeting, I exceeded my own expectations and qualified for the final – only to fall off after passing Rickardsson! I just was stuffed. I didn't appreciate how much the previous days and weeks had taken out of me and simply could not hang on.

To be honest I was not 100 per cent for the first three or four GP rounds, but that's how it goes. In all sports you often have to keep going even though there may be some injuries niggling away. If you stopped every time that happened, nobody would ever get on a bike so I won't cite that as an excuse.

In the first five rounds, I made the final three times (Hamar, Bydgoscz and Stockholm) without placing once, Rickardsson won in Norway and Sweden, in between times Ryan Sullivan went back to back in Cardiff and Krsko and it looked very much as the championship was going to be all about those two, even after Tomasz Gollob as usual was the man in Poland.

Most of the riders were excited about the extension of the series but not all of the new venues were that flash. The Krsko track is okay but the pits are the worst anywhere, with no room, and everyone herded into a very low roofed area. It's like a concrete cavern, the fumes are terrible and the roar when the bikes are warming up is deafening. A definite case for the Health and Safety people to check out.

At the halfway point in the championship I'd had two unsuccessful semi-final appearances including a tapes exclusion in Slovenia, after which I was down to fifth and still behind Leigh Adams, which left me as the third-placed Aussie in the top five.

It looked as if I had done my dash but then I felt the pleasure of winning in Prague which narrowed the gap between the top two and myself to 17 points. However, Leigh took out his first title, the Scandinavian GP at Ullevi and although it wasn't the best day for me I did close the gap on Sullivan.

My former King's Lynn team mate Nicki Pedersen came from absolutely nowhere to win the GP of Europe in Katowice with me second. Rickardsson (148) was growing in confidence, making the final for the eighth time out of eight. Sullivan (134) had his chances, and his shoulder, damaged in a crash and now I was up to 128 points.

When Tony won in Vojens, where I had my fourth unplaced final of the year, it was enough to have him crowned as the champion again with the Australian round still to come.

By now I was just three points behind Sullivan, and by qualifying for the final in Sydney – where Greg Hancock became the season's sixth different winner – I managed to move on to 162 points to Ryan's 158. Tony didn't make the last race of the series but still finished with 181 points.

So there I was ... runner-up again.

Once more, I couldn't be too devastated with second. In truth I was really proud of having been able to make any sort of a challenge after injuries threatened to derail the entire year.

Frankly I had no business to even be riding in the first couple of rounds which meant that anything I did achieve was always going to be a bonus.

And there was another major drama to contend with after Jimmy Nilsen didn't see out the year. Fortunately Wlodek Skudlarek, whose LNB company had come on board as the major sponsor, did the right thing by me and it turned out to be the start of what has continued as really good, strong relationship.

It was an unsettling time and it was a big relief that he undertook to sort out the situation.

In fact, he did much more than that. The way he treated me then, and since, has been a huge help. Nowadays I leave virtually all of my business dealings in Poland to him, he's very straight, and he and his wife Jola have become our friends.

FAVOURED VENUE ... Jason soaks up the atmosphere after winning the Czech Republic Grand Prix in Prague, 2002 – the first of three consecutive victories at the Marketa Stadium

He is a very successful businessman and you wouldn't pick him as a speedway sponsor in his elegant suits and distinguished appearance. But he respects what I do and is such a major support.

Second in the world again wasn't bad and in another respect the 2002 international season followed the pattern of the previous year as Australia again won the World Team Cup. Our first big hurdle was a semi-final at Sheffield in which we got the upper hand over Great Britain and put them on the verge of going out of the competition.

With the final at Peterborough, a track most of the boys enjoyed, and no home team to contend with, we felt right at home. The Danes and Swedes loomed as our strongest challengers and Poland and the Czech Republic had riders capable of making life difficult. We all pulled together, though, and ended up winning by half a dozen points from Denmark.

Everyone came to the party – Leigh and Ryan Sullivan grabbed 17 apiece, I got 14 and Todd 13. Australian speedway had never had it so good. We didn't realise that for the next few years, it would never be so good again.

Because of the injury problems my first season at Belle Vue was not all it might have been. I finished up doing fewer official meetings than in any other year in the UK, but still scored 394 points in 26 matches and had a 10.44 average so they were pretty happy.

It was an interesting team. Sam Ermolenko, who I'd enjoyed watching so much as a kid, then crossed paths with a few times on track in more recent times, was still going strong. Brian Karger was there – another blast from my past – and Steve Johnston, one of the most outgoing Aussies who has always been up for anything.

Mr Belle Vue though was Jason Lyons, who was coming up for his 12th season with the club and still knocking in an eight-point average. We had been on the World Team Cup wins of 1999 and 2002 but my connections with him went back much further than that.

I remember watching Jason and Leigh Adams, both Mildura boys, winning the Australian Under 16 pairs back in 1986. We had ridden together and against one another loads of times and it was good to hook up again.

He's the ultimate club man, Lyonsy. Back in Mildura he has been a very big contributor just as his dad was from the beginning. He likes nothing more than to ride there on the weekend and then come back to help out on the working bee when all the volunteers clean up the place and get it ready for the next event. The prefect day for him is rounded off by having a few beers and a yarn with everyone in the clubroom.

You don't get many people like that with such a close affection for a club but he's been like it at Belle Vue, too. It's not at all unusual for him to roll up hours before the start and help out around the track, watering or doing some other job. No wonder he is one of the most popular riders the Aces have had.

John Perrin was a top bloke to deal with. You couldn't have anything but respect for the way he fought for the club. It was good to get to the end of the year and shake hands straight away on a deal for the following season.

Poland, after the injury, was not the best scene. I missed a lot of matches, then missed a few more because there were problems with the club. In the end I did only seven matches, winning 22 races, but it was not a great time.

This also was a year in which a few cracks started to appear in the situation at Norrkoping. In all the time I had been with Vargarna you could usually rely upon them to start the year well, even though the standard was getting tougher each season.

This time, with Jimmy Nilsen retired and much missed, we lost our first five meetings including three at home. There was a knock-on effect with attendances which meant that for financial reasons, the club didn't always field the best team and this, in turn, affected the league position which slipped to eighth.

The bright spot was provided by Krystof Cegielski, who looked to be a fast-improving rider. I did 13 of the 18 fixtures and placed third in the Elite League rankings with a 10.65 average, beaten only by Ryan Sullivan and Tony Rickardsson.

It was tempting to stay on in Australia after the Sydney Grand Prix and chill out for a while, but I decided to resist the idea. After my early-season injuries I wanted to give my body the best possible chance of getting back to peak fitness and in any case, I wanted to leave no stone unturned in my preparations for the following year.

If I started each of the three preceding seasons with a high degree of confidence in my ability to win the world title, it's fair to say I was if anything more optimistic about 2003 than before.

That is not to say that I didn't have doubts, of course I did. Experience had taught me that you might think you are looking at a good thing, but destiny takes a hand. There always is the possibility that something will spring up and bite you. My ambitions in 2002 looked to be well-founded, until that crash in Poland. After that it was a question of re-grouping.

CLUB MAN ... Jason Lyons, another Mildura old boy, has been a Belle Vue stalwart

But little did I know that the following year would provide me with the greatest test of all. I had to come from behind – again – but managed to do that and found myself in the box seat going into the last round of the year in Hamar.

Tony Rickardsson for once had not quite stayed the course and was a dozen points adrift. He hadn't won since the opening round and although you could never rule him out, the vital statistic was that I went to Norway a point ahead of Nicki Pedersen and, barring an absolute shocking meeting, needed to finish in front of him – as I had done for the past three rounds.

That's where, famously, it all unravelled with the grand prize almost within touching distance. I had got to the last Grand Prix of the season leading the championship, looking good, feeling good. But not for the first time in my life, I couldn't deliver when all the world seemed to be convinced that all I needed to do was turn up. Hamar, 2003, should have been the greatest day of my life, but for whatever reason, the script didn't play out.

Afterwards, and for some time, I felt as if I had been in a train wreck. I just could not comprehend that such a chance had come and gone. All you ask for in sport is to have an opportunity to shoot for the big awards. This was a golden opportunity and I stuffed it up.

Don't ask me why, I've asked myself a few times but each time put it all in the 'down to experience' basket. I was sniffling around all week, didn't feel that great, and on the day just seemed to lack the energy or the ability to do anything about it.

It was weird, because there is no doubt I had put myself in the position I wanted to be, I was excited at the prospect of being world champion, and yet at the same time I tried very hard – maybe too hard – not to count my chickens or to put too much pressure on myself.

Subconsciously, no doubt, I did exactly that. There is not any other logical explanation, I just didn't feel comfortable when it came to it and whatever it needed to make sure I capitalised upon my position, I didn't find it that day.

I was making what seemed to be solid progress, had a morale-boosting win over Pedersen and made it through to the semis. He was still on my tail, though.

People have quizzed me about my take on that exclusion in the semi-final when the referee Marek Wojaczek excluded me after Rune Holta fell as I came up to make an inside pass at the end of the first lap. He left the door open and in such circumstances you don't think twice – you just go for it. But we tangled as he came back down towards the line. I can think of other occasions when I wouldn't have been penalised, but often these are desperately tight calls and some you win, some you don't.

Of course I desperately wanted to be given the benefit of the doubt, but even as my guys were getting the bike sorted out I just knew the exclusion light was going to come on in a minute – and it did.

Nicki Pedersen had snuck up from the shadows and he was the world champion. I was bridesmaid ... again!

In the final count, Pedersen had 152 points, I had 144. Tony Rickardsson pipped Leigh Adams for third by a single point – seriously frustrating for Leigh whose previous four years had seen him move from seventh, to sixth, to fifth, to fourth.

Somehow I managed to keep it together. I even stayed calm when Steve Brandon came over wanting an interview for Sky TV. Mind you, it helps when people treat you with consideration, as he did.

He said "Mate, I don't suppose you want this at the moment, but we would like a few words."

Put that way, what can you do but grin and do it ... it was a much better approach than some I've had.

Speedway loves its publicity, the access television has in the pits is probably unlike any other motor sport, or any sport for that matter. When you have just had a bad race or a bum decision the last thing you need is a microphone stuck in your face and timing, as they say, is everything.

But you can beat yourself or keep going. I knew I had to keep my head up, to cop it, and congratulate the guy, even it was through gritted teeth.

For a while there, though, I was shot. So much effort and emotion had gone into the world championship campaign. To be so near and yet so far was devastating. It isn't easy to think logically at such a time.

At different stages of a career there will be a crisis point, and this was mine. That's when the questions start. Is this really what you want to be doing ... is the tension and the heartache really worth it? There must be more to life than this.

All this sort of irrational stuff courses through your mind. I suppose it's a sensation most people experience at some time in their life, the sportsman's equivalent of a mid-life crisis. I defy any elite athlete to say that they haven't been there.

The bitter disappointment of falling at the final hurdle apart, this wasn't a year to be fondly remembered. For a variety of reasons, the atmosphere around the pits and among several of the rival camps was pretty ordinary.

For most of the time, allowing for the intensity of the Grand Prix and what is at stake, most of us get along well enough. I'm not bosom buddies with any of the other riders but there are not too many that I don't get on with at some reasonable level.

Competition inevitably generates various degrees of passion in all sports. Very often, as I found way back in my junior days, it's the people around riders rather than the riders themselves who can stoke up a lot of bitchiness, tension, argument and controversy.

I'm not saying that every speedway rider in the GP is cool, calm and collected all the time, or unaffected by personal considerations – but we have to try to work together in a reasonable manner, to give respect to our colleagues, because we're all in the same boat.

Racing is not like an everyday job but we still want to go to work in a good environment. Nobody wants to be caught in the middle of politics involving opposing countries or ill-feeling caused by riders whose behaviour on or off the track goes over the top. When that sort of stuff threatens to get out of order, it makes for a less than ideal situation.

In so many ways 2003 was the world title which got away. What added to the frustration was the fact that after a so-so start to the year I had kept it all together and gradually fought back.

I didn't make the main final at the European GP at Katowice (won by Tony Rickardsson) and was even further off the pace in the Swedish round which Ryan Sullivan won. This meeting was held at Avesta because a public sector strike caused it to be switched from Stockholm.

However it went much better in Cardiff where Nicki Pedersen won his second Grand Prix – following a second place in the opening round – and at least I made it into second which dragged me into seventh in the standings. Then came the first meeting at Copenhagen's spectacular Parken stadium where it all came together for me and Rickardsson followed me home.

It was great to christen speedway's latest big venue with a victory. Going to Cardiff a couple of years earlier had given the whole concept a lift and while Vojens had the history, staging a GP in another seriously modern stadium seemed to be a confirmation of the growing status of the series.

Tony at this stage had 76 points with Pedersen on 69 and my situation improving to 61. But that was followed by a shocker in Krsko, running out of

HAPPY RETURNS ... Another win in Prague for Jason at the 2003 Czech Republic GP

fuel on the last bend of the semi-final when lying second. It was Nicki who profited, securing a final place which he hadn't expected, and what a crucial twist that was to turn out to be. Leigh Adams was too hot for him in the final, though and did his chances a lot of good.

It pushed me back to fourth and my bad luck continued in the Scandinavian GP in Gothenburg with a broken rocker arm on the start line in the final. Sullivan won there as he had done at Avesta but in all the other meetings that year he was way off the pace. The real turnaround though was from Tony who was eliminated early and picked up only half a dozen points.

All of this drama unfolded after the first attempt to run the meeting ended in shambles. We had three heats in which riders had little or no chance to race properly on a track that was the worst-prepared I have seen for a major event.

Then the decision was taken to scrap the whole thing and run it a week later. It was a huge blow for the credibility of speedway, never mind SVEMO whose responsibility it was to produce a track fit for the occasion.

Gothenburg has a long and proud history of staging world championship meetings, including some of the great World Finals. This was a farce. Certainly there had been problems during the week, rain on the two days before the meeting, and practice had to be cancelled. But nobody expected this.

Ole Olsen's track-building team who had made a good job of the Parken meeting were called into take over and seven days later, we were all back at Ullevi. It was another unwanted interruption to a season which was full of tensions.

In spite of everything, I was on 88 and that result at Ullevi left me trailing Adams (96), Nicki Pedersen (96) and Rickardsson (95) with three rounds to go. The hassles made me all the more determined to give it my best shot and my chances received another boost when I won again in Prague from Tony and Nicki.

This was after I had broken the tapes in an early race, but got my head together quickly and rode really well – my riding was back to the level of the last couple of meetings of 2001.

Now the top of the ladder as we set off for Bydgoszcz showed Rickardsson 115, Pedersen 114, Crump 113, Adams 107. Leigh had a disappointing meeting and he slipped further behind in Bydgoszcz where Gollob produced his usual party piece. But I got second, going past Nicki in the final, and Tony had another six-point shocker and I was able to slip into the top position for the first time on 133 points.

Nicki's third put him a point adrift, and surprisingly Tony was suddenly struggling with 121. He was right in there until Poland but his second below-par performance in three meetings effectively left him with a mountain to climb in the final round. Adams was back in the picture, just three behind.

The stage was all set. After those two second places, it did look as if it might be my time. I felt I had the wood on Nicki, but at the same time was very nervous about getting too far ahead of myself. To the neutrals Hamar promised a finale to delight the organisers and the fans but in the event, Norway was the stage for disaster for me.

Before an occasion of such importance, it's so important to keep a sense of balance, to maintain focus without being consumed by the magnitude of the moment. But I was edgy, distracted, if anything a bit listless in the days leading up to the deciding GP.

And as if there hadn't been enough drama, before setting off for the meeting, we had received death threats which said that if I won the title, I'd be for it. The media made a meal of that when it became general knowledge and I have to admit, it was scary, very unpleasant indeed. What we do for a living is a tough gig, and it means a great deal to lots of people. But this was way, way over the top.

The police took it all pretty seriously and we never found out who was behind it. It was quite unnerving though. If the intention was to scare me, it succeded. It didn't stop me from going out to race with my usual 'let's get stuck in' attitude, but it was scary.

Ideally, you go to a big meeting telling yourself that it's just another day at the office, something you have done countless times. Much as I tried to be on top of everything going into that Hamar GP, it was a big ask.

Never had the world title seemed so tantalisingly close. A thousand scenarios went through my mind. No way could I convince myself that it was all business as usual, because, obviously, it wasn't. We went through all the usual routines to try to make sure everything was the same – easier said than done.

When it all went wrong in that semi-final in Norway, I didn't have the energy in me to blow up. The emotion of it all, the enormous letdown, left me completely drained.

For a while there I honestly didn't care if I never sat on bike again. People later complimented me on having taken the disappointment in a dignified way but I think I was just too stunned to blow up which was the reaction many might have expected.

World No.1, world No.2, it didn't matter too much to Mia and Seth. They still loved me at the end of the day.

And Mel, as usual, said all the right things and we simply considered our blessings and vowed to get on with life.

It was not easy to keep things going to the end of the season, but that's part of the deal. Professional sportsmen are expected to front up and do their very best day in, day out, and there was the rest of the schedule to deal with.

But it wasn't a year to remember too fondly. There was no Australian World Team Cup win to celebrate this time. The Danes started favourites in Vojens but Sweden chose this occasion to string together one of their most convincing performances for years and beat us by five points.

I had the chance of finishing the season with a consolation prize in the Elite Riders' Championship at Coventry on the last night – and blew a motor on the line in the final. It was kind of symbolic, although everyone would understand me saying that winning the ELRC wasn't really my priority for the year.

My entire thinking, even before the end of the previous season, had concentrated on what to do to maximise my chances of becoming the world champion. That's not to suggest that the rest of it was unimportant. Clubs and promoters put it a big effort to run their show and there always is a responsibility to them, your team mates and supporters.

Before the 2003 season I was looking to cut down on the number of meetings, to keep myself fresh and up for the entire year. I suggested to Vargarna that it might suit both parties for me to do fewer matches, but as it happened I ended up doing all but a couple.

Sweden was ultra-competitive by now and to achieve a 9.95 average, third behind Tony Rickardsson and Rune Holta, was not too bad.

The team's results generally were better but still a mid-table position was the best we could accomplish, with a bad injury to Krystof Cegielski throwing a cloud over proceedings. Crowds continued to be good but there were increasing financial problems which meant that by the end of the year the club's future was in some doubt.

But at least I managed to land on my feet in Poland, following a switch to Torun. They were keen to have a real crack at winning the title and signed Tony Rickardsson and myself to spearhead that challenge.

It went well from the start and I went through the card at Leszno. Both of us had one or two ordinary meetings but Torun still had a decent shot at the championship and picked up half a dozen away wins. We had to settle for second place at the end of the season, though.

It was good to be able to deliver a bit more for Belle Vue. For the fifth British season in a row my average was in double figures and I actually upped it to 10.79, my best so far.

Technically I was still on loan but to all intents and purposes I felt 100 per cent about being there.

John Perrin included me when it came to talking about the team, what riders were doing and how things might be improved. Once again we didn't pull up any trees but there was the feeling that there was some improvement in the wind and a chance for the fans to look forward to better times.

But my priority as soon as possible after that Elite Riders meeting at Coventry meeting was to be out of there and on the plane to Disneyland with Mel and the kids. I'd had enough speedway for one season.

MANCHESTER travel agent Gareth Parry has helped oversee Jason's international schedule for many years and managed to place a good working relationship at risk when the Pair were chatting before a Belle Vue meeting.

"Somehow the conversation came round to the good old days at Hyde Road and I happened to say 'I used to hate your dad'," said Parry, a longtime Aces follower.

"Jason gave me a long hard stare, one of total disbelief. I suppose if someone said the same thing about my dad I would be less than happy!

"Then I began to explain where I was coming from.- it was because Phil was one of only a very small handful of visiting riders who could come to the old track and really test PC and Mort.

"As a kid growing up in Manchester, if anyone dared to take a single point off either of my heroes it ruined the weekend.

"I went on explain to Jason that as I got older(and possibly wiser) it was only then that I really appreciated just how talented people like his dad and Michael Lee were.

"As if to get his own back Jason called over his dad who was working on one of his bikes and said 'tell him what you have just told me' and with a red face I began relating the story again.

"Phil smiled and threw in his own little ditty, fondly remembering the night he came north and took the Golden Helmet off Peter Collins, thus ruining yet another weekend."

We had an absolute ball, no one knew us in America, nobody expected anything of me and all we did was behave like eight-year-olds for a week.

We came home to West Hunsbury, and then we were on a plane again, this time headed for Australia and some more serious relaxation. We spent a couple of months at Mel's folks place, and I enjoyed going out with her brother Lincoln on the moto cross bikes.

I definitely wasn't too bothered about riding in many speedway meetings. I did one at Gosford, one at Newcastle and the Queensland titles on the Gold Coast.

The first two were pretty much like local events, and although by this time I wasn't living on the Coast I had maintained the relationship with Bob Cowley and was happy to combine a meeting there with a ride around Bob's country property at Kyogle on the New South Wales–Queensland border. He had just bought a 30-acre spread out there with its own track and of course this was too good to resist.

Blasting around with a dozen or more guys, then sitting round the camp fire sharing racing stories and a couple of beers at two in the morning under a brilliant starlit sky was just magic. It was about as far removed from the hubbub and stress of the Grand Prix as you could imagine, as close to heaven as you can get without actually going there.

GOLD Coast Motorcycle Club president Bob Cowley is one of Jason's greatest supporters. He has been around speedway as a Queensland and Motorcycling Australia official for 20 years and a backer of numerous young hopefuls.

While speedway has been his favoured discipline, he also put a lot of time and effort into backing Mick Doohan, particularly in the early days when the five-time world champion's career was an uphill struggle.

"Mick was an example to others because he absolutely loved what he was doing. He was never happier than when he was racing, and that included stepping up on to the podium after winning another race.

"You have to be hungry. Loads of kids look good when they're flying around on their own, but the determination which goes with being a racer and a winner, that's what stamps a few of them as being different from the rest.

"The thing with speedway is that to be successful, you need to have something between the ears. Jason has always been a bright kid, with a sense of direction. His sort of professionalism intimidates some people, especially in Australia. Some have mistaken his attitude for arrogance, but I don't think that's right. He is just very, very focused, ultra-serious about what he does, and it's been the case since he was just starting out."

I had no particular ambition to do the Aussie titles, which for the first time were run as a series of three meetings. There was the usual criticism from certain quarters over that, but what a lot of people in Australia do not appreciate is that after eight months of non-stop action in Europe, most of us like the idea of having a break.

You get back and want to catch some sunshine and generally kick back, free from the workload and routine of hours in the workshop, more hours on the road or flying around Europe, and three, four, sometimes five meetings in a week.

It's easy to get to October and be absolutely stuffed and especially after the pressures of the previous year or two, that is exactly how I was feeling at the end of the 2003 season.

Of course Motorcyling Australia could have made us an offer we couldn't refuse but contrary to widespread belief, it isn't and wasn't about the money.

Any and every time an elite sportsperson goes out to perform, the paying public expect – and have a right to expect – that they are going to see a fully committed performer. To me it is far more honest and morally correct to knock back an unwanted invitation rather than simply saying you'll take the money and run.

Anyway, being based in Charlestown meant that I wasn't under the same sort of pressure as, say, Leigh Adams who goes home to Mildura in between European seasons, and for all I know Leigh, Ryan Sullivan and some of the other guys are only too happy to have a ride when they're back.

Sully won that 2003-04 series in a canter and Leigh chalked up an incredible eighth Aussie title (only one short of Aub Lawson's record) in the 2004–05 version which ran over four rounds.

The people who complained that I didn't do either of them chose to overlook the fact that I had not done that many of the one-off Australian championship finals of recent years. So it wasn't anything much to do with the title being decided over a series of meetings rather than just one, either.

It was purely and simply about wanting a break – and at the end of 2003 in particular, I felt I had never needed one more.

www.Speedwayworld.tv
speedwayworld.tv
Castrol
SGP
SWEDISH MATCH
www.Speedwayworld.tv
LNB
POLAND
LNB
POLAND
KEYNE EXPRESS
DELIVERIES
ADRIANA
REGINA
Mitas
K&N
SYSTEM EDSTRÖM
WINNER

Moment of truth

Champion of the world ... at last

> When he had those three years of finishing second anybody could be excused for wondering if he would finally crack it, but, from way back, I felt he could
>
> – Phil Crump

SATURDAY, October 2, 2004, is a date I will never forget. This was the day on which I became world champion, fulfilling a personal dream and guaranteeing myself a place in the history books which no one can take away.

The Viking Ship stadium in Hamar, Norway, is one of the unique venues in speedway. It was built for the 1994 winter Olympics and in 2003 was the scene of my most devastatingly disappointing moment in speedway.

Ten years earlier, I had to bite the bullet in Norway when a World Under 21 title I was expected to win – at Elgane – failed to materialise. But I did come back to make amends the following season. That was one thought to sustain me as we prepared for the return to Hamar.

And nine years from that first entry on the FIM gold medal honour board, 13 years on from my first official ride on speedway, I achieved the goal with which every rider – if they're honest – comes into the sport.

With so much baggage, so many near misses and testing times, it was so difficult to stay calm in the lead-up to the final round of a 2004 GP season in which, at last, I'd managed a level of consistent scoring which is a requirement of being in the mix and also done it without too many of the panics and dramas of previous campaigns.

Even arriving at this stage with a 17-point lead over the second-placed Tony Rickardsson, however, it was impossible not to feel a few butterflies, and

ELATION ... Champagne all round for the 2004 world champion, thanks to Tony Rickardsson and Greg Hancock

to be aware of everyone tiptoeing around the subject, conscious of how much it all meant to me.

Some people appear confident all the time, but most performers get nervous before a big event. It's not just racers ... I could have been a lawyer, a cricketer, a singer or actor, the nerves do kick in beforehand and I defy anyone to say otherwise. It doesn't matter whether you have been in this situation many times, or never. The trick is to handle it, deal with the moment, concentrate on the essentials, maintain as much of a level of concentrated calm as possible so that you can go out there and do what you have to do.

Now I was at the point I had dreamed of, in pole position and apparently on the threshold of that world championship. It hardly bore thinking about. I'd been there before, of course, but had spent 12 months trying to erase from my brain the scars of the previous year's massive anti-climax.

This time, surely, nothing could go wrong.

After the desperate ending to my bid in 2003, I was determined to try to start the 2004 series with some decent results. Too often I had under-performed in one or two of the early rounds and then left myself way behind the eight-ball with so much to do that I was constantly in a pressure situation.

My ambition for the year was to get my act together straight away and if possible establish a lead so that it was the turn of the other guys to do the chasing and the stressing. The bookies seemed to think I could do it. They had me at 15-8 favourite to win the title. And with a low-key off-season and plenty of time in which to prepare I felt quite calm about things and sure enough, I had a good start.

Leigh Adams, who had won a GP in each of the two previous seasons, took out the opening Swedish round at Stockholm but I was more than happy to collect second.

I was happier still after winning in Prague, in terrible weather conditions, my third successive victory at the Marketa stadium and a result which nudged me into first position. It's one of the best venues, and pretty familiar territory for me because of the Jawa connection.

Wroclaw wasn't that clever as I went out in Heat 21 and Tony – third in the final as he had been in each of the first two meetings – took over the series lead by a single point. Most of the other obvious contenders did not fare so well and Bjarne Pedersen claimed his first GP.

The British round in Cardiff is always a highly-powered affair and this was no exception. There was a tremendous atmosphere as usual with more than 40,000 in the place and as ever it was a great advertisement for the sport. Greg Hancock collected the win, Leigh was second and I had to settle for fourth behind Lee Richardson. Now Adams and I were tied on 69 points, with Rickardsson, who went out early for once, seven points back.

The mid-season Danish Grand Prix in Copenhagen was the crunch round. It couldn't have gone much better for me as I won the meeting from Andreas

GETTING CLOSER ... Victory in Copenhagen sent Jason off for a 2004 mid-season break holding a valuable world championship lead

Jonsson, Hancock and Nicki Pedersen, making the final for the first time in the year.

It wasn't uneventful, though, as I had to do a lot of work from the back in a few races, and also got on the wrong end of Nicki's rear wheel in Heat 19 as I was shaping to go round him. He was not happy and nor were the Danish crowd when he was excluded for bringing me down, but it didn't affect the outcome for either of us.

More important in the overall scheme of things, Leigh and Tony both had a poor night and so heading into the summer break, five rounds gone, four to go, I was on 94 points with some daylight between me and Adams (80), Hancock (75), Rickardsson (70) and Pedersen (63).

With a break of four weeks between rounds, there was a perfect opportunity to get away from it all. Belle Vue had a gap between home

LOST IN THOUGHT ... Series leader JC contemplates his hour of destiny before the start of the final GP of the 2004 season

meetings and so Mel and the kids and I all shot off to Marbella in Spain for a week. We lazed around, played on the beach, and simply acted like holiday makers.

I couldn't pretend that I didn't think about speedway while we were there – it was good to re-focus, think things through, take stock of where I was at and what had to be done in the remaining four rounds of the series. My conclusion was that now I had to be responsible, consistent, and know when to measure risk against possible reward.

It was back to business in the Scandinavian GP at Gothenburg, second behind Hans Andersen, the year's second first-time winner. No damage suffered there as I finished ahead of Hancock and Rickardsson and now had 114 points, with Adams and Hancock back on 91.

I was not about to start counting my chickens but it was a very reassuring situation to be in. If I kept my nerve and produced consistent results over the remaining meetings, I would give myself the best possible chance of becoming world champion. I could have spent a few anxious moments leading up to the seventh round in Krsko in a fretful state but instead I could afford to let the others do the worrying.

Sooner or later Tony Rickardsson was bound to make a move and he did by taking out the Slovenian round where I blew out in the semi-final. It had been a long time between drinks – it was his first GP win in 15 meetings. But with two rounds remaining I still felt good, with 127 points to Tony's 112 and 111 for Hancock. Leigh's challenge appeared to be on the wane when he failed to reach the semis for the third time in a row.

It was up to me to ensure that there were no such slips in Bydgoszcz and all credit to Leigh, he was really supportive when he could see I was getting edgy. Despite my lead, past experience had made me nervous. He spotted that I was putting myself under pressure and came over to offer some encouraging words.

Tomasz Gollob has such a terrific record at Bydgoszcz and he was the man to beat. Suffice to say that as usual none of us could better him but I was pleased with second, again ahead of Rickardsson.

Just one round to go, and now I had 147 points. Tony was up to 130. Everyone else had gradually fallen off the pace. Here we were again.

And at last the script writers got it right. Fortunately, they didn't forget the happy, if slightly bizarre ending!

Once again it was desperately difficult to keep my emotions in check. And once more, who should come up with the right move at a critical time but Leigh Adams. Again he made a point of coming across to my pit to asking how I was feeling.

"Not great, really," I said.

We had a chat about our moto cross bikes, our plans for the off-season, anything but the most important meeting of my life. Then he said "Come on Ginge, let's go for a little run" so there we were, the Mildura connection, jogging up and down out the back of the stadium where within a few minutes it would be on for one and all.

He didn't have to do this, he'd had another strong shot at the title himself and come up short, and at such a time he was prepared to do what he could to help settle my butterflies and get me up and ready for the final chapter.

Tony, of course, kept right on to the end in Hamar and collected another win – even after I'd had my celebrations and then bowed out after a semi-final ride in which I was in auto pilot. Typically, it was his reminder that come 2005, you could bank on him being there or thereabouts once more.

And Hancock just kept his nose ahead of Adams to claim second on the night and third overall. I could identify with Leigh's disappointment. It was fantastic of him to show such warm appreciation towards me at a time when he must have wondering what he had to do to get on to a world championship podium.

Another year, but what a year for me, one I would remember and replay with so much pleasure and pride. And what an unbelievable contrast to 12 months earlier when I was at my lowest ebb, completely gutted, not convinced I even wanted to sit on a bike again after things went so totally wrong in Norway.

Fortunately I coped with it. Our trip to the States was a great lift, and the months off to re-group helped me come to terms, not so much with what had happened, but with what needed to be done and how I had to prepare for the 2004 campaign.

Staying away from speedway was part of it. We enjoyed our trip back to Australia but it never was the intention to do much more than wind down from a tough year and clear the mind.

Nothing against the concept, but the new three-round format of the Australian titles didn't particularly excite me. I rode in a couple of meetings which appealed and that was enough. Apart from that I spent plenty of time out with Mel's brother Lincoln, riding our moto cross bikes. The neighbours must have thought we were a couple of bums with nothing better to do because day after day we would load up and drive out into the bush.

But as any bike rider will tell you, there is nothing better! It's just a blast, doing your own thing with nobody around and the whole emphasis on having a good time. It's escapism, pure and simple.

JOHN Perrin, who kept the Belle Vue flag flying for 17 years after the historic Manchester club's enforced relocation, might be excused for having less than fond memories of what were, for the most part, extremely tough and turbulent times.

Trying to convince the public that the greyhound stadium at Kirkmanshulme Lane was a worthy successor to the big open spaces of Hyde Road – so beloved by the sentimentalists – never was going to be an easy task.

And for much of the time, in between battles with his landlords, the BSPA, stock car operators, television and all manner of other people who did not appreciate his bluff and blunt demeanour, Perrin had to front up with teams that lacked depth and crucially, did not have a charismatic presence in the mould of past icons such as Peter Craven, Ivan Mauger or Peter Collins.

His signing of Jason Crump from Nigel Wagstaff's King's Lynn in the off-season of 2001-02 failed to immediately produce dividends, but it was arguably his most important legacy for the club before he sold out to Tony Mole after the 2004 season.

Jason didn't come cheaply, a £36,000 transfer fee simply repaying Wagstaff what it had cost King's Lynn to acquire him, and his personal terms and conditions were those of a 21st century champion. Perrin, pointedly, insists he did not begrudge a penny.

Of course, you have to get back to the real world – and as far as 2004 goes, I managed to do that quite satisfactorily. When we got back to England, I felt stronger in mind and body, determined to put past disappointments behind me and to get set for a new campaign which, as it turned out, made up for everything that had gone before.

With so much focus on the world championship, anything that happened in domestic speedway was always going to be a bit of an anti-climax. In fact it was a really difficult year, especially at Belle Vue where it never seemed to stop raining. I lost count of the number of meetings we had called off.

On top of that, the Aces struggled for a long time. We started off with a team that looked reasonable under the newly-introduced grading system but didn't start performing until it was too late to make a real impact on the season. But I didn't allow myself to be knocked out of whack and in fact was pretty pleased with the way I kept my form going.

I totalled 500 points in 36 matches for the Aces, chalked up my 400th Elite League appearance during the year, scored 12 maximums and had an 11.11 average.

Jim Lynch, who had finished his involvement at Peterborough, came in to help John Perrin and acted as team manager on away meetings. We also signed Kenneth Bjerre who had been showing a lot of promise with the Panthers and

"I have nothing but praise for the lad and what he has done for Belle Vue," said Perrin.

"There were people who told me not to sign him, that he was hard to work with, only interested in himself, too expensive and carried a lot of baggage. I really wasn't that bothered because most of the things they said about him were the same sort of stuff people said about me. It suited me fine.

"I had found him good to talk to when we spoke at meetings and a couple of times he'd said he would like to ride at Belle Vue. I just said to him to talk to me properly when he was ready. When he did, we got on straight away. We never had a problem about anything. He had this hothead image but I've always found him dead quiet and polite. I never had a bad word with him.

"Jason Crump is my sort of speedway rider. Sure, he costs money but if you want the best, you have to be prepared to pay for the best. You could pay for a couple of mediocre riders with the money he gets, but you get so much from having one rider like him.

"It's the same as paying top dollar in football, a top man might cost as much as three ordinary players but you don't with anything with just ordinary people. Jason is completely focused on speedway, he doesn't mess about. That's what he is here for."

his performances, and those of Rory Schlein, doubling up from Edinburgh, suggested much more hope for the future.

The big problem was in fitting in the fixtures – which in the end, we didn't because of all the postponements. It's no fun getting prepared for meeting after meeting only for the weather to intervene. It leaves everybody feeling flat and of course, it's pretty ordinary from a financial angle.

Times were tough in Sweden as well, with Vargarna struggling to field a competitive team. They did agree to my earlier suggestion that we pick and choose the meetings in which I rode – it helped them financially and lightened my schedule – but it wasn't a great way to go after eight seasons.

It was sad to see one of the country's great clubs so far off the pace and although I averaged 9.86 in seven matches there were times I felt I was fighting a lone battle. I got 19 of our 42 points at Vastervik and 15 against Indianerna at Kumla where at least we picked up a rare bonus point.

The last of my 120 matches for Vargarna was in the home fixture against Piraterna, our local rivals who were back in the top flight for the first time since 1949. It was a must-win match as both clubs were flirting with relegation. In front of the biggest crowd of the season, we won 54-42 and I signed off with 15 points from six starts.

It got a bit emotional in the end. I had built up a really genuine rapport with everyone there over the years, especially the supporters, many of whom had become personal friends.

It was special to see so many Vargarna fans cheering me in Hamar and I would like to think that my success there brought a lot of pleasure to the people who had been supporting me for years.

ALMOST an ever-present member of Jason's world championship crew is his uncle Adrian Street, known to all as Drew. The 41-year-old has missed only one of his nephew's 68 GP events and been in his corner for countless other meetings.

"I'm just there to make sure everything is looked after, that he has all he needs – and sometimes as a peacemaker when he and Phil are having an argument. Even after all this time they still manage to fall out and have blazing rows which isn't really ideal, especially if you are trying to keep your head together at a vital meeting," he says.

"I try to watch everything and Jason can bounce ideas off me, about gate positions and things like that. At the end of the day though, he's seeing it all too, so it's his decision.

"And whether it's been a good night or not, I try to keep things going. That's easier said that done if the meeting has been a disaster. We've had a few quiet trips home."

Drew can't help but remember some of the down times, even though they have been outnumbered by the good ones. The disappointments, he believes, played a crucial part in strengthening Jason's resolve and shaping his eventual path to world title success.

The Torun fans were behind me all year as well, which was great because I'll admit there were one or two matches in which my mind was not on the job quite as much as it might have been.

Despite losing four matches at home in my second season with the Angels the team finished fourth. The slip from the previous year was not so surprising as we had lost Tony Rickardsson to Tarnow. There still were plenty of good moments and all told it was not a bad year's work.

As far as other overseas commitments went, I also got a lot of joy out of winning the Golden Gala in Lonigo, always a favourite meeting for the boys and a good one to add to the collection.

Our most memorable overseas trip, however, had little to do with speedway. It was to Mauritius for our wedding, on October 17.

Chris Van Straaten, who was chairman of the British Speedway Promoters Association at the time, gave me a bit of a lecture when I opted out of the Elite Riders Championship which had been rearranged after a rain-off the first time round.

He and others were unhappy when I told him that our arrangements had been locked in. Speedway takes up enough of your life, you have to make room for some special things which are entirely personal and hopefully he, and everyone else, understood.

Mel and I had lived together for seven years, we had two wonderful kids, and from a professional and personal view, our lives were fantastic. It was the right thing to do and the right time.

I'm a believer in timing. When you are ready to do something, that's the moment to do it. In some instances – like winning a world title – there is only

"The GP Challenge in Prague in 1996, the qualifier at Bradford in 1997, they were meetings in which we all expected so much and it went pear-shaped. Before that there was the Second Division Riders Championship at King's Lynn in 1993. Jason was far and away the best rider in the league that year, he'd had an exceptional run but on the night it didn't happen for him. He so wanted to sign off by winning it and was very disappointed to let the chance get away.

"Then we had 1994 when so many things did fall into place, three world finals and all that – but even the individual final at Vojens was a downer really, because he should have qualified for the top 10 and a place in the first Grand Prix, and didn't do it.

"I do believe Jason has been a bit unlucky that he should be around at the same time as Tony Rickardsson who is one of those 'best of a generation' riders. His turn may well come, after all he is five years younger than Tony, but we will have to see.

"I think 2003 was the world title that got away. He had a bad meeting in Sweden, his fuel ran out in the semi-final at Krsko – and that was the moment the title went to Nicki Pedersen, every bit as much as at Hamar in the final Grand Prix."

so much you can do to influence things. But for whatever reasons, I wasn't ready before 2004.

And we didn't see a pressing need to get married until then. We had been quite happy living our life, developing our relationship, building the family, as couples do. It wasn't much different from what millions of others do these days. We were never uncomfortable with any aspect of what we were doing, who we were, or where we were.

But when the moment came to officially and properly tie the knot, we knew, absolutely, that it was right.

We also felt, instinctively, that we had to make sure all the vibes were 100 per cent positive. Since my parents split up, they have had virtually no contact with each other and much as it hurt me, we decided that we couldn't invite one and not the other. To have had both of them there in a very small gathering would have been just too stressful and uncomfortable for all concerned.

If we invited one or the other it would have suggested taking sides, something I wanted to avoid. So in the end, we limited our numbers to just 14. Mel's folks Bob and Jannene and her brother Lincoln came from Newcastle, Neil Bird flew in from Melbourne, and six Streets flew out with us from England – my uncle Graham, his wife Eddie, their kids Lucy, James and William, and Drew.

Mauritius was all we hoped it would be. It's a beautiful tropical island a million miles from anywhere, with a luxurious resort and plenty of absolutely nothing to do but relax. I don't have anything to compare it with ... but as honeymoons go, it was the best.

After the realisation had sunk in that not only was I the world champion but also a fully paid-up member of the married brigade, the last thing I wanted to do or even think about was riding speedway.

Our trip back to Australia was the break I had promised myself, a break we all deserved. There were some people in Aussie who apparently didn't appreciate that once again I was not bothered about doing the national titles – over four rounds this time – but the intention all along was to relax, kick back, have a great Christmas and New Year and re-charge the batteries.

Years earlier, you could ride in a dozen or more decent meetings in Australia and in any event, at 20 you're keen to do it all. As a married man and a dad, it's not top of the list, especially at that time of the year. For eight months I'm all over the place, Mel and the children are lucky if they get to see me two days in a row, and it's tough for everyone. I owe them and myself some proper time and attention over the holidays.

For Mia and Seth, it's a chance to get out in the sunshine and enjoy some of the delights I experienced as a kid growing up in Australia. For Mel, it's an opportunity to catch up with family and friends, without having to worry about the various routines which rule life in the UK.

But I did make a couple of exceptions. I rode in a farewell meeting for Mick Poole, who has been one of my greatest mates in the sport for years, and

HAPPY COUPLE ... Mr and Mrs Jason Crump after they tied the knot

attended a special dinner his dad Terry and the people at Gosford laid on the recognise my achievement in winning the title.

It was really cool, made all the more special to have old friends such as Boycie, Todd Wiltshire and Craig Watson along for the night.

And I had a civic reception at Mildura, organised by Brendon Gledhill and the local club officials, followed by a meeting at Olympic Park in which what would have been my appearance fee was put into the pot to assist with the continued development of the junior section. It was kind of paying my dues for all the support and encouragement people in Mildura gave me when I was starting my career and over time.

I enjoyed those occasions and bike riders being bike riders, didn't manage to stay out of the saddle for too long even though I was giving official competition a miss for a while. I did put in a few more sessions during that break – on the motor crosser with brother-in-law Lincoln, riding around Craig Wallace's backyard track. Mick Poole introduced us way back in around 2000 and it's gone on from there.

SUNSHINE VACATION ... Jason racing with Adam Shields and Jamie Stauffer at the Shields family property in Kurri Kurri,. NSW, 2005 and (inset) with Matt Shields, 75

Craig, who is a distant relative of Billy Sanders's family, has a place of something like 10 or maybe 15 acres alongside the Pacific Highway between Newcastle and Sydney. Using his bobcat and digger equipment he carved out a very good, fast, challenging moto cross track and as the word spread, more and more of us have gone out for a ride.

Speedway wasn't forgotten completely either because I also had a blast around at the property Adam Shields'folks have in Kurri Kurri, near Cessnock, which is just outside Newcastle. There's a really cool little banked track there of about 250 metres, hacked out in the middle of nowhere.

The Shields family have speedway in their veins. Adam's father Brian and grandfather Matt both used to race and so did his uncle Dave who was a pretty useful rider with Oxford some years ago. They have an afternoon riding speedway like most people have a barbeque.

Adam and I had a few battles along with Jamie Stauffer, a Kawasaki road racer who is Adam's brother-in-law and likes to dabble with speedway engines. The real highlight though was some match races against his grandfather who is 75 and was riding an old two-valve Jawas – it was a real hoot.

It's good to remind yourself that this sort of thing is the fun part of motorbikes, which is how almost all of us got into it in the first place.

But it was straight back into reality when we returned to England. With a new season coming up, I was not sure what would be expected of me as world champion and it soon became evident that everyone wanted a piece of me.

No complaints about that – I can stand being introduced as 'world champion Jason Crump' as many times as you like, and the day the telephone stops ringing and people don't want to know is something no sportsman likes to contemplate. But I did not anticipate just how much busier things would become, with requests to give my opinions on television, radio, to the newspapers and magazines, to attend functions and so forth.

I was very grateful for the interest, very conscious of the responsibilities which go with being world champion, but at the end of the day I had to start knocking back most of the enquiries and invitations. There just wouldn't have been time to be a speedway rider otherwise, and, that after all, had to remain my focus.

MICK Poole remains one of Jason's best mates in Australia and they enjoy nothing more than going out on their motocross bikes to relax far from the madding crowd.

"When Jason is at home we try to hook up as much as we can," says Poole.

"It`s pretty hard as we are both fairly busy at that time of year.

"Jason likes to ride motocross a lot to stay fit and have some fun and, as with speedway, he only knows two speeds – flat out and stop.

"After he had won the world title, he came to Craig Wallace`s farm to have a ride with his brother-in-law Lincoln and had a fall in a fairly quick part of the track. He went head first into a tree, wrecked his helmet and took skin off his forehead so Lincoln had to drive home."

Jason did venture into the public domain a few times.

"We went to Parramatta city raceway to watch the sprintcars which we both love," says Poole.

"He had a ride in a two-seater with multi-Australian title winner Gary Rush.

"It was nice to see the car fraternity treating him like royalty."

After spending several years trying to get the balance right, to ensure that the preparation and organisation gave me the best possible chance of doing well, it would have been crazy to put everything into reverse. At the very minimum I wanted to give it a good shot at winning again.

You never really know how something will go if you haven't experienced it before. And being world champion and having that No.1 on my back, such a long-time ambition fulfilled at last, threw up its own new set of challenges for me.

At the start of the year if someone had offered me two GP wins, and qualification for seven finals, I would have taken it. In 2003 I made five finals and nearly won the world title. In 2004 I made six, and did win it. Up to this point seven final appearances in the 10-round series of 2002 had been as good as it got.

As events panned out, despite a couple of victories and seven finals in 2005 I still had to settle for another second place – and it really wasn't any more acceptable than some of the earlier runner-up years had been.

FINETUNING ... Getting down to the job at Cardiff, 2005

It would be too easy to say that one unbelievable night at Cardiff screwed my world title defence – but it went a long way to doing so. In its own way the British Grand Prix of 2005 was almost as much of a downer as Hamar 2003 or any of those other, earlier disasters had been.

Right from the start of the GP series it had been obvious Tony Rickardsson was going to take no prisoners. He set such a pace from the beginning, and was winning with such style, it was clear it was going to be a hell of a battle to contain him.

Even so, the Grand Prix these days is a marathon, not a sprint. I had a win, a third and a fourth from the first three rounds, and didn't feel remotely close to having produced my best. I certainly wasn't too fazed to be 11 points adrift, feeling reasonably hopeful of pegging back the deficit at some stage.

That was until Polish referee Marek Wojaczek excluded me from three of my five qualifying rides in Cardiff. The first two of those decisions were extremely harsh.

I was thrown out of heat six after Hans Andersen fell off and again in heat 10 when Greg Hancock and I came down in the first corner, a classic first bend bunching if ever there was one. Then I was out again after a final bid for a last-race win that still could have earned a place in the semi-finals.

I've never been excluded three times in a league match and for it to happen in a Grand Prix was a disaster. A few of the referee's decisions were wrong, although I couldn't argue with the last one. In different circumstances on a different night I could have been in re-runs of both of those first two races and, possibly, even on the final occasion.

Of course I kept my head down and most of my thoughts bottled up inside, but short of Tony hurting himself or getting caught up in some unimaginable drama, you might as well have given him the championship there and then. The record book shows that with such a huge cushion to protect, he was able to sail through the rest of the year, going on to take his total of wins to six out of nine rounds.

It didn't take Einstein to work out before the series began that he was likely to present the greatest threat. And as it happens he really lifted the bar, producing a string of almost unstoppable performances. Fair play to the guy, he just was on a different lap to the rest of us for most of the summer.

A third place in the European GP in Wroclaw had been an encouraging way for me to start. I won three of the five qualifying races before taking out the semi-final but was not quite there in the final. In fact it was not a particularly convincing performance although miles better than I usually seem to do there.

Right from the off, Rickardsson was exceptional, winning all of his races. and Leigh Adams finished second. My feeling afterwards was that Tony was probably at 110% whereas I was at about 80%. Quite simply, I just couldn't get my starts. I got gate two in the final and made another shocker of a start, and it was really hard to reel in Antonio Lindback. I had to give him a hard time on the back straight on the last lap to get by, but by then it was too late.

Lindback was a bit of a surprise package in only his second Grand Prix – he was a wild card at the Scandinavian GP in Gothenburg in 2004 and got into the series by working through the qualifiers.

I squared the ledger by winning in Eskilstuna, my 11th career GP victory, taking advantage of a stoppage in the final when Tony looked as if he was going to win. Some people might suggest I was lucky but I had to work for it.

They changed the track a lot from practice the day before and I basically made the wrong bike choice for the conditions. It wasn't until I came last in my fourth heat that we made the changes to get me back and in with a chance.

In the semi-final I finally made a good start but I let Nicki Pedersen through because the way he was riding it was better to have him in front of me so I could see him as when he was behind me he could've done anything to ruin my night.

The final had to be restarted after Nicki was excluded for slamming Bjarne Pedersen into the boards and bringing him down, which suggests that my caution in the semi-final was well-founded.

In the re-start I got away to a bad start, trailing Rickardsson and Bjarne for a lap or so and then managed to pass both of them. It was extremely satisfying to be able to pass Tony. It's better to beat him in Sweden in front of his home crowd than anywhere else.

Eskilstuna does not have the grandeur of Stockholm or the history of Gothenburg, but I like the place – it's a real speedway town, the track is a purpose-built affair out in the middle of a forest and it really is a different setting. We love riding in the big venues but you get just as much atmosphere, and sometimes more, in the smaller stadiums with a packed crowd.

The run to the first corner there must be the longest in speedway. The start is way back towards the fourth bend and the Smederna club decided to do it that way when they had to relocate from their own stadium in town. They reckoned it would produce a much fairer outcome and reduce the emphasis on winning that first bend dash.

A fourth place in the Slovenian round was a bonus for me – Krsko had never been kind as I had not made a final there before, and that kept me within 11 points of the series lead. Tony Rickardsson claimed his second win, followed by Nicki Pedersen and wild card Matej Zagar.

A good confidence boost was beating Rickardsson in the semi-final but to tell the truth I made a lot of mistakes in the meeting and possibly chose the wrong gate in the final. Once again I didn't make good starts and I didn't do myself any favours in the final by getting another one. I got chopped up in the first corner so basically it was over from there.

Obviously I would've liked to have done better but I could not allow myself to be disappointed. The result proved that the championship was definitely not a two-horse race between me and Rickardsson as Nicki Pedersen was right in there as well and there were others who you would never make the mistake of under-rating.

At this stage of the proceedings, however, without having really hit my straps I still felt comfortable about my chances of being there or thereabouts right to the end. It's handy if you can get results without necessarily producing your best form and that's part of the art of mounting a decent GP campaign.

Sometimes, though, it's not just the guys on the track who can spoil your chances. It sounds like sour grapes if you blame anybody but yourself, but most people would agree that the performance of Mr Wojaczek in Cardiff virtually cost me my chances of retaining the title.

While I held on to second place in the overall standings, suddenly I was a massive 32 points behind Rickardsson who helped himself to another win, seeing off Jarek Hampel, Bjarne Pedersen and Hans Andersen in a different-looking final race.

There were a few other controversial decisions on the night, other riders, supporters and the press guys were mostly supportive and sympathetic, but what can you do? Absolutely nothing except dust yourself down and get ready for the next one in Copenhagen.

Denmark had been so good for me in 2004, and it was all going well there in the qualifiers. In fact it was probably as good as I had ridden all year – until I picked the wrong gate in the semi-final and got cleaned up. The frustration of missing out was compounded when Tony won the final once more.

If I had some lingering hopes that he might slacken off, he dispelled those by winning again in Prague, despite damaging a thumb and bending his first bike in a heavy heat five fall. His record-breaking fourth GP win in a row extended his lead to 54 points. It wasn't a great night for me, needing to win my last qualifying ride to scrape into the semis, and then coming last in the final behind Rickardsson, Bjarne Pedersen and Jarek Hampel.

At least I was able to halt Tony's triumphal march by winning again in a rain-delayed Scandinavian Grand Prix at Malilla. It's always a buzz to win in Sweden. Andreas Jonsson and I both scored 13 points in the qualifying heats and in the final I wound on the gas to go round him and deny TR a fifth successive GP victory and delay the inevitable. He finished third.

The start of the meeting was held up for nearly an hour because of rain, but the Malilla track staff worked wonders to produce a track surface that served up some thrilling racing. It was every bit as good a meeting as any in earlier years in Stockholm, reinforcing the point that the small stadiums sometimes produce terrific speedway.

The result meant that Tony needed only four points in the Polish GP in Bydgoszcz to complete the formality of a record-equalling sixth title. Within two heats he had made sure, though he didn't go on with it on this occasion.

Tomasz Gollob – on a Jawa instead of his usual GM – maintained his astonishing record by winning at his home-town track for the fourth year in a row and I managed a third place in the final, behind Lee Richardson and ahead of Greg Hancock.

Tony, on 171 points, was home free. My total was now 134, and with Nicki Pedersen on 97 it meant that I couldn't be caught either.

That didn't mean to say that I went to Lonigo for the final round any less motivated to do well. Another GP success at any time would have been welcome, but it was the same old, same old – second to Rickardsson in the heats, second in the qualifying scores and, after winning my semi-final, second in the final as well.

Tony racked up 196 points from the nine rounds which will take some beating. I got to 154, which in almost any other year might have been enough to win the whole thing. I also took a great deal of satisfaction out of seeing Leigh Adams make it into third spot overall, after finishing fourth for three years in a row. This time I could identify with his pleasure!

Leigh just managed to inch ahead of Nicki Pedersen, 107 points to 102, with Greg Hancock on 100 reminding everyone that he still is a very useful performer.

Another season, another second. Apart from Cardiff, I'd again produced the sort of consistency which, in any other year, would have put me in with a very realistic chance.

Could I have narrowed the gap but for that disastrous British GP ... would Rickardsson have started to feel a little sensation of pressure ... it's all academic.

One of the big stories of the GP year came a few days after Lonigo when Tony announced that he would be retiring at the end of the 2006 season. He had arrived at a place in his life where he is happy with who he is, happy with what he has done, grateful for what speedway has done for him. When you're hot, there is the temptation to keep going but seriously, what more has he got to prove?

So we got two Aussies on the world championship rostrum for the second time in four years, but the World Team Cup was a downer. We were pipped for top spot by just one point in the elimination final in Eskilstuna, but still had another go in the final play-off. Unfortunately I was sick and missed the next meeting and we just didn't have enough depth to compensate.

For much of the year, it looked as if at least one of the three clubs with which I was associated would provide some form of consolation. Disappointingly, all of them caught the 'second-place' syndrome as well.

Belle Vue led the Elite League for most of the season, finishing on top after the home and away programme, only to lose out to Coventry in the play-offs. Missing Kenneth Bjerre, who broke his leg in a Danish League match in September, was the key.

ACES HIGH ... a good way to start the 2005 UK season with victory in the Peter Craven Memorial Trophy at Belle Vue ... and a great ending, triumph in the KO Cup Final, left to right: Andy Smith, Jason Lyons, James Wright, Simon Stead, JC, Ian Thomas, Joe Screen, Rusty Harrison

TACTICS ... Jason talking with VMS Elit team boss Bo Wirebrand

Torun placed second in the Polish Extra League but a rain-off in the first semi-final meant Andy Smith and I had to miss the re-staging the next day – that's the system in Poland. Czestochowa proved too much of a handful, demolishing our hopes of doing anything in the return leg, and we ended up playing off for third and fourth.

VMS Elit also finished second on the Swedish Elite League table, made it through to the play-off final but still missed out on the title against Vastervik which completed a rather unwanted sequence!

For a couple of years I had been looking to cut back on my Swedish commitments, just to keep the calendar a little less congested and the demands on bikes, body and brain slightly less hectic than in earlier seasons. Vargarna understood where I was coming from and I appreciated that they wanted someone who was going to be around on a regular basis – but it was good that Bo Wirebrand was happy to let me sign for VMS Elit on a very loose and open-ended arrangement.

Like most of the clubs there, they were operating on a squad system, which enabled them to call upon me when they wanted some more top-end strength for certain meetings and which fitted my schedule. It worked pretty well and I ended up doing six out of my seven matches away from Vetlanda, which isn't a track I particularly enjoy.

They even went for more balance at home in the final and I rode in the second leg – good in theory but we came up just short on aggregate.

The team had an up and down start and Bo called me up for the important derby meetings against Luxo Stars. The first match at Vetlanda in front of a 5,029 crowd ended 48-48, but the return a week later was much better, a 53-43 away win and I won my last four races.

I got 14 at Smederna in the semi-final which set up the decider against Västervik, a team that was not among the pre-season favourites, but had won the league and beaten Luxo Stars in both semi-final meetings.

In the first final at Vetlanda, watched by a record 8,703 crowd, I was in the pits as a spectator as VMS Elit opted for a really strong reserve duo. With half of the heats completed, Västervik led 28-20, but the home side managed to pull it back to win 49-47.

Despite heavy rain which delayed the start for an hour and a half, the title decider at Västervik was watched by 7,264 fans, another attendance record. for that venue. The meeting was delayed for 90 minutes. By Heat 8, Västervik led by 32-16, but I then won three straight races and with one heat to go, we could still have forced a run-off for the title if we could grab a 5-1. Unfortunately Ales Dryml was excluded for bringing down Sebastian Ulamek, so we had to settle for second ... again.

ALL SET ... last minute preparations before a Polish Extra League race

It was close to a dream start to the year in Poland, after a false start when the first fixture weekend was scrubbed because of the death of the Pope.

Torun lost at Leszno the following Sunday and then won five in a row. In three of those meetings I only dropped a point and in the last of them, against Czestochowa, I was paid for a maximum.

Then some of the impetus disappeared, and the final placing of fourth after the play-offs was not quite what had been hoped. My record of 230 points and a 9.45 average was not too bad though – it's tough going to maintain a figure around nine and a half to 10.

Most satisfying of all was the massive upsurge at Belle Vue, with new promoter Tony Mole and team manager Ian Thomas enjoying some of the good fortune which so often had escaped John Perrin. It was the best year there for ages, certainly since I had been with the Aces and for a long time before that.

There had been rumours floating around that John was on his way out after a long run. We had a good relationship based very much on trust and on being honest with one another in our dealings and it was a shame he hadn't had more joy from it all in recent years. The 2004 season was an absolute nightmare for him with endless problems, mostly caused by one rain-off after another.

Once more it looked as if I might have to be looking for a change of surroundings, dependent upon what happened to the promotion. Coventry, with their new boss Avtar Sandhu obviously very ambitious to do well, were keen to know what was happening but in the finish, when Tony Mole took over, he didn't take long to sell me on his vision for Belle Vue.

BELLE Vue manager Ian Thomas rates the 21-point maximum Jason Crump scored at Coventry in last season's British Elite League play-off final first leg as one of the finest individual displays he has seen in domestic racing.

Thomas has witnessed some outstanding performances from stellar stars down the years and while a year working with Crump had reinforced his opinions, this was the best he had seen of him.

"It was one of those nights where nobody as going to beat him," he says.

"We could have run a 50-race meeting and he still wouldn't have lost a race. He kept us in with a chance of the title, a chance we didn't take advantage of in the second leg.

"He's a very bright young man as well as being one of the all-time top riders. The influence he had on the year Belle Vue was enormous.

"In terms of preparation, Jason is a lot closer to Ivan Mauger than Barry Briggs. He knows what he wants and he is very, very professional.

"He's not always the easiest bloke to deal with. I can't say we are buddies, we had a few spats during the year, but I think there is mutual respect and we work well together which is what it's all about."

He is a very smart businessman who has made a big impact at various tracks and Ian Thomas has the reputation of being one of the shrewdest team managers in the business. It really did look as if between them they knew what to tip into the mix to produce a team capable of winning something and that certainly appealed to me.

I wanted to be riding in the big end-of-season play-off meetings and cup finals and in that respect, at least, we were in the hunt right up until the last minute, topping the points table before losing to Coventry in the play-off final. The team gelled together pretty much from the off, had a little stutter midway through, but fired up again with one highlight a 51-39 win at Wolverhampton.

The start was delayed for an hour because the track looked very dodgy following a lot of rain over the weekend. And when we got under way it was Wolves who fired up first, taking a 31-23 lead after nine heats. Then we really got down to business. Simon Stead was in a hot form from reserve, I got the lot and we managed to completely turn things round to pull of what was our sixth win in eight days.

We led the table for almost the whole year and, until Kenneth Bjerre got injured, we were the best team running around. It stretched our resources just that bit too much when he was out, but that's speedway. It's pointless complaining. Topping the table doesn't equal winning the title nowadays, you have to prove yourselves all over again in the play-offs and we did not do that.

We did our chances in the play-off final no good when we lost 54-41 at Coventry. I went through the card but there was not as much back-up as there might have been. Coventry had been going well, but if we could have limited them to, say, eight points, I think we would have fancied our chances of pulling back the deficit at home.

But too many of the riders didn't believe we could do it. And if you don't believe, you're no chance. There were a couple of bits of bad luck, I blew an engine, and in the end the Bees even beat us on the night, so you couldn't argue with the nature of their win. I still think we could have done better. And it was a shame for everyone who had worked so hard, and, especially, for guys like Screeny and Andy Smith who went back such a long way with the club and would have loved a title win.

Screeny, who started with the Aces, and came back there in 2003, my second season in Manchester, has turned out to be a great clubmate. We have always got on well although in our early days people tried to build up a rivalry between us because he was the emerging young English hope and both of us were flat out to make an impression.

We talk most days, and it is good to have someone who is of similar age and has been through it all with whom to compare notes on what's happening, or just pass the time. There's not a bad bone in his body and he is very well liked.

It was only right that after our league performances, there was some major consolation to be had when we beat Eastbourne in the KO Cup Final. This time, we laid the proper foundation in the away leg where we lost by only a couple of points. Nicki Pedersen was just back after injury and as usual made life difficult but we got it together as a team, and won on the night to take the trophy with a 97-83 aggregate. I got the lot at Belle Vue which was a nice personal plus.

It was absolutely brilliant to see what it meant to so many people in Manchester, to win something for the first time since 1993. Apparently you had to go back even further – to 1975 – for the last time the Aces had won the Cup.

Nobody was more pleased than Alan Morrey, who has been part of the furniture for years, first at Hyde Road, then Kirkmanshulme Lane. Riders and promoters come and go but Alan had been clerk of the course for a lifetime and he was so chuffed to be asked to present the trophy.

It was a reward for everyone at the end of a season which really put Belle Vue back on the map. We're not up there with the all-time greats yet, but it's a beginning.

Legends like Jack Parker, Dent Oliver, Peter Craven, Ivan Mauger and Peter Collins had brought glory and distinction to the club and featured in some tremendous team successes down the years. To have our own little piece of history alongside guys like that means an awful lot.

And on a personal note, I posted a higher average away from home than at Belle Vue – 10.32 to be precise.

It's always good to put on a show on the road, a matter of professional pride as much as anything.

A lot of guys rack up the points when when they're on familiar ground at home. Maintaining anything like the same sort of scoring record on away tracks doesn't come quite so easily.

Our third and last chance of silverware was in the Craven Shield and we did well enough to reach the final, but then ran out of steam. The meetings were quite enjoyable, though. Just to be involved in something meaningful right through to the middle of October was a definite improvement on previous years.

So often in the past I have got to the end of a European season and felt absolutely stuffed but even though 2005 was quite a year, I ended it feeling pretty good. Part of the pleasure was being involved in more decent end-of-year action including wins at Peterborough's ASL Freight Trophy and Leigh Lanham's testimonial meeting.

Additionally, the way the new GM engines were performing (late in the year I'd decided the time was right to switch) gave me a lot of satisfaction when I tried a few things in the closing weeks.

So that's me, pretty much up to date.

And what do speedway riders do when another season draws to a close?

Well, in my case it was off to America again – a family holiday at Disneyland is always a highlight and each time we go the kids are a bit older and can appreciate it more. Whereas of course I'm desperately trying to hold on to my youth and I enjoy it more each time too.

Mel, Mia and Seth flew back to England a couple of days ahead of me because I also had some work to do, leading a World side against the USA in the 'fast Friday' finale at Auburn in California.

This was a blast as well, with our team including old mates such as Armando Castagna, Joe Screen and John Cook – in by virtue of the fact he won the Swedish title one time – outpacing the Yanks 86-59.

Even then there was no immediate slow down. I wasn't home for more than a few days before heading off to Lonigo for more testing. The exercise was one of the best of its kind that I have had and set me up for the new season in an optimistic frame of mind.

One unexpected highlight of that trip was when Armando took me to the Milan Motor Show. There were lots of top road racers there, but speedway also got a great plug when the television guys cottoned on to the fact that I was at the show and spent several minutes doing a piece with me.

It was an encouraging sign of the times. The Grand Prix has increased its profile so much in the past few years. More than ever, it's good to be a part of it – and who knows what other frontiers there will be to conquer in coming seasons.

Behind the man MEL'S STORY

Being a speedway rider's wife is never dull. But it's great. I could write a book about my years with Jason. Well, almost.

From the speedway point of view, it's been tough, but rewarding, especially after we went through a lot before he finally became world champion. Since achieving that goal he's become much more relaxed and we try to enjoy everything to the full these days. There are more smiles on race day than ever before and that tense underlying feeling has left the air.

We met in the Australian summer of 1995-96. I had just finished my HSC (higher school certificate) and was working part-time at a surf store in Swansea.

I was waiting for the summer break to finish and college to start. I had enrolled in a Japanese language and tourism course at Newcastle TAFE college and had my sights set on being a translator in the tourism industry.

If I wasn't at work I was usually at the beach. Newcastle is a good surf town and still one of my favourite spots.

I was at work one morning and the owners Wayne and Kylie McCormick said this guy was popping in on his way through to say hi. Wayne's brother Darren previously had a surf shop and had sponsored Jason for years, and after selling up he sent him to the one where I was now working for some free kit.

WE'RE IN THIS TOGETHER ... Jason betrays his relief and delight after winning the Czech Republic Grand Prix in 2003

They both seemed quite excited but I didn't understand the fuss as I'd never heard of him or had any idea what speedway was. That was obviously a 'Westy' sport and I was what is affectionately known as a 'Weed' in Aussie. Jason hung out far from the surf 'out west' and I did things at the surf and coast. Weed has something to do with the seaweed thing, growing up at the beach.

Anyway later that day Jason and his uncle Andy (Street) turned up. Jason and I hit it off instantly and by the time they left for a race meeting down south he had my number and was trying to figure out when we could see each other again.

He had a full schedule of racing over the following month before he went to England so it wasn't going to be an easy task. He was living just out of Surfers Paradise and I was north of Sydney so we had about eight hours between us by car. It wasn't going to be a day trip.

He stopped in my area on his way back through again before heading off for another race but that was it and he wanted me to fly up to Queensland before he went back to the UK. "I don't think so" was the answer he got. As keen as we were on each other I hardly knew him and I certainly wasn't doing that. I got the impression he found me a bit of a challenge.

We spoke quite often on the phone and he had started talking about me going to the UK for a trip to see what I thought. It was 'No thanks' to that idea either. We said goodbye, good luck for the coming year and maybe we would see each other in about 10 months time if we're not doing other things.

I heard a little about what Jason was up to through the year from friends at the surf store but I soon left once my course had started and also began work relief managing for a large surf company. I cracked on with the Japanese and didn't give much thought to the following summer.

Around Christmas time I got a phone call from a friend saying that Jason was back in the country and would like to see me. We met up a few times round my area and he was talking seriously about me going to England with him again.

This time I also met Neil Bird, who was Jason's manager at the time. 'Roy', as he's always been known to me, was a real laugh and did all he could to try and encourage our relationship. He had helped Jason in every way possible since he was quite young and he meant a great deal to him. Roy is someone he considers as family and we don't get to see him anywhere near as much as we'd like as he now lives in Aussie full-time.

Jason didn't really explain a great deal about his racing to me in terms of how well known he might be in certain countries. I had someone tell me about that and to say it made me less keen on him would be an understatement. I told them I didn't like the sound of that and they passed my thoughts on to Jason.

MEET THE FOLKS ... Jason and Melody at the Johnston home at Charlestown near Newcastle

He cottoned on pretty quick that could be the end of it and soon started talking things down and keeping the subject off the racing. I don't think he was used to doing that – but he can tell a good story, so it probably came to him naturally.

In the end I basically believed that he raced speedway once, maybe twice a week and lived in the UK for eight months of the year because he wasn't able to do much riding in Aussie at that time of year. I remember asking repeatedly what else he did as I couldn't understand what his 'job' was.

He finally satisfied my questioning by telling me he did some building work doing up old houses with his uncles as well as picking up some money through racing. All of which wasn't lies but just a slight bending of the truth.

He couldn't really win as he knew I'd be waving goodbye if I thought he was in the public eye. But he knew I was wondering whether or not he was just a 'try hard' who rode his bike around fantasising about getting his picture in a 'racers' magazine.

Too soon it was time for Jason to return to the UK and I just couldn't go. I had things sorted with my course and my job and didn't want to give them up as we weren't exactly what I'd call serious.

A few months after he left he was still trying to get me to the UK. I had a phone call I think almost every day from him and every time he'd ask when or if I was going to go see him. It was pretty obvious he wasn't going to throw the towel in and he finally got the better of me after having a pretty cool delivery made to me at my work. He was proving to be a bit of a romantic and his efforts didn't fail him.

The next phone call was from me telling him what date I would arrive in the UK.

Two weeks later I took off out of Sydney after convincing myself and everyone else this was only a short trip.

By this point my parents and brother Lincoln had heard plenty about Jason and although they didn't want me to leave, they all gave me their blessing and waved me off.

It was a daunting venture. Nobody close to me really knew Jason, my family hadn't met him and I was travelling on my own to the other side of the world to see how this might turn out. No wonder my parents were in tears at the airport. You don't realise what you put your parents through until you have your own children.

I arrived at London Heathrow at the crack of dawn on a beautiful sunny day, thankfully.

As soon as we met up I knew I'd done the right thing, we were going to have a blast!

That day was a bit of a blur, my first international flight and I needed a good night's sleep to get my bearings. We went go-karting, checked out Northampton and then I insisted on seeing the red meat in England. Mad Cow disease had had a lot of publicity in Australia at that time and everyone told me not to eat the stuff or else!

That night Jason told me he had to go to Sweden the next day to race. What? I didn't even know he raced in Sweden, ever! He then showed me his schedule and I nearly fell over. It was that full it was ridiculous and he said he couldn't have told me about it as he knew there was no way I would have come to England if I had known.

True, and if we hadn't picked up where we left off so well there's a good chance I would have been back in Sydney for the following weekend.

As it was I went to my first speedway match that Friday at Peterborough. I didn't understand much of it but Jason had someone sorted to look after me and it was really cool fun although very daunting. Everyone was really friendly and couldn't do enough for me. I made some great friends there that I still have today.

Immediately after the match we jumped into the van, then

affectionately known as 'hotel le transit' and headed for Poland. It was another long trip and when we finally reached the Polish border we were ordered out of the van by a few scary, very pale-looking guys with guns like I'd only seen in the movies.

Jason's mechanics had spent many hours winding me up with stories about being locked up at the border. I didn't know whether to laugh or cry when they marched us across the road toward the most dilapidated building I think I'd ever seen. After about 15 minutes they returned with a few more guards all looking chirpy and proceeded to take great pleasure in shaking Jason's hand over and over and getting what seemed like a ridiculous amount of autographs.

I'll never forget the sigh of relief I had or the smirk on his mechanics' faces as they knew they'd got me a beauty. The only word I understood was CRUMP and of course those of Jason's mechanics telling them what they thought of them for holding us up.

By the time we got to the hotel in Gorzow I was gobsmacked. Once we were over the border the first thing I saw was endless prostitutes on the side of the road, for hours. They were just appearing out of the forest and as amusing as the boys made it as we drove past them I couldn't help but wonder how much of a state the country must be in.

The hotel goes down as I think the worst ever, just behind one in Katowice when I lined the floor with the blankets out the cupboard as the carpet looked too disgusting to stand on even with shoes while we waited for our travel guy to 'get us out of here ASAP.'

I couldn't wait to have a shower after spending the night travelling but when I turned it on the water came out brown so I decided to give it a miss after all. I poured a few bottles of water in the sink and bird-bathed. There was no way I was washing in that, let alone brush my teeth in it!

Fortunately the water colour cleared up after a while so the shower was finally tempted but Evian water became my best friend and still was in certain places until a few years ago. Running water was ok for a shower but that was it. Thank goodness Radissons are now world wide!

We had a few meals and went to the best local club. This was when I realised how big the sport was in Poland. We couldn't go anywhere without Jason being hassled if not mobbed. Getting a table was not a problem though and somewhere at the back was and still is always cleared for us for a bit of privacy which is nice.

We've had to do a runner quite a few times over the years. You can walk around for a while with nobody being any the wiser but as soon as someone recognises him it's like a swarm of bees coming. Sometimes we get a good laugh out of it and they usually cop a few kicks and punches but it's usually a complete pain and quite intimidating.

My first taste of Polish speedway was let's say 'interesting'.

It was not unlike the first few miles after leaving the border but apparently these weren't necessarily paid prostitutes, this was standard dress for females wishing to 'catch' themselves a rider and a ticket to a better life.

Blimey! I'd never been to King's Cross, the infamous red light district in Sydney, but figured this was probably coming pretty close.

On reaching the pit area gate there was a huge amount of chanting, only the same word I'd heard at the border 'CRUMP, CRUMP'. There was a quick scramble to check all doors were locked and windows up. The van had stopped bumping around because of the bad state of the roads but started rocking from side to side instead. The chanting was right outside the windows and all I could see were people everywhere around us going wild. Everyone in the van seemed to get great amusement yet again out of the look on my face, Jason must have asked me if I was all right about 100 times that trip.

Finally we got inside the pits and it was like a different world, with everyone just going about their business. It was calm and everyone was polite. My advice from Jason before he went off to prepare for the meeting was "don't have anything to do with anyone you're not introduced to, leave your handbag in the van and if all hell breaks loose stay where you are and I'll come and get you."

"What?" was my only reply I was not exactly feeling confident about what may be on the horizon and would have quite happily stayed in the van with doors locked. Where I was to stay during the racing was basically within a large seated cage on the side of the pit area, I was escorted over, asked where I'd like to sit and then left alone as the racing was about to start.

I seemed to attract a lot of attention as the new half of 'CRUMP' and I'm sure for the fact I didn't fit in there at all which was again really daunting. The interior of the cage was pretty dismal, wooden slat seats, covered in dirt and a lot of broken concrete, plus a lot of faces pressed against the outside looking in and a distinct smell of madness in the air.

There were however some people I felt more comfortable with within the cage, though a smile was our only form of communication. I had begun to notice two completely different groups of people here and I started to find the country fascinating.

The meeting went fairly smoothly apart from security having to escort a few out and seeing some supporters spitting on the visiting team's riders from above as they passed under a tunnel that led from the track to the pit area. They take their speedway very seriously!

Jason came and checked on me a few times which was reassuring as I was definitely feeling like I was at the zoo but the animals weren't the ones locked up.

CROWDED HOUSE ... thousands watch as Jason takes command in the Extra League third-place play-off, Torun v Czestochowa, 2005. Also in shot are Slawomir Drabik, Wieslaw Jagus and Grzegorz Walasek

The finale was just before the last heat. Anticipating a final result which didn't please a lot of the fans, security kicked in ten fold and a swarm of men in black from head to toe (balaclavas included) entered, machine guns in hand and dogs that looked and sounded like they were ready for their first feed of the week.

I didn't understand what was going on in the match, but the sight of these boys seemed to tip the crowd over the edge and almost as soon as the heavy security appeared so did the chaos. The last heat was almost finished as I looked over to see most of the stand to my right covered in black smoke and my side of it there were people literally belting the living daylights out of each other.

Some of the heavies had gone into the crowd and the dogs were sounding as savage as ever, I turned around to see a group of men at the back of the cage wielding what looked like the planks off the seats at each other just before Jason appeared to get me out of there.

Within about two minutes all hell had broken loose and while the crowd were being sorted out and taken from the stadium we were on the other side of the fence being treated to a barbeque Polish style! It was ridiculous and I still shake my head thinking about it now.

That was without doubt my most memorable trip, maybe because it was such an eye opener, and I still haven't seen anything again quite as severe as that day. I think that's probably a combination of the crowds mellowing a bit and me becoming accustomed to their antics.

Our children have only ever been to about three Polish league matches and only those we felt were safe to go to. The Polish people are very different, there is a huge distinction between those that have spent a substantial amount of time abroad, dealing with western people and countries and those who haven't.

We have made some fantastic friends from Poland but are always wary of who and what's going on around us. I still feel uncomfortable with the children there, even at the Grand Prix events. Saying that though the Bydgoszcz GP is without doubt the best of the series every year and that's purely because the fans there are so fanatical and love their speedway so the atmosphere is always awesome.

After we returned from that trip I got into the swing of things. I spent most of that season working on a hotel reception but my shifts clashed all too often with what we wanted to do together, Jason enjoyed my company at races so we started travelling together as well.

Before the following season I had quit and signed up as a promo girl after Simon Wigg's wife Charlie put me in contact with a good company. That suited me fine and I was able to pick and choose which jobs I did and Jason's racing then became the centre of attention.

As well as things had worked out I really started missing home after a few months. I have always been quite close to my brother and missed being able to hang out with him at the beach. I wasn't enjoying being so far from the surf and the

Saturday ... Grand Prix day

way of life is seriously different from that in Aussie

It was starting to feel claustrophobic in England. I had never really been a home body but was pining to get back to Australia and see my mum and dad as well.

The biggest event of the year was going to Bradford for a qualifying round for the following year's world championship. I didn't really understand how the system worked but there was a lot of talk about it by everyone that we came into contact with and I didn't feel that comfortable hassling Jason about the ins and outs as he seemed to have had enough of everyone else doing it.

All I knew was that he needed to have a good day and qualify. This was what he was expected to do.

I had become someone that he could relax with, no pressure, I didn't care whether he was winning or losing. I just enjoyed our time together and we joked around a lot and didn't talk 'speedway' which I think was a welcome relief to what I didn't realise then was a huge amount of pressure he was under.

That Bradford round didn't go to plan. I don't remember the races, only someone saying to me on my way back to the pits 'that's too bad, he should be in it.'

Once I reached the pits Jason was nowhere in sight and I was told he was in the van and he would probably be best left alone. I don't think so, we had become very close and I wasn't going to sit on one side of the door while he was on the other.

I jumped in the back of the van with him and didn't say a word at first as I didn't know what to say. I just sat and hugged him. He said he'd missed his chance and it's another two years now before he'd get another.

I couldn't help but start asking questions I didn't understand exactly what he meant and I needed to. This was the first time I'd seen him unhappy and hugely disappointed. He wasn't angry or agitated at me asking. I think it probably did him some good to talk about it. He may wear his heart on his sleeve at times but he also soldiers on without burdening everyone else with how he feels.

Thinking about it now, for me that day was a big turning point in our relationship. We had become very close in every way but the 'speedway' thing was not something we'd gone into that much.

That day though, Jason told me exactly how he felt and how much being world champion meant to him. He also explained how the qualifying system worked and that his only chance to be in the world championship series the following year was if one of the guys that had reached the final round pulled out as he was now the reserve.

I remember telling him he'd get a spot, I just knew he would. I did my best to lighten his mood! He told me I was mad, but was grateful for someone to give him a laugh at that time.

SHARING THE JOY ... Vastervik, 1997

It's one thing to be there for the build-up, wish people good luck, tell them they can do it and all the rest of the stuff you hear from everyone. But the real support network are the people that are there immediately after a failure or disappointment as well.

And I discovered the only other people Jason could really, comfortably speak to were his mum, Roy Bird, and his uncle and auntie (Graham and Edina Street) none of whom were geographically close to him.

I was finding out pretty quickly how shallow some people can be and how important some others are to surround yourself with. Everyone loves a winner but only a few love the loser.

A few weeks later Jason had a phone call after which he sat there grinning like a Cheshire cat telling me I was right. Dean Barker had broken his arm and was not going to be fit to race in the final qualifying round so Jason was in after all. This was his chance!

We went to Sweden, he qualified after all and that was my first taste of a victory as such. He didn't win the round but that wasn't the goal, it was about qualifying so he was rapt and so was I.

He had a Swedish league match a few days later where he was presented with among other things a huge bouquet of flowers. I remember it was packed in the stadium and the crowd were standing as he did a lap of honour. He stopped when he got to the stand where I was and climbed the fence to give these flowers to me.

It was really embarrassing but a beautiful gesture.

The entire crowd were watching us and I was bright red in the face I'm sure. I had to clamber to the bottom of the stand so he could get the flowers to me and the entire parade was held up in the process. That was a really cool thing for him to do and I'll never forget it.

Towards the end of that season he also got a wild card entry into the Swedish Grand Prix. He'd been a wild card the previous year in Britain where he had become the youngest ever rider to win a Grand Prix and he couldn't wait to have another go at it and a warm-up to the following season with his place now secure for every one of them.

I remember things off the track more than those on it from that trip. The hotel room we had was absolutely huge and we thought they'd made a mistake and went to check what was going on. We were reassured that the price was as quoted and we were just lucky we'd been allocated the largest suite they had for some unknown reason. We had a ball checking the place out and made the most of it. It's nice to remember that as it makes you appreciate things more if they've not always been something you're accustomed to.

There was an FIM dinner the night before the meeting which all the competitors and their wives were at. Afterwards there was a group of them sitting drinking coffee and another group at the bar as full as could be. They were all riding the next day and I could see those that were taking things seriously and those that weren't.

That image has stayed with me and the same things go on to this day. It doesn't mean you won't win on the night if you're blotto 24 hours beforehand. Some of the guys that have achieved the greatest results are the biggest drinkers in the field. They can obviously just handle their alcohol a lot better than others.

We had an early night as has become custom for Jason before a big meeting. He doesn't drink much anyway, but for a week before a Grand Prix he won't touch a beer.

Sunday ...
on duty in Poland

Jason didn't do as well as he would have liked in that GP but he made the headlines anyway. A story got round that he and his mechanics had such a big night at the casino that they'd had to fly home barefoot the following day because they'd lost everything including their shoes on the black jack table. We had no idea where the story had started but we went along with it anyway for a laugh and it still gets a mention to this day!

We finally returned to Oz and spent four months travelling, spending time with family and I took charge of dragging Jason to the beach at every given opportunity. We had a great summer. I had my 21st and we had loads of parties to go to, at some of which Jason absolutely cleared the dance floor.

The following season was the start of a long road to number #1. Jason won the British GP again that year and just managed to finish in the top eight riders which gave him an automatic Grand Prix place for the following season without any qualifying rounds.

The main aim that year was to stay in the top eight and I don't know how many times I must have added up scores that year so I knew what was going on and who was where and who Jason needed to finish in front of to stay in. I got to know most of the riders' wives and it was great the way everyone looked out for each other.

That year we had also been doing a lot of talking about babies. Jason has always loved kids to bits. He's always been really close to his cousins, Lucy, James and William Street and spent a lot of time with them when they were younger.

We decided that we would like for me to be due at the end of the season so there would be no major stresses about him being away racing at the due date. So I spent the next season pregnant and Mia was born in October 1999. We were both thrilled to bits and much of the year had been spent waiting for her to arrive.

Jason's priority was again to stay in the top eight that year. He didn't win a GP but was gaining experience, and consistency was what he needed to get some real results.

His English club Peterborough however did extremely well and won the treble, all the three competitions possible. The main thing I remember about that was not the winning of it but the way Jason was treated through it. There were major problems within the promotion at the club and bickering had become a constant occurrence. He left the club at the end of the season.

That year's highlight was the birth of our first child and the love we discovered we had for her was unbelievable. It also put things into perspective and it was now about us as a family. We had a beautiful baby and getting the best for her and ourselves was now priority.

The next year Jason finished the world championship in fourth. He had made a huge leap from his previous two years of scraping in at eighth place and was happy to finish just behind Tony Rickardsson. I remember him saying he didn't want his first podium to be third. He had this thing about believing that third place for your first ever world championship rostrum position would never give you a first in the world championship.

It was just a little thing he couldn't get out of his head and he rattled off some names that had been there in that position and never gone on to win it. So he was happy to settle for fourth. He made a few finals and won the Swedish GP so that was a good year for him.

Now he was looking to that ultimate goal as it was getting closer and he now had the consistency he needed. This had become serious business and everything started revolving around the Grand Prix for us.

The 2001 season was a different year altogether and mainly taken up with Jason's family being the biggest issue. Jason's youngest sister Gabrielle came to England to stay with us for the year after just finishing school and his father Phil followed about a month later. His parents were looking to separate and it proved to be a difficult time for all of us.

His father spent some time with us, had a brief trip back to Aussie and then returned to stay with us for the rest of the season. His parents did separate and we were left to pick up the pieces on both parts.

Phil said he had no real reason for staying in Aussie, he was happier being around the speedway but he needed an income and so we created a job for him. We set up an engine servicing business for which Jason and I did most of the organising, and his dad started servicing some Conference and Premier League riders' engines and going to the speedway.

There was a lot going on and Jason and I had a lot to deal with off the track. Despite everything going on Jason still managed to move up the ladder in the GP again with a third, two second places, and two wins and only one bad GP result that year. He finished second this time round – getting past that unwanted third podium position.

He had become a real threat to taking that No.1 position and raced Tony for the points to the final GP that season. Jason had proven to himself that he could come close. But that's not good enough, anyone can come close, anyone can win it. He wanted to earn the victory and talked a lot about people who were better riders than others that had won it but just didn't quite get there. Now he just needed to step up again and try and take that spot.

That was also the year Jimmy Nilsen retired from racing and started his own Grand Prix team up. Jason had known him since he was a child and Jimmy wanted Jason in it. He had some serious sponsorship and wanted the best guy he could get. The main sponsor was a Polish company so he needed someone from Poland as well and that's where Krzystof Cegielski came into the team.

It wasn't a team as such that they were there to help each other, it was more that they were just racing under the same banner. We did however become good friends with Krzystof and his partner Anita. They were great to be around and Mia loved them both to bits.

Unfortunately for one reason or another Jimmy and family decided to leave the UK towards the end of that season and before the world championship was decided. With the management gone all of a sudden things were left up in the air to say the least and nobody seemed to be able to get hold of him. A few people he'd had working for him ended up just keeping things running for the last couple of GPs.

This was also the start of another great friendship – with the team's main sponsor,Wlodek and Jola Skudlarek from LNB Poland. We hadn't had a huge amount to do with them but Jason had got on really well with them so when the middle man disappeared Jason was left doing the business with Mr Skudlarek himself.

We have always done all Jason's contracts with clubs and main sponsors ourselves so it was no big deal as we don't like the idea of a middle man taking a cut when it's not necessary. If I ever see Jimmy again I'll be sure to thank him very much for disappearing like that!

By the following season Jason and LNB Poland had a great relationship and the 'team' as such was scrapped with the sponsorship pool being directed entirely for Jason and Krzystof's benefit.

MAJOR SPONSORSHIP … Jason pictured at LNB headquarters

We decided we should think about some sort of hospitality vehicle to look after a sponsor that was so good in looking after us. But when Jason mentioned it to him he insisted it was as we'd always thought a complete waste of time and money. Buy another house instead was his reply. And that was the closest we came to ever doing the motor home thing.

We don't enjoy hanging around at the track – we prefer to stay in the comfort of a good hotel as do the mechanics and our sponsors. We go to the track for the race and then to the hotel for a meal and drinks so we'd decided years ago it was not for us.

Mr Skudlarek has over the past few years played a huge part in any dealings Jason has had in Poland and really does look out for him and us as a family which we are extremely grateful for.

The 2002 season was a year split into two halves. The first was an ongoing of the problems of the previous year with Jason's mum and dad and I don't remember it fondly at all. To say we could have done without it is a major understatement. The second half of the year was great though and things had become about us again rather than everybody else's problems.

The highlight of that year for us was having another baby on the way, Mia was an absolute little angel and had given us so much enjoyment we wanted another one. Mia was about two when we decided to try again but with all the stuff going on with his parents the season before we wanted a calm atmosphere around before I got pregnant.

Thankfully that happened and I found out just before Jason's birthday that year I was pregnant. Although I decided to tell him as a surprise I couldn't help myself and we had something new and great to look forward to again. To top it off we also moved into a lovely new house at the end of the season.

On racing Jason did extremely well with his world championship result that year and managed another second place behind Tony. The series finished with the first ever

Monday …
it's Belle Vue

Aussie Grand Prix and although he would have loved to have won there he managed a third on the podium that night so he was pleased to have at least got a result in his home country.

We started 2003 season with another baby, Seth. He was born in a hurry. I called Jason who was then 20 minutes away. He had just pulled apart an engine he'd been having trouble with and was going over it when I rang and said "I think you'd better come home."

His reply was "Are you sure? I'm just getting somewhere with this thing. Give us a ring in 20 minutes if you still reckon it's time."

"You've got to be joking" I thought, but I humoured him. My mum had come over from Aussie to lend a hand and she told me not to mess around and quick labours were common in our family.

About 10 minutes later I called him back and he was home about 10 minutes after that. I knew this one wasn't hanging around in there either. My labour with Mia lasted only five hours but Seth decided he'd better that and managed it in only three. Jason knew I wouldn't have called back if I wasn't 100% sure so he got me to the hospital quick smart.

Jason's reaction was a classic and it still makes me laugh. We didn't know the sex of either of the children before birth and really didn't care but when Seth came out Jason's face lit up like a picture: "It's a boy! And he's got red hair!!" The doctor thought it was fantastic and obviously so did Jason.

The rest of that year had some pretty frustrating memories. There was a huge rift within the GP camps and a lot of people weren't happy with some of the goings-on that year. There was a pretty unhappy and unfriendly atmosphere in the pits. The respect for other riders' safety disappeared.

I remember watching the look of pleasure of all but a few in the pits as certain riders got excluded or didn't make finals. It was like a huge amount of the field had a common bond because of the issues at hand. I would have loved to have a video of some of those meetings, not on the track but on the pit area. It was great to watch although it should never have been an issue.

The season came and went and Jason finished second again. He was dogged by bad luck that year, unbelievable bad luck, even down to his gates being flooded by freak puddles of water throughout the meetings. He was accused of cheating and given endless hassle at scrutineering.

Then the famous 'no fuel' incident occurred and he didn't make a final in Slovenia. He'd been having trouble with one of his mechanics and that night was the last one before he planned to let him go. It was one night too long though as Jason's bike stopped short. Those points could have proved to be the ones he needed that year to clinch the world title but that wasn't even worth thinking about. The mechanic

LNB
POLAND
speedway
LNB
POLAND
POLAND
Silkolene
ADRIANA
LNB
POLAND
LNB
POLAND
ADRIANA
HAGON
SHOCKS
GRAND
PRIX
2004
SCOTT

disappeared and we have not had contact with him since.

It didn't matter what Jason did something came up and stopped him being able to make it. We just accepted it in the end. He wasn't to win. The only consolation was the support he had from other riders in the field.

The year finished with an anonymous letter. In short Jason was told to 'back off' and not to win the world championship that year or else. We were all threatened and it was made public because we were blowed if we were going to take that crap from some sad case that couldn't handle Jason winning. It was a threat that the police took seriously and we were really shocked by it.

We had so much support from such a huge amount of riders and other people throughout that year and even more so after this incident. It was interesting to see the people that came up to us, and could look us in the eye and offered their support in a situation like that and a minority that didn't. Actions do speak louder than words.

We were asked a lot of questions from the police about it. They took it away and did all the usual tests. Obviously the FIM were wary about the trouble that could have ensued afterwards. Having investigations go through riders and anyone else thought necessary was not what we wanted.

It had been a bad enough year for speedway getting negative press without us dragging this through the mud as well. We made it public as advised by the police so that the sad case that sent it knew we weren't going to sit back and hide – then we put it out of our minds.

Our attitude was: "Let's go and win it next year and put them in their place."

We left the country and had a couple of really good holidays that off-season. Then we got ready for a new year and a win!

I don't know what else to say about 2004.

Jason Crump – speedway world champion.

It was like most other seasons but there had been extra fire in it. Jason had it pretty much sewn up at the second last round. He only needed a few points in the final GP and it was his.

He and Tony were yet again the two main contenders but this time Jason was in the driving seat.

At the final round he did what was needed, got the points and got himself out of the meeting. The job was done – finally! When he realised the points were in the bag and the pressure was off he let go of the bike on the track and lay on the ground. For me that summed up all the emotions we'd had. He 'just let go' emotionally as well as physically. The pressure was gone, the stress was gone. My thousands of prayers were finally answered.

"He's done it, it's over, that's it" was all I could think for a long time. It really was like a huge weight had been lifted.

Our entire lives had revolved around that goal. Our children don't know anything apart from trying to win. Try explaining to a young child that it doesn't matter if you don't win a running race when all they see is their father constantly trying to win. Mia has seen disappointment in Jason as well as me and she knows that has come from not winning.

It's a difficult situation to be in, Mia goes to school one week and cuts short every other week during the Grand Prix season to travel. Her teachers say she's the only one that can keep the kids' attention for more than a few minutes because she can tell them all about the racing.

She loves it and is proud as anything of Jason. We were lucky to find a school not too far from us that specialises in sports and there are quite a few other professional sportsmen's children going there so the school are really understanding of our situation and unusual schedules.

Our children have done about 40 flights a year since they were born. They're extremely lucky to have some of the opportunities they have but it can be really hard for them as well at times.

Travelling and missing out on things isn't that much fun for a young child but at the same time they love being with Daddy and watching him race. It's funny the things kids get a kick out of and even at two years Seth will ask me when he sees me packing our bag 'we go hotel, we get room service?'.

Jason has always liked us to go to big meetings with him. I've only missed two, the first when I was almost due with Mia and the second when the children were ill a couple of years ago. I even tried to get them to catch chicken pox at a 'convenient' time for us which sounds a bit bizarre. They finally got them by chance last English summer so that turned out all right anyway and didn't require us to miss a GP.

Those meetings have become something we do as a family. Jason's results mean a lot to him. I wanted him to reach his goal almost as much as he did and it was fantastic

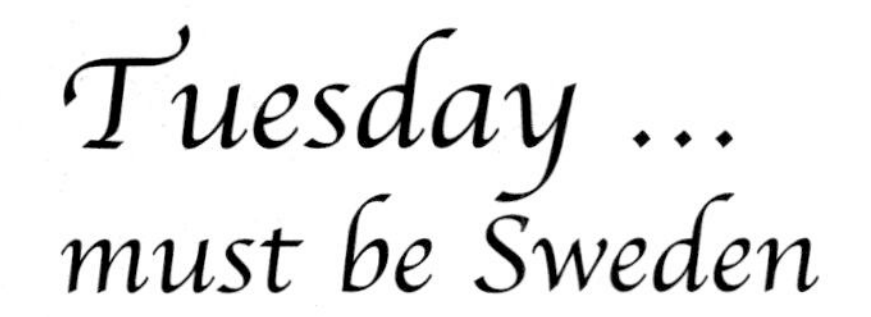

'The kids love being with Daddy and seeing him race'

COME ON DAD ... Jason takes the long route to pass Scott Nicholls in the Scandinavian Grand Prix of 2005

AWESOME FOURSOME ... The Crump family: Jason, Melody, Mia and Seth in Mauritius, October 2004

SMILE PLEASE ... The wedding party in Mauritius

we could grow and share all those experiences together.

Jason is great with the kids and has hidden emotions very effectively from them but Mia has sat with me in the stands at almost every Grand Prix there's been since she was born. She knows it's about winning and she has a wild streak that appears at the GPs when Jason's in a race. It's fantastic to watch and Seth is learning from his sister.

They constantly want to win things all the time. I'm sure all kids do but I get the impression from other parents we know that our two are obsessed with it.

We flew to Mauritius a few weeks after Jason won and got married. It was something we'd planned for quite a while but had decided we wanted our children to be part of. We are both really pleased we did it that way. It was unconventional but really special. We do everything as a family and getting married seemed to require the same plan. We had a brilliant time and spent it with some of the people closest to us.

The past year has been pretty cool. Of course we would have liked Jason to have won the world championship again. Who wouldn't want to win again just like that?

He has kept his form though and without the problems with the referee in Cardiff he would have probably chased Tony down to the last GP yet again.

There's no doubt he's been a huge threat for some years to that No.1 spot and he's been in the top two for five years running which is a huge achievement in itself.

You hear a lot of talk about the pressure put on a new world champion. I can agree with that completely but I think for Jason it's a bit different. He doesn't need to prove he was worthy to win it. He's done that undoubtedly but he has only just turned 30 and has a lot left to give.

He has grown a lot through the past few years and we have learnt a lot. We have always looked after ourselves and I think that has helped us grow and mature immensely.

Jason has always been very generous and at times people have really taken advantage of that. He will help people out no end, when he probably should be doing things for himself instead. That's Jason though and a lot of the reason I fell for him in the first place.

He's always messing around at home and joking and I've enjoyed watching him the past year at the track.

The pressure he had put himself under to win that world championship has gone and the Jason from at home and the one at the races are slowly merging together.

He has relaxed immensely which is great to see.

CW
Race Products

SGP

SGP

After climbing Everest the question is ...

> Jason learned a lot last year and I think he has a very big possibility of being right at the very top once again
>
> – Bo Wirebrand, VMS Elit team boss

What next

IN AMERICA, baseball and basketball players are out there doing their thing four or five times a week. Not many other sports demand so much of the participants, but speedway riders are able to identify with that sort of schedule.

At the height of the season I might ride half a dozen times in a week in three or four different countries. It's a hectic and sometimes exhausting lifestyle. But then, at 6.30 or seven o'clock when it's time to compete, I just put on my race face and my weariness goes away for a while.

When the Grand Prix series is in full swing it's flying followed by practice followed by the race and back to the airport again. A successful season in England can involve 50 or 60 meetings. Then there are around 20-odd trips to Poland and Sweden during the year. I've been to Prague 30 times but, though people say it's one of the most beautiful cities in the world, I've never seen the sights.

But there should be time for that later. Mel and the kids get glimpses of some of the exotic locations because we've made it a habit to treat the GPs as our opportunity to travel as a family. It will be great to go back to some of those locations in a few years' time and have a proper look around.

In the meantime, it's business as usual. It would be a mistake to look too far ahead because in sport you never know what might happen next. My game plan for the start of 2006 was never going to be much different from previous years. I want to win the world championship. I hope to be capable of challenging for a few years yet.

The fact that Tony Rickardsson has announced that it will be his last season before he moves on to four wheels isn't going to affect my mindset too much, other than to say that this probably will be the last chance of beating him. We have had so many fantastic battles in recent years and if and when you get the better of him, you know you've beaten one of the all-time great riders.

No one can take anything away from Tony and the manner in which he went about winning his sixth world championship. His performances in the first half of 2005 raised the bar to another level, a level which was just too much for the rest of us. But experience is a wonderful thing.

When I was washing his bike in Mildura all those years ago, few would have realised that he was going to be around, let alone so consistent, for so long. Tony was second in the world around the time I had my first professional ride, so for him to still be such a force in the sport is pretty outstanding.

What has made him one of the top riders of all time? Well, he has a stack of natural ability, loads of determination, and great confidence in what he can do. He came to last season's GP series with a plan and was completely prepared. Even at that stage I think he recognised that he might not have that many more chances to win the world title and he went for it.

From time to time in sport along comes someone who produces a freakish run of form and however energetically everyone gives chase, it's all over. At times, all of us in the Grand Prix last year felt like the Formula One guys must have done in all those years Michael Schumacher was virtually untouchable.

Mick Doohan and Valentino Rossi have done it in the 500cc championship, golfers at the majors turn up knowing as often as not they're shooting for second behind Tiger Woods, and Roger Federer is doing in the tennis world what Pete Sampras did before him.

Maybe nobody has been more dominant in his own sphere than the cyclist Lance Armstrong, who bowed out of the Tour de France last year after seven successive victories which would have been remarkable enough even if he hadn't had to overcome life-threatening illness along the way. What a legend, what a man, absolutely inspirational.

But nothing is for ever. Rickardsson starts 2006 level with everyone else on no points. If he performs this year as he did last, he'll be the benchmark again, but hey, several of us will go into the season determined to show that he can be beaten, that he's just another guy, that maybe it's time for a changing of the guard.

I have learned not to get too far ahead of myself. It's one step at a time. This year is yet another season in which, hopefully, a lot of little steps may take me to where I want to be. I'm encouraged by the thought that last season, things went a lot better for me in the later GP rounds, and need to focus on that. You

MOTIVATION ... In a world of his own at the Polish Grand Prix, Bydgoszcz, 2005

win things by getting your own act together. Get that right and the consequences can take care of themselves.

Of the current crop of Grand Prix riders, Nicki Pedersen is the only other one to have won a world title and all credit to him, he did what he had to do and was the guy in the right place at the right time.

From a personal angle I can't help but remember the 2003 season as anything other than the one that got away, but that's not to suggest that Nicki was not a deserving champion. A couple or so years down the track, he's a much improved rider.

He always has been a very determined racer and takes no prisoners, which has divided opinions among other riders and supporters. Some think of him as a terrific all-action entertainer and others consider he can be a bit too exuberant for his and everyone else's good.

Off track he is a good guy but on it he's a different beast. I guess I've heard that said about some others, too.

The Danes continue to come up with decent riders and I've got a lot of time for Bjarne Pedersen, who has won a Grand Prix and comes across as a good professional, well turned out and very capable.

He seems to have improved steadily, and is one of those riders who if the track conditions are right for him and he gets things going on the day, he can be a challenge to anyone on the circuit.

The Swedes, too, continue to produce likely candidates and probably their next major hope is Andreas Jonsson, who's a bit in the Tony mould ... very self-contained, doesn't give a lot away, and a strong, resourceful racer who is keen to maintain the traditions set by so many of those class-act Swedes of past years.

Andreas also has one of the best set-ups among any of the GP riders, with terrific sponsorship and a great back-up team.

Observers who have claimed that there are not enough good newcomers coming through got quite excited about the prospects of Antonio Lindback,

DESPITE a much more mature image than that of his early years, Jason still is widely regarded as one of the sport's hard men, always a crowd puller but not necessarily a universal favourite. Everyone on the Grand Prix bandwagon has an opinion and most are complimentary.

Among his peers though he is generally well liked, as Coventry skipper and Grand Prix racer Scott Nicholls confirms.

"You always get the nice guy and the bad guy in any sport and Jason seems to have this image. He's very aggressive and doesn't have the razzmatazz. He's happy as long as he's scoring points. But he's not unpopular with the other riders, who respect him."

Sky television presenter Kelvin Tatum, a former friend and rival, has witnessed Jason's growth as a rider and an individual and followed every step of his battle for top spot.

"He is not the easiest of people but he's actually a smashing guy. He's got the monkey off his back by winning the world title.

"He's very intense but a little more relaxed these days and I think that helped him win it. I think Tony has the edge on most things but they both know how to win ugly."

Tony Steele, who has taken charge of more GPs than any other official and is a long-serving member of the British refereeing panel, has his own take on Jason.

"Private and a devoted family man – not many riders in my recollection have I seen wheeling the pushchair around the shops on a Grand Prix weekend, talking patiently to fans whether in support of him or not. Who would have thought a man who has nurtured such a hard man image would be a significant supporter of a children's charity."

who was in the GP last year by virtue of having won the SGP qualifying final at Vojens in 2004.

He had one or two quite notable results, especially early on, but I think the expectations placed on him were a bit too high. It is tough, adjusting to the demands of the Grand Prix series, and as the year developed Antonio started to find out just how difficult it can be.

Even in league matches you never quite know what he is going to do next – it may be spectacular, it could be highly unpredictable. It might be great for the fans to watch but as far as success in the longer term, he is probably going to need to develop a fair bit more consistency which comes with time.

You only have to look at a rider like Greg Hancock to realise that there's much to be said for experience. Herbie has been going around for a long time and it's 10 years since he was world champion, yet he is still there or thereabouts in most of the Grands Prix.

He is one of my favourite characters in speedway, going all the way back to when we were team mates at Rospiggarna in 1995 and I ended up riding his bike as much if not more than he did!

He is still a very good, committed and effective rider and although the American influence in the sport has diminished over time, he remains really good value.

If it's experience we are talking about, and respect, Leigh Adams more than meets the necessary criteria on both counts.

Leigh of course was one of my childhood models in Mildura and although we always have had a fair bit of rivalry going, there is, I think, a lot of mutual respect.

He has paid his dues in the world championship, getting so close to a rostrum place for several years before his third in 2005, and he has been a credit to Australia and the sport in general.

The year he and I rode together at King's Lynn was one of the best and we pushed and helped one another – he's one of those guys you ride alongside with millimetres between you and still be totally confident of what's going on.

The Poles have made their mark on the world championship and in the GP era Tomasz Gollob has been one of the most enduring performers. He's perhaps not quite the threat now that he was when he went so close to winning the title in 1999 – he was injured before the final round and ended up losing his series lead to Rickardsson that year.

Nevertheless you always know you're in a race when he is around, and his record in winning at Bydgoszcz four years in a row is going to take some beating.

On the other hand he really doesn't fancy the one-off tracks like Cardiff and Copenhagen and I think he has convinced himself he won't do anything at places like that.

One to look out for is Jarek Hampel, who is representative of a whole new breed of Poles. He's smart, he's skilful and something of a trend setter.

He learned a great deal at Pila when Hans Nielsen was riding there and it is easy to see him becoming quite a force in coming seasons.

I find him a good guy, not a clown at all. He keeps himself pretty much to himself but when the chips are down he is very determined and definitely one to watch for.

For various reasons it's probably good for there to be three Poles in the championship although Tomasz Chrznowski really struggled on his debut year in 2005.

It would have been a steep learning experience for a rider officials over there have earmarked as a very promising prospect and time will tell whether the year did him more good than harm.

It can be depressing scrapping for the odd point or two while the best riders in the world are going by at a million miles an hour, but having come through it he may well reappear as a more serious contender in the future.

The English have been waiting for a while for someone to come along to put up a major challenge after Mark Loram faded out of the picture.

A lot of people see Lee Richardson as a rider for the future. He has come up with the goods in a few major meetings, including winning the Elite Riders title a couple of years ago, and he had an outstanding second place in the Bydgoszcz round last August.

The thing is though he probably would have done a lot better to have had a string of top six places rather than just the one big meeting and a lot of rather indifferent ones. My feeling is that he could move from the fringes to the mainstream but he has a bit to do yet.

On the other hand Scott Nicholls has the ability to be a genuine challenger for honours.

After he got his move to Coventry last year he had a few issues to settle, and once he got into a groove he was very hard to beat.

He didn't properly carry that form through to the Grands Prix, or particularly the later stages of those meetings, but he's fast, strong and talented. There are a few areas he needs to polish up but for me he is an excellent rider, not ever so far away from becoming an outstanding one.

The last three places awarded to permanent wild cards open up a few new possibilities for 2006 and it will be interesting to see just how great an impact the guys coming in – Matej Zagar, Piotr Protasiewicz and Niels-Kristian Iversen – will make. Nobody should underestimate the desirability of having some rotation in the series. It's especially significant for the long-term welfare of the GP and the sport that some new faces get a chance.

It was disappointing to see Mark Loram, a former world champion, out of the reckoning last year. Ryan Sullivan and Hans Andersen are two more formidable talents who will also be missing this time. All of them paid a heavy price for failing to maintain a consistent level of performance.

But that's speedway. Mark didn't really get the results he wanted in 2004 and that was his lot. Ryan, who won twice in 2002 and again in 2003 and was looking a real contender at that time, was battling with his health and mostly off the pace last year.

Hanging on the possibility of a wild card is abolutely no fun.

It's good to see the return of a proper qualification system which will come into play this year.

Unlike motor racing, commercial considerations are not the major factor in how the Grand Prix line-up is put together – but people need to understand that they do have a bearing on things. If it helps sell the series rights to have a strong representation from certain countries then that can't be ignored.

At the same time, guys who are striving to get into the world championship need to see a pathway and as far as possible, they expect it to be fair to all. However, when a place was handed to someone like Zagar from a country such as Slovenia – not exactly a big deal in speedway terms – there could be no complaints because he had a very strong case.

Zagar, who is 21 and has all the goods to make an impact in Elite League racing, might just turn out to be a significant player in 2006, a bit like Lindback did early on last year. We will all be keeping an eye out for him, that's for sure.

While Australia will be down to two riders – our lowest representation since 1997 – Danish and Polish numbers are unchanged. Pepe Protasiewicz will be stronger than Chrzanowski, who tried hard but rarely got off the bottom of the scoring charts in last year's championship. But it's a big challenge for Iversen to show he warranted a place ahead of Andersen.

Hans won the Scandinavian GP in 2004, he's only 25, and form suggests he's more of a rider on the rise so most people sympathised when he made public his obvious disappointment. At the same time, he is not the first rider to be rubbed out of the championship for the simple reason that he did not do enough to earn a guaranteed start for the following year.

With Peterborough's new boss Colin Horton forking out a big fee to sign him, though, he will be fired up for a big year in the hope he can have another shot in 2007.

Even so, neutrals would not have too many complaints either about the inclusion of Iversen who at 23 is the latest of the bright young Danish prospects running around. It's a bit of a twist that he's going to Peterborough, too.

There was more debate over the nomination of Protasiewicz, who is 31, and been in the series before without making a tremendous impact. There was a strong push for Krzystof Kasprzak, nine years younger, and the Under 21 champion (even if it was on the toss of a coin) and he would have been frustrated to lose out.

For a variety of reasons, there was a need for the return to a qualification system. You have to give the ambitious up-and-comers a target and it seems reasonable that riders who have missed making it into the top eight plus selected seeds should still have a second chance, if they want it.

Anyway, it is a strong group which will go into 2006, all of them fired with ambition and looking to either improve or consolidate their status in the world. All any of us ask is a trouble-free run and there will be a few other more specific items on everybody's personal wish list.

Experience has taught me that you have to make the most of whatever cards you are dealt although I suppose it wouldn't hurt if we had a year without any major controversy. That's not going to happen, of course. It's like hoping that referees will be consistent!

One important change for me this year will be getting back on to GM equipment. I have never chopped and changed for its own sake. I rode GMs from when I started up to the end of 1999. Then there were six years with Jawa, and I value the association I had with them..

In the final analysis both makes have characteristics which distinguish them and it's very much down to the tuners and the rider as to how to have bikes set up. I just feel it's time to try a few different things and going back to GM gives me a little bit more freedom to experiment and to have things tailor-made to my specification and satisfaction.

A lot of people whose advice has proved sound in the past helped me make an early decision. I managed to get in a few meetings at the end of last season on the new engines and felt very comfortable. We also spent some quality time testing in Lonigo in November and it was a great feeling to be getting pretty well organised so far in advance of the next campaign.

On the international front this year – and in the longer term – it would be good to see Australia coming back as a major force. After winning the top prize three times in four seasons, we have had a couple of lean years.

It may hinge upon whether the likes of Adam Shields and Davey Watt continue to improve and some of the other young guys coming through such as

TRADITION ... Jason is the latest of several world champions to wear the famous Belle Vue colours

Rory Schlein and Travis McGowan can jump from being good, promising riders into something more.

Schlein impressed me when he did a number of meetings for Belle Vue in 2004 and everybody hoped he would move up full-time last year. He did, but opted to go to Coventry and had his season wrecked by injury.

In the latter part of last year McGowan was one of the form riders in the Elite League. He's served a lengthy apprenticeship and seems to be improving in a lot of ways, which is encouraging.

It's essential to have fresh talent coming through. Leigh Adams and I have worn a fair chunk of the responsibility for a while and even if Ryan Sullivan comes back strongly, it is time for someone else to step up if we are going to be competitive with other nations who have always had more depth of numbers.

Four or five years ago was a once-in-a-generation coming together of top riders, a bit like it was back in 1976 when Phil, Billy Sanders, John Boulger and Phil Herne won the World Team Cup for the first time.

Three years ago we had four in the Grand Prix, in 2002 we had three of the top four, and suddenly, or so it seems, we're back to just a couple. It's a bit of a lottery, really. You can be around at the right time or the wrong time. It's quite different from domestic competition in which teams and their riders are changing on a regular basis.

At a club level, I am very keen to win a few more titles. We went so close at Belle Vue last year, winning the KO Cup and being pipped in the play-off final after being the team to beat in the league.

Going to Belle Vue was a challenge. There is so much history about the place, several of the best riders of all time have ridden for the Aces, and I would like to think I can do a job for them on par with all those other world champions.

I don't have any real recollection of the Hyde Road track and what you can see on video or DVD doesn't necessarily convey the full picture. A lot of the fans there still love to reminisce about how it was when Ivan, Peter Collins or even before them, Peter Craven ruled the roost.

Fortunately, the success we started to enjoy last season means that an increasing number of fans have a current team to excite them rather than having to rely on past memories. They happen to think that what's going on now is as good as it gets and I'm with them.

Maybe in 20 years' time they will be sitting around longing for the good old days of 2006, but it doesn't matter. That's sport.

John Perrin battled for years to give the people of Manchester what they wanted and there were a lot of reasons why it didn't happen for him as he would have hoped. He was a straight shooter who I must say was very good to me, always backed me 110 per cent in any and every situation, and riders appreciate having a promoter like that.

Tony Mole has been responsible for reviving and resurrecting more tracks than it's decent to recount, but you sense he is getting as much pleasure from the Belle Vue revival as anything else he has done in the sport in the past. And if an owner is going to put his trust in an experienced promoter to front the show, they don't come much more canny than Ian Thomas.

Sure, I have a two and a half hour trip just to home meetings but no complaints about that, the place suits me in so many ways. The fans are good, they want access and that's understandable, but not being based in the city or even nearby does give me and the family the breathing space and privacy we like and to which we are all entitled.

It can be quite different in Poland, which often tends to be pretty hectic. The fans are there in such numbers and they do like to get involved. It's definitely inspirational if you have several thousand of the crowd cheering for you and it has the ability to be a bit intimidating if you are at an away track and there's a close-to-unanimous disapproval rating going on.

POLE POSITION ... The Torun 2005 team, back row, left to right: Mariusz Puszakowski, Miroslaw Batorski (club chairman), Andy Smith, Jason Crump, Piotr Nagiel (team manager), Jan Zabik (coach). Front: Adrian Miedzinski, Karol Zabik, Wieslaw Jagus, Marcin Jagus

Last season Torun rode at Bydgoscz which is pretty much a local derby – there were 18,000 there including maybe a couple of thousand who had come across from Torun and needless to say, the atmosphere was absolutely on fire.

And I mean that. A group of Torun supporters were chucking flares and some of them landed in the area between the terraces and the track, setting the grass alight. The start was held up for a quarter of an hour and the locals, let me say, were pretty hostile.

But whether they are for you or against you, the Polish speedway fans love to be entertained. If you put on a real show, they appreciate that. They've had a tough history, they appreciate people who put themselves on the line and for the most part the energy and excitement that's generated at meetings there is something special.

The Torun arrangement isn't going to continue though, as my major sponsor in Poland wants me to be based at a track which can give his business maximum exposure. In the coming season I'm going back to Wroclaw, who have popped in and out of my Polish career. They are an ambitious club and that's the sort of environment I like.

Hopefully it should be a really good experience, with Marek Cieslak as the coach and Jarek Hampel one of my team-mates. Cieslak rode for White City when they won the British League in 1977, and by all accounts was a popular character. He's a successful businessman himself as well as being a well-respected trainer.

Riding full-time in three leagues, as I did for several years, is a huge commitment. Particularly with my GP ambitions in mind, it is something I simply did not want to continue to do indefinitely. Some people think you can lock into automatic and keep on doing the business day in, day out, in one country, then another, without a break. It's not as simple as it appears.

I am fortunate to have a great set-up, people around me who help organise my affairs, keep my schedule in order, make sure everything is ready to go on any given day of the week. But I've felt better since scaling back in Sweden and cutting my meetings from around 100 a year to something like 80-odd. And I'm certain it has helped me as far as the world championship is concerned.

As things stand, I enjoy racing in Sweden as much as I have done in the past, but if I was going to cut down on my schedule, this was the league which had to go. It suits me very well to do a limited number of meetings there and Bo Wirebrand at VMS Elit has been able to accommodate my wishes and still serve the best interests of his club.

Obviously if they are involved in a particularly important phase of the season and want me to do an extra meeting here or there, then I am going to do the best I can to help. But it's not smart to do someone else a favour if it can rebound on you and you end up doing yourself a disservice.

That might sound selfish, and to an extent it is, but that's the nature of elite sport. Don't forget, though, that a lot of people invest a great deal of time and effort into giving me the best possible chance of achieving my goals and it's only right that their take on it has to be considered as well.

I love Sweden. I like the country, I've made many very good friends there and it's a civilised place to be. My uncle Ian – Phil's younger brother – lived there for a while, and at one time we even had thoughts of doing so ourselves.

My years at Vargarna added up to the longest unbroken spell I have had at any club, anywhere – so far – and will remain right up there among my career highlights.

ON THE GAS ... Jason is leader of the pack for VMS Elit in the 2005 Swedish Elite League play-off against Smederna

Soon after I went there in 1997, they asked if I would commit to a long-term arrangement. I ended up signing a 10-year contract although circumstances at the club eventually meant that I only did eight. It was great to know I had a fantastic club that treated me well and it also gave the supporters a permanent team member.

It was something special when Jimmy Nilsen also signed with Vargarna a couple of years later. There was so much history with him yet this was the first time we had ridden together on the same team and we had some great times.

One of my most vivid memories was the time we were travelling together from London and due to get into Stockholm with loads of time to spare to do what normally is a two-hour road trip to the track. For some reason our plane thundered down the Heathrow runway to take off – and then dropped down again straight away.

We never did find out what the problem was but had to sit through a huge delay, By the time the plane eventually did get going time was slipping away fast. When we landed at Arlanda there wasn't much more than an hour before we were due at the stadium.

There was no way we could get there in time without breaking every speed limit and road rule in the book but Jimmy had the answer. He insisted that I should drive! His reasoning was that if we were stopped by the highway police they would throw the book at him whereas I was a foreigner and stood much more chance of getting away with it.

Believe it or not we got there in time and Michael Schumacher himself would not have covered the distance a moment quicker ... although possibly he would have been in control.

There was a really genuine rapport with everyone at Norrkoping over the years, especially the supporters, many of whom are now personal friends. I won't forget that when I won the world title, there were as many Vargarna flags waving in the crowd as there were from anywhere else.

Wherever it is, you try to fit in, to help and influence teams and riders. These are your workmates, pulling together in a common cause. Speedway isn't all about personal glory. A huge part of it revolves around team competition, with all that means to so many people And if you have a role as the No.1, and. as I do at Belle Vue, the captaincy, that brings with it extra responsibilities which I have always welcomed.

As long as I am with the Aces, though, it's always going to be a tricky one to do the Swedish League on any sort of regular basis. There are plenty of good reasons for doing Poland, and after going to and fro for a while, Belle Vue have made Monday nights their own. That makes backing up on Tuesdays a big ask.

There's Poland every Sunday – sometimes arriving from a Grand Prix, other times flying out of England on the Saturday and stopping over in Copenhagen before completing the trip next day.

Then there is the return trip to Manchester, as often as not getting in there in the afternoon and grabbing half an hour's rest before going off to race. You can never reckon to be back home and in bed before midnight and more often than not it's 12.30 or later.

When I was doing Sweden on a regular basis it was a case of setting the alarm for seven in the morning, off to the airport again – and rocking up at Norrkoping or some other track about six feeling like doing almost anything but getting on a bike to race.

It is too easy to end up knackering yourself, failing to turn in the performances you expect of yourself and others expect of you, and it was getting out of order. Of course we have a limited career span, there always is the temptation to take every opportunity you can, but in the final analysis it wasn't doing me or my speedway any good,.

I am sure it knocked some of the edge off me during the Grand Prix campaigns and honestly, I'd prefer to be doing 80 meetings and feel keen about all of them rather than doing 100 and wishing I was somewhere else on perhaps 30 per cent.

A lot of people who have to go to work five days a week probably think that pampered, overpaid sports stars shouldn't complain about their lot, and that's fair comment. It doesn't mean to say, though, that we should be held prisoner 24/7 by the expectation of the public or officials.

It was no coincidence that the consistency and the staying power which got me to the world title at last coincided with the first year in something like seven or eight seasons in which I hadn't chased every meeting.

Domestic matches are the bread and butter for fans at clubs in various places, and it is important to keep things bubbling along there. We are the fortunate ones who might be in Prague one day and Poole the next but the vast majority of speedway fans follow just the one track, and we owe it to them to put on a suitable show.

Realistically, it is impossible to keep yourself up time after time for the intensity that the Grand Prix demands. That is not to say that league racing is ever anything short of challenging. But whereas every one of what could be seven races on a GP night will be against the very best in the world, in a league match you'll meet Tony or Nicki or someone else a couple of times in the night and it is that bit easier to maintain a pretty constant standard of high scoring.

Even so, you cannot take anybody for granted and every team has a reserve or a second string who will be keen to take the chance to make a name for himself by collecting a 'big name' – it keeps you honest.

I go to race with every intention of winning but I think it is important to keep everything in perspective. A few years ago I would blow up if I dropped a point in a league match, but in the end you have to accept that that is going to happen.

Kelvin Tatum told me long ago that he tried to ensure he was on the ball for domestic meetings but had something in reserve when it came to the bigger events – in his case, increasingly on the long tracks rather than conventional speedway.

I tried to adopt something of that philosophy and nowadays league matches are the fun meetings. I wouldn't and couldn't do what I do if I didn't love racing and you can still love it when the stakes are not quite so high.

In the overall scheme of things, it isn't going to have quite the same impact on my career if, say, Joe Average beats me in Manchester or Bydgoscz or Malilla as if one of my great rivals sees me off in a GP final.

WHILE the Jason Crump of recent times is a more mature, measured and politically correct presence than in his headstrong youth, from time to time he still manages to have the mother and father of all arguments with his dad.

Phil Crump, who was and still is renowned in speedway for his laidback demeanour, accepts that the collision between the generations is not unique to father and son motorcycle racers.

"We have plenty of disagreements and sometimes I'm the scapegoat but we both want the same thing which is for Jason to be successful.

"I am sure Jason accepts that anything I suggest to him, or Neil (Street), we're only trying to help him to do better and to win more races. When you are watching there are so many things you can see that a rider might not notice or be aware of.

"What is important is to give information and a point of view for him to consider and then it's up to him to make the final decision."

While Jason has made only fleeting visits to Australia in the past three or four years, Phil routinely closes down his tuning workshop at the end of October and heads back to the Gold Coast.

The pair maintain regular contact – frequently discussing the latest technical ideas and plans for the forthcoming season – before Phil flies back to Europe in February.

He then spends a month working alongside Brian Karger in Denmark as final touches are applied to the mechnical preparation for a new campaign.

Riding league matches on just one day of the week, as happens in Poland (Sunday) and Sweden (Tuesday), works well for those countries but I don't see it ever happening in the UK. Many of the British tracks share facilities with other sports such as greyhound racing, stock cars, football and rugby league, and the flexibility with dates just does not exist.

The way things are, most promoters base their business on running a speedway meeting every week for at least six months. I doubt there are any in England or Scotland who would be able to run at home one week, and do an away match the next – they simply would not make ends meet if they ran only a dozen meetings.

Even so, you can bet there are some who would love to do as the Poles and Swedes do, because not only would it reduce their workload and expenses, but it should concentrate all the meaningful business into a much more compact schedule.

When the Grand Prix came along, and especially when it stretched from six rounds to nine (and 10 in 2003 and again this year) there were lots of complaints from British promoters who reckoned their whole operation was being jeopardised.

But most of them have found a way to keep the interest ticking along and the supporters coming, even though it has meant some radical changes for many of them. When I first rode in the top flight in 1994, Coventry, Cradley Heath, Bradford and King's Lynn ran on Saturday nights.

Nowadays only Eastbourne run at the weekends and they have to juggle their fixture list around the Grand Prix dates. Traditional Saturday night operators such as Coventry (and Belle Vue for that matter) have had to educate their public to accept a different, midweek staging date.

From a rider's point of view, one night is much like any other. For fans though, the traditions of following a team on a particular night die hard. And there is little doubt that the trend away from weekends – which the development of the Polish scene as much as the Grand Prix has done much to influence – has presented British speedway with some problems.

It is much more difficult for fans to travel to midweek matches, unless it's a real local derby ... and there are not many of them these days. In any case, it is not cheap following your favourite team or rider to two or three meetings a week, especially if you're talking about a family. You need to take out a mortgage to fill the car with petrol, never mind travelling to and from the tracks, and getting some refreshment en route or at the stadium.

It has a remarkable knack for survival, mind. People have been writing off British speedway for years and years and yet it still keeps on going, and throwing up some surprises.

Who would have thought that Belle Vue and Coventry, two of the poor relations in 2004, would revive echoes of their great days and be the two best teams in the country last year? Improved performances on track obviously generated a lot of renewed (and in some cases, new) interest off it.

I have got a few ideas and a bit of experience which hopefully might make some constructive contribution in the Speedway Riders Association and I always look forward to having a sensible dialogue with promoters who care a great deal about the direction in which the sport is headed.

But don't ask me for any easy answer as to how to double crowds overnight!

I know they don't charge so much to watch speedway in Poland. The crowds there are fantastic although the average wage isn't that special. I don't think reducing prices in the UK would achieve anything, though. Any business has to charge a going rate and by comparison with other top forms of sport and entertainment, speedway isn't that much more expensive.

The promoters are constantly required to understand what the public wants, and to do whatever it takes to feed their need. Riders also have to understand that we are all part of the deal. We are in the entertainment business.

The team thing is an ingredient everybody has to be aware of. I have become much more conscious of the need to be a team player. I've been fortunate to ride in some outstanding sides and at the risk of offending people elsewhere would have to put the 1994 Poole experience at the top of that list.

Someone once said there is nothing more entertaining than winning, which is fair comment – but supporters also want to see a show. The least they are entitled to hope for is good racing which depends to a considerable degree on the attitude of the promotion, how they go about preparing their race strip and how they look after the interests of riders ... and I don't just mean money.

Most riders do what they do because it's an inbred, instinctive thing. It's the same with most sports people. The financial angle does come into it if it's your living but good tracks, a decent atmosphere, supportive management, a meaningful occasion – they are the essential ingredients which can fire everybody up.

I have been around speedway long enough to see it through different eyes and I have tried never to forget the sense of excitement and enjoyment I experienced when seeing it as a kid. Today's supporters, especially the young ones, need all the encouragement we can give them. And if that means doing a

WILD ... celebration after Apator Adriana Torun had beaten Unia Tarnow, 2005

HAGON
ADRIANA
HAGON

couple of wheelies, an extra lap of honour, signing loads of autographs or just taking the time to acknowledge the fans, then that is part of what we're paid to do.

The higher you go in the sport, the greater the emphasis on the individual. There's nothing wrong with that. Pride in your own performance, the way you go about pursuing your goals, that's what defines you as a person.

I've always made a point of trying to be my own man, to do things my way and not be a clone of anyone else. Sons of speedway fathers can be a pain in the backside, anyway. I would never complain about the connections I had, the fact that I grew up in a speedway family and racing environment, and know that it's only right and proper to acknowledge help, wherever it's come from.

It's a bit irritating, though, to read or hear suggestions that you have achieved certain things for which others are given an undue amount of credit. There are riders past and present who have been unfairly labelled in this way and I know it bugs the hell out of them, too. The fact is that when the flag drops the bullshit stops as they say in car racing.

The rider is responsible, the buck stops with him. You make decisions about your off-track support group, your machinery, how you live your life and at the end of the day a lot of factors can influence whether you are successful or not. But the real business is how you handle yourself in the sixty-odd seconds from go to whoa, when the race is on.

These days I get myself organised before the start of the season with about eight new engines which Brian Karger then plays with and tunes to my specification. We hop over to Denmark to collect them. Apart from the fact that he does a great job, Brian is a really good guy too – I've known him for many years and it is good to have him as a friend as much as a super-tuner.

During the season the engines are mostly maintained by Phil, who has a workshop at Ted and Helen Jarvis's place at Newton Longueville, near Milton Keynes. It's half an hour through the country lanes, far enough away for us not to be clashing, close enough if motors need to be delivered or collected. Peter Johns also helps out. His base in in Southam, near Daventry, so that's just a 20 to 30 minute drive, again pretty convenient if there's a last-minute drama over anything.

I get the motors back to Brian on a fairly regular basis and constant attention to detail is important. Most riders are so competitive these days, they all have their own specialists and a set-up which suits them and you always have to try to be a step ahead if possible.

Bikes and engines have always interested me but I wouldn't describe myself as being particularly cluey or hands-on. Nor would I see myself as someone who is going to spend hours, days, weeks or even years wrapped up in engines. I've always preferred to have someone who is a specialist doing the work on the bike and I'll do the bit I'm best at, which is riding it!

At Grand Prix meetings I'll usually have three guys in the pits – my uncle Drew, my father and Dariusz Sadjak, known simply as Jack.

Drew Street is the person who has spent more time and done more meetings with me than the rest of them put together. I've acknowledged the fantastic support of my grandfather and it is only right to add that Drew's hands-on, unselfish and unstinting help has been equally important if not more so.

Starting out, wherever I needed to go, he was the chauffeur. But he was, and remains, much more than that. He's a terrific loyal friend and confidant, a trusted mate. He's witnessed and felt all the ups and downs. He doesn't flap, and there have been many times when he has known exactly how to handle me and my often up and down emotions.

We've had fun and adventure, heartache and pain and he has shared the lot. If a job needs doing Drew will fix it. If I need to talk, he'll talk and if I want peace and quiet on the way to or from a meeting, or during it, he just lets me be.

For years he was prepared for his work and his social life to run a poor second to the time he spent with me, at or going to and from speedway meetings in Europe and, on several occasions, in Australia.

Phil can be good or, sometimes, a pain. Fathers and sons don't always make a great team and we always have had our ups and downs. When we're on a downer we can be pretty pissed off with one another for some time.

When he thinks about what he is saying to me, he makes a lot of sense and of course I will take notice of his opinions and take them on board. Sometimes he just gets wound up and that's never the best way to convey advice.

I've also learned from his mistakes. When he was riding he had loads of bikes. At one time he was switching from GM to a Godden, then a Jawa, then back again. I would never do that. You have to have stability.

When I started I rode a GM for quite a few years, nothing else. Then I was with Jawa from the year 2000. This season I've gone back to the GM. Not too much chopping and changing there over 14 years.

But Phil has been an important contributor to my career, particularly over the past five years during which he has been based in England during the season. He's got great experience to draw upon, both as a rider and with engines.

To be honest, our relationship nowadays is almost exclusively professional, strictly business. It has to be that way. It's not perfect, but it works, although it hasn't been that easy, separating family issues from speedway, especially in the time after he and my mum split up.

Then there's Jack, who as well as all the GPs does Poland and Sweden. He is based in Torun and in addition to looking after everything there, he'll pick me up from the airport, drive to meetings and get me back in time for the return flight. It's a similar sort of arrangement when I do Swedish meetings – what he does is take a ferry from Gdansk across to Karlskrona and then we link up for whatever meeting is on.

He's ridden a little too so he knows what is required. And you don't need to tell him what a tough business it is. If you want to get a racing licence in Poland there is an exam to pass, which includes demonstrating that you can go round within so many seconds of the track record. Unfortunately on his big test day the Torun track was wet and treacherous and he crashed and broke his collarbone.

After that he decided to limit his involvement to off-track work and he's been associated with a few riders, including Tony Rickardsson. He was Tony's full-time mechanic in the year we rode together at Torun, but tired of always being on the road. Now he can live at home, still be involved, but without as much traveling as before. He joined up with me in 2004.

Strider Horton, who's ridden a bit of speedway and long track in Australia, joined me as a full-time mechanic last year and it's working well. He helped Newport's Craig Watson before that and knows his way around.

We had a chat when I rode as a wild card in the New Zealand round of the long track championship at the end of 2004 and decided to hook up. There was an opening because Mick Day, who had been with me for a few years in the UK, decided he'd had enough.

Strider lives at Kettering so he's pretty local and he does all the British meetings for me.

He is another genuine guy, a good worker, and does really well – especially when a couple of hyperactive kids threaten to take over the workshop and disrupt his routine.

ENGINE tuner and former Danish international Brian Karger is confident Jason will add further world titles to his CV.

"He's going to be very hard to beat. He's always been fast with a lot of talent, and so much focus."

Karger, a friend since his riding days at Swindon, has an easy-going relationship with him and finds Jason an understanding customer.

"We try lots of things with the motors and he's good, if something doesn't work quite as well as we hoped he doesn't react as some riders do – he is happy to move on and try something else."

These are the people who keep the show on the road in practical terms. Whatever combination is on parade, we're a team. We work together. I've had different people alongside me and over time you get to know who's there for the right reasons, who you can always trust.

Equally important in the overall scheme of things is to be sure my head is in the right place. The mental side of things is such a key area for a successful sportsman and it's something I have tried to improve upon over the years.

My aim is to continue to improve, and a lot of that is in the mind. After a while you don't necessarily make giant leaps forward as a rider, and so much of it is about attitude.

Anything you can do, however small, could be the difference between success and missing out.

There are people who don't pay much attention to sports psychology but I am a believer in it. I have had a lot of help in this area and believe it has made me a better person and a more rounded individual as well as a better speedway rider.

I have always liked being a winner and a believer in giving it all you have got. Sometimes you need more. It started to change for me when I learned to train my mind to work in different ways and to curb my bad traits. Instead of going like a bull in a china shop, I try to be aggressive in the right way.

Then again I probably wouldn't have achieved half as much without the wisdom and non-stop, unconditional support of Bill Street. Although he'll pick and choose his meetings these days, he has always been there for me and he still is. He's my grandad first of all, and over the years he has been a best mate.

I could not begin to properly acknowledge all he has done for me. There is no way I could have come to England and done what I did if it was not for him and Mary, as they and the boys – Graham and Drew – all made me instantly at home.

Bill is one of the wisest brains ever associated with speedway. He was a decent rider, a terrific tuner, a great innovator, a massive source of help to my dad when he was racing. He's been Australia's team manager through thick and thin, and done so much to encourage and bring along young riders.

This book is not long enough to list the people who have helped me along the way. There have been riders, officials, team managers, promoters, sponsors, supporters. In their different ways they have all been important at various times. If I mention a few I'll be bound to leave out someone else who has been really significant.

When you're trying to be the best and to beat everyone, it can be difficult to form close friendships with other riders. You find that some of the older guys are more likely to share their thoughts and compare notes and from that angle I've been fortunate.

Simon Wigg, Kelvin Tatum and Jeremy Doncaster are guys who spring to mind who gave me the benefit of their advice and experience when I was finding my way – being in close contact with them when I was long-tracking was invaluable.

What they had in common was knowledge of various forms of racing in all parts of the world. Mick Poole is a guy with whom I probably have the longest-running relationship. Most recently, Joe Screen is someone with whom I talk a lot.

Jimmy Nilsen and Per Jonsson were important role models for me, too, especially early on. Jimmy helped and encouraged me in many ways, and it was a shame the Grand Prix team, a great idea in theory, didn't work out so well in practice.

For me, though, Per was the king, the main man. I only got to ride against him a few times and it was an honour to be in the same race. The end of the world as Per knew it happened when he crashed riding for Torun against Bydgoszcz in 1994, and crushed the fourth and fifth verterbrae in his back.

He was 28, and a lot of people reckoned he was a big chance for the world title, to go with the one he won at Bradford in 1990. He's been in a wheelchair since then.

There are riders whose career has been wrecked by injury who wanted no more to do with speedway but Per has retained his interest and he's always been great with me. He helped get me organised with my equipment when I first rode in Sweden and we still keep in contact to see how things are going.

Per is a very remarkable person, to have stayed involved and so enthusiastic about speedway after it dealt him such a terrible blow. The way he handles himself is inspirational.

I was such a big fan of his when he was first in England, an impressionable kid no doubt but you could not fail to be impressed with how he went about his business. He was a class act right from the beginning, you never saw him crash, and that made his accident all the more difficult to take.

As a young rider at the start of my career it affected me a great deal, made me stop and think a lot about the whole business. It doesn't hurt to pause and consider what you are doing. From time to time everybody needs to assess their goals, establish their priorities and evaluate where they're at.

People in the past have accused me of being a whinger but overall, please rest assured I am very happy with my lot and with what speedway means to me. That doesn't mean to say that I will be backward in coming forward with an opinion if it needs saying. That is something I have always done and if I'm now in a position in which more people are prepared to listen and respect my point of view, then I'm pleased about that.

My philosophy is that if you have decided there is nothing you would rather be doing with your life at any such moment, what comes with the territory is the recognition that there's good and bad in everything. What is more important than anything is for all the pluses to outweigh the minuses.

I don't spend too many idle moments wondering about retirement. It just isn't the done thing and anyway, there isn't the time.

But I recognise that within another 10 years I'll probably be another ex-speedway rider. Just how long I continue racing depends on a few considerations, far and away the most important one being the enjoyment factor.

And remaining competitive probably is the key to that.

Although some of the critics have suggested that there is a shortage of good riders coming through, it's obvious to me that quite a few of the young guns going around have the ability to make an impact.

None of them will particularly relish the prospect of having to wait for years before they can have a pop at the highest honours. In recent times though speedway hasn't been a sport for overnight sensations. They pretty much went out of fashion years ago when, to be fair, the standards were quite a bit different.

This is a topic you can argue indefinitely but what has been happening over the past decade, especially at Grand Prix level, is in my opinion the hottest, toughest and most competitive speedway has ever been. And you won't see it getting any easier.

But I don't do what I do because it's easy. Rather the opposite. If becoming a world champion was easy, everybody would be doing it. What makes it special for me is that I joined that select band after a massive amount of effort and what at certain times seemed to be an unreasonable amount of struggle.

Knowing all of that, I'm still up for it again, very much so.

It would be good to think that down the track I might be able to retain some connections with motor sport, because this, after all, has been my life so far – although it is difficult to speculate on what sort of role there could be. When the time comes it also would be nice to know there were a few other options.

Choices are what we all want to have as time moves along. I hope to have done well enough from racing to have a few possibilities open up for me, and I realise that, too, may not be easy.

The trouble is, there is no structure in speedway to prepare anybody for life after racing. There are some sporting codes which spend a lot of time and money educating and preparing people for the time when the applause stops and reality bites. Speedway, unfortunately, really doesn't.

I believe that the challenges you have to meet, the hard work and discipline which is involved if you want to be an elite sportsman, do give people some life skills which may be invaluable later on. There have been plenty of 'normal' people who have made a huge success of their business and personal lives, drawing directly upon the lessons learned in their sporting career.

But there probably have been many more who found it desperately difficult to adapt. While most people are used to the routine of regular employment, organisation in the workplace and regular social activity, speedway riders, footballers, cricketers, and the rest spend years in a privileged but often unreal world.

Speedway differs from a lot of the other sports though, with many performers being entirely dependent on the way they fit into the scheme of things with one club, or team. And we don't get involved with the sort of pampering and physical conditioning that, say, David Beckham does, the detailed psychological planning which is part of the deal if you're an Australian Test cricketer, still less the lives of the rich and famous baseball or basketball stars.

Everything is done for these guys, they're clothed and fed and transported and fussed over to such an extent that it is no surprise many of them end up with a completely distorted opinion of who they are. No wonder some have a very blurred view of the real world.

THE doubters who are yet to completely embrace the Grand Prix concept appear to be diminishing as the series continues to seek new frontiers.

As one of the most experienced of GP campaigners, Jason Crump is supportive of the event's continued expansion.

"For riders and spectators, it's exciting to be back to 10 rounds for 2006 with the addition of Daugavpils," he said after the programme for the 12th season was finalised.

"Latvia isn't the most obvious destination right now, but who knows how things will develop as the Grand Prix spreads its influence.

"If the series can get into places like Cardiff and Copenhagen and fill the stadiums then that's fine, but the idea of going into other venues has a lot going for it too.

"Both Eskilstuna and Malilla put in additional stands to cope with their rounds last year, Lonigo installed extra floodlighting. If existing tracks can grow and improve their amenities in tandem with the GP series, that's all good."

As one who sampled all manner of drama in his early years on the fringes of the world championship, Jason also identifies with the FIM/BSI

Against that, there is a speedway fixture list which controls a rider's movements for eight months of the year and many of us serve different masters. At least at the end of the day, you're the one who calls most of the shots. And you stand and fall by the decisions made and the choices taken.

That does not guarantee an ability to carry those decision-making processes into life after speedway. I know a lot of guys who are decisive on the track and inventive in the workshop but hopeless in lots of other areas. And the sport has a long list of ex-riders who seriously failed to successfully make the adjustments necessary when they stopped racing.

There is not much chance to prepare yourself, however. As long as you're riding professionally it is a job which demands a huge level of commitment. It isn't as if we get four months' holiday, either. For weeks before the start of a new season it is all systems go, getting equipment and 101 other details sorted out ready for the off. And around the end of the year, what with Christmas and new year, the time quickly slips away.

When Phil first came to England he was, in effect, the only full-time rider in what, admittedly, was a Second Division outfit. Even when he moved up two or three years later, he was the exception rather than the rule.

I believe it was Ivan Mauger who did most to start the trend which transformed the identikit speedway rider from the 1970 stereotype with one bike strapped to the back of a Ford Cortina, and, in most instances, a full-time job, to the modern-day version.

Of course everyone can't be world champion or even a Grand Prix rider but almost everybody wants to try. And for those who attempted to catch up with

initiative whereby many more riders from around the globe will have an opportunity to claim a place in future seasons.

"By re-introducing a qualification series for 2006, BSI and the FIM have moved in the right direction," says Jason.

"In some ways I don't envy the guys who will be on the edge, trying to get in (or back) because it's going to be really hectic – great for the sport, though."

Jason continues to dream of the day when Australia again hosts a grand prix but accepts it may not happen within the next few years.

"All the boys loved the opportunity to race in Sydney in 2002 and it would be great to see something like that happen again."

The ultimate 'dream' venue, however, is Wembley, which for almost half a century was regarded as the spiritual home of the world championship.

"With the place open again, what a sensational location it would be," he says.

"I would love to see a situation in which we had our usual 40,000 at Cardiff for the British GP and then maybe twice as many in Wembley for the season finale. Now that really would be something."

LNB
POLAND
Speedy
Speedy
FIAT
COMMERCIAL
VEHICLES
FIAT
COMMERCIAL
VEHICLES
VEIDEC
SGP
speedwayworld.tv
POLAND
POLAND
POLAND

Ivan, right up to the current crop, it soon became routine to travel to a meeting with two or three bikes, to employ a mechanic, and to concentrate more or less exclusively on speedway.

Another era's bike rack is today's custom-built and fully-equipped van. There is so much more to be learned about machinery, too. It's always been a key element of the sport and there is some really exciting cutting-edge technology involved nowadays. Striving for improvement from yourself and your bikes makes for a big challenge on several levels.

I can see that some of the old-timers might have a point when they talk about it all being 'more fun' way back then. Riding speedway, even though it's only in the past few years that it has become such an international affair, would have appeared to be a terrific adventure set alongside the day-to-day business of doing an ordinary job.

Probably it was easier to have some sort of balance, something which is difficult to achieve for most riders nowadays as they tend to have speedway breakfast, noon and night. There is very little escape. That is fine when everything is going well, but when there are problems, sometimes you need a break, some kind of relief, and a chance to step back to get some perspective as you try to analyse what is happening.

And very often, there is no such opportunity.

The flip side is that if a rider has a poor night then he probably won't have to wait long for the chance to have a good one. If you're going badly in one league, going off to another meeting a thousand miles away might just be the change of environment to help turn things round.

So when you boil it down, there are lots of lessons to be learned from elite sport. We don't take our good fortune for granted. Some things you learn the hard way. However organised or experienced you may be, it isn't realistic to expect everything to go like clockwork.

But I've got to this point without too many regrets.

Racing offers a great life, a very different lifestyle, a decent standard of living, and opportunities to visit places most people know only as names on a map.

It's really cool and I don't expect to tire of it any time yet.

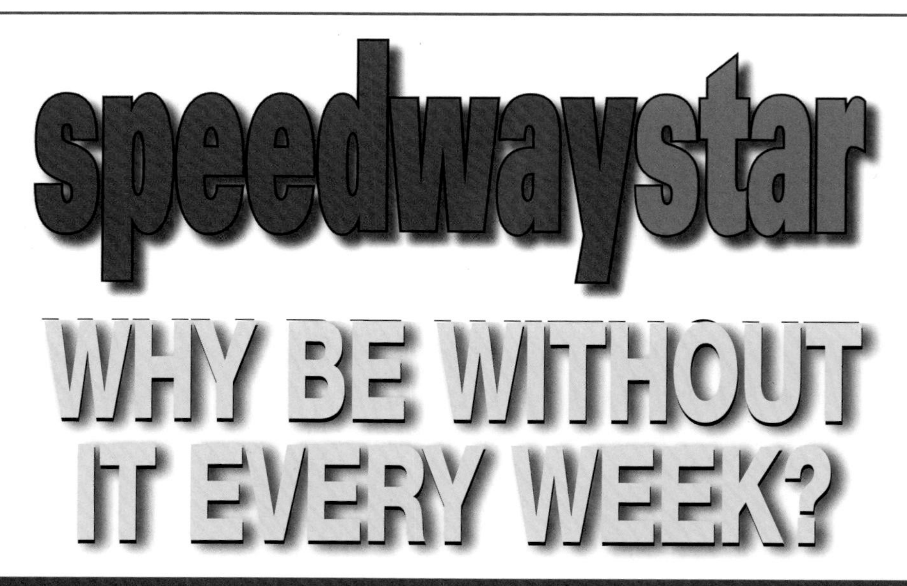

speedwaystar
WHY BE WITHOUT IT EVERY WEEK?
Call: 020 8335 1113
for subscription rates worldwide